THE HUTCHINSON GUIDE TO WRITING RESEARCH PAPERS

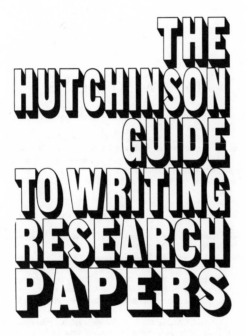

THE HUTCHINSON GUIDE TO WRITING RESEARCH PAPERS

HELENE D. HUTCHINSON

Kendall College

Glencoe Press
A division of Benziger Bruce & Glencoe, Inc.
Beverly Hills

Glencoe Press
A division of Benziger Bruce & Glencoe, Inc.
8701 Wilshire Boulevard
Beverly Hills, California 90211
Collier-Macmillan Canada, Ltd., Toronto, Ontario

Library of Congress catalog card number: 72-86030

4 5 6 7 8 9 KPt 80 79 78 77 76

ACKNOWLEDGMENTS

Acknowledgment is gratefully made to the following authors, artists, photographers, and publishers who have granted permission to use selections from their publications.

AMERICAN HERITAGE PUBLISHING CO., INC., *for:* The entry "druid" from *The American Heritage Dictionary of the English Language.* © copyright 1969, 1970, 1971 by American Heritage Publishing Co., Inc. Reprinted by permission.

ANTIQUITY MAGAZINE, *for:* Reproduction on p. 73 of photographs by John Palmer, "Rock Temples of the British Druids," from *Antiquity*, vol. 38, Dec. 1965 (Plate LII, opposite p. 285).

ART EDUCATION, INC., *for:* Woodcut showing the tree of knowledge from *Art: Of Wonder & a World.* Copyright © 1967 by Art Education, Inc.

ASHOK ANAND, *for:* Photograph entitled "Trees" on p. 228.

AVANT-GARDE MAGAZINE, *for:* "Nude Pregnant Woman," photograph by DeWayne Dalrymple on p. 12, from *Avant-Garde*, issue of January 1969.

A. S. BARNES & COMPANY, Inc., *for:* Two drawings by Rombola, man made up of typewriter characters on p. 171 and "I am to fat" on p. 227. Both from *Rombola's People* (1970).

LLOYD M. BEIDLER, *for:* Photographs of the eye of a fruit fly, magnified 180, 2240, and 11,200 times. Reproduced by permission of Lloyd M. Beidler, Department of Biological Sciences, Florida State University.

R. R. BOWKER COMPANY, *for:* Bibliographical entries, reprinted from *Books in Print* (pp. 53 and 56) and the *American Book Publishing Record* (p. 50) by permission of R. R. Bowker, a Xerox company.

CARNEGIE INSTITUTION OF WASHINGTON, DEPARTMENT OF EMBRYOLOGY, *for:* Photograph by Richard Grill on p. 4 of 44-day-old human embryo.

THE CHICAGO DAILY NEWS, *for:* Photograph of Archie Clark of the Philadelphia 76ers and Jimmy Collins of the Chicago Bulls that appeared in the *Chicago Daily News* of October 13, 1971. Reprinted by permission from the *Chicago Daily News*. Photo by Don Bierman.

COMPIX, *for:* Photograph of Chicago's Mayor Richard Daley on p. 10;
Photograph of Robert Kennedy campaigning on p. 14.

CROWN PUBLISHERS, INC., *for:* Gustave Doré's drawing entitled "Farinata Degli Uberti," from *A Doré Treasury*, edited by James Stevens. © 1970 by Crown Publishers, Inc. Used by permission of Crown Publishers, Inc.

DANISH NATIONAL MUSEUM, *for:* Reproduction (on p. 51) of Plate I in Stuart Piggott's *The Druids*, New York, Praeger, 1968. Published by permission of the Danish National Museum.

DARGAUD EDITEUR, *for:* "The Unheroic Druid: the Druid Panoramix," from the modern French comic strip series "Asterix le Gaulois" by Goscinny and Uderzo, as reproduced by Praeger in Stuart Piggott's *The Druids* (Plate 31). Copyright Dargaud Editeur 1968.

J. M. DENT & SONS LTD. PUBLISHERS, *for:* Photograph on p. 38 by Jean Roubier of Rock Fortress of Rocsaliere, West Wall of the Druid Temple, from *The Art of Roman Gaul* by Marcel Pobe. Copyright 1961. Reproduced also by permission of the University of Toronto Press.

DOVER PUBLICATION, INC., *for:* Drawing and verses appearing on p. 33 of *Topsys and Turvys*, by Peter Newell.

DRAEGER FRÈRES, IMPRIMEURS, *for:* Three paintings by Salvador Dali, entitled "Dali at the Age of Six . . ." (on p. 36), "Automatic Beginning of a Portrait of Gala" (on p. 125), and "Las Meninas" (on p. 100). Reproduced by permission of Draeger Frères.

E. P. DUTTON & CO., INC., *for:* Untitled verse on p. 11 from the book *Boss: Richard J. Daley of Chicago* by Mike Royko. Copyright © 1971 by Mike Royko. Published by E. P. Dutton & Co., Inc., and used with their permission.

JULES FEIFFER, *for:* Drawing of Julius Hoffmann, reprinted from *Pictures at a Prosecution* by Jules Feiffer. Copyright © 1971 Jules Feiffer.

ANDREAS FEININGER, *for:* Photograph of man with test tube, from *Family of Man*, p. 126. Photograph by Andreas Feininger.

BENEDICT J. FERNANDEZ, *for:* Photograph entitled "Newark, 1967," frcm *In Opposition*, by Benedict J. Fernandez, Da Capo Press, 1968.

FIELD MUSEUM OF NATURAL HISTORY, *for:* Photograph of model of Neanderthal woman on p. 16.

RALPH GINZBURG, *for:* Excerpts (three cartoons and selection of jokes on pages 172–73) from "Why Automation Is a Laughing Matter," article by John Dempsey from *Fact Magazine* (October 1966). Reprinted by permission of Ralph Ginzburg.

GROSSET & DUNLAP, INC., *for:* Photograph on p. 82 of "Zulu Maiden with Fertility Band," reprinted from *African Image* by Sam Haskins. Copyright © 1967 by Samuel Haskins. Published by Grosset & Dunlap, Inc.

GROSSMAN PUBLISHERS, *for:* Cover illustration by Paul Bacon, from *The Accidental President* by Robert Sherrill. Copyright © 1967 by Robert Sherrill. Reprinted by permission of Grossman Publishers.

HILL AND WANG, INC., PUBLISHERS, *for:* "Santa Claws," from *Black Pow-wow* by Ted Joans. Copyright © 1969 by Ted Joans. Reprinted by permission of Hill and Wang, Inc.

JOHNSON PUBLISHING COMPANY, INC., *for:* Photo of Len and Toni Frazier on p. 147, top right (from *Ebony*, November 1970).

KAISER ALUMINUM NEWS, *for:* Line drawings of dogs, from *Communications: The Transfer of Meaning* by Don Fabun, p. 33. Kaiser News © 1965, "Communications."

OMAR LAMA, *for:* Drawings of eyes (p. 68) and black Christ (p. 114). Reproduced by permission of Omar Lama.

LICK OBSERVATORY, *for:* Photograph of the Diffuse Nebulosity Near Cygni on p. 77.

MAGNUM PHOTOS, INC., *for:* Two photographs by Ernest Haas, "New Mexico" on p. 72 and "The Graceful Dancing Girls of Bali" on p. 105. Reproduced by permission of Magnum Photos, Inc.;

Five photographs by Dennis Stock from *The Alternative: Communal Life in New America:* "Trio," p. 129; "Boots," p. 147, center right; "Man with Hoe," p. 147, top left; "Man with Goat," p. 147, bottom; "Man Planting Seed," p. 169. Reproduced by permission of Magnum Photos, Inc.

THE MIAMI DAILY NEWS, INC., *for:* "H-H-Herbert Hoover," cartoon by Don Wright on p. 88.

MODERNA MUSEET, STOCKHOLM, *for:* "Marilyn Monroe in black and white" by Andy Warhol, on p. 98.

MUSEI CAPITOLINE, ROME, *for:* Photograph on p. 91 of the statue "The Dying Gaul," as reproduced in *The Celtic Realms*, by Myles Dillon and Nora Chadwick. London: Weidenfelf and Nicolson, 1967, p. 165.

THE NEW AMERICAN LIBRARY, INC., *for:* Excerpt from Dante's *The Inferno*. As translated by John Ciardi. Copyright © 1954 by John Ciardi. Reprinted by arrangement with The New American Library, Inc., New York, N.Y.

NEW DIRECTIONS PUBLISHING CORP., *for:* 115 lines from "Thou Shalt Not Kill." In Kenneth Rexroth, *Collected Shorter Poems*. Copyright © 1956 by New Directions Publishing Corporation. Reprinted by permission of New Directions Publishing Corporation.

PETER LEE INC., *for:* "A-maze-zing Maze" (on p. 19) and "Scorpio" (on p. 17) by Peter Max, from pp. 55 and 61 of *Peter Max Magazine No. 1*.

PHILADELPHIA MUSEUM OF ART, *for:* Reproduction of "Prometheus Bound," painting by Pieter Paul Rubens (eagle painted by Frans Snyders). Reproduced by permission of the Philadelphia Museum of Art: The W. P. Wilstach Collection.

PAUL POPPER LTD., *for:* Photograph of Stonehenge (p. 63) appearing in the McGraw-Hill *Dictionary of Art*, ed. Bernard Myers, vol. 5, p. 239. Reproduced by permission of Paul Popper, London.

PUBLISHERS-HALL SYNDICATE, *for:* Three articles by Sydney J. Harris from the *Chicago Daily News*, entitled "A Challenge to True Dog Lovers" (July 7, 1971); "Timeworn Phrases for Quiz Fans" (August 24, 1971); and "At Last a Simpler Harris Quiz" (December 6, 1971). Reprinted by permission of Sydney J. Harris and Publishers-Hall Syndicate.

G. P. PUTNAM'S SONS, *for:*Excerpts from quizzes on pp. 20–21, 85, and 122–23 in *The Potboiler Quiz* by Robert Kilbride. Reprinted by permission of G. P. Putnam's Sons from *The Potboiler Quiz* by Robert Kilbride. Copyright © 1969 by Dillon Press, Inc.

RANDOM HOUSE, INC., *for:* "Movie Actress," poem by Karl Shapiro. Copyright © 1943 by Karl Shapiro from *V-Letter and Other Poems*. Reprinted by permission of Random House, Inc.

RIPLEY ENTERPRISES, INC., *for:* Drawing of "The Living Tomb of the Suicides" by Ripley (insert in drawing on p. 24), from Ripley, *Believe It or Not: Tombstones and Graveyards*, published by Pocket Books, a division of Simon & Schuster.

SATURDAY REVIEW, INC. *for:* "Dad, tell me the facts of life . . . ," cartoon by Joseph Farris on p. 83. Copyright © 1971 by Saturday Review, Inc. Reproduced also by permission of the artist; excerpts from bibliographical essay "Everything You Wanted to Know . . ." by David Glixon. Copyright © 1971 Saturday Review, Inc. Reprinted also by permission of the author;

"I distinctly ordered a *reclining* nude," cartoon by Paul Peter Porges on p. 75. Copyright © 1971 Saturday Review, Inc. Reproduced also by permission of the artist;

Quiz and answers entitled "Your Literary I.Q.: Their Majesties" by David Glixon. Copyright © 1971 Saturday Review, Inc. Reprinted also by permission of the author.

GARY SNYDER, *for:* 8 lines from *Cold Mountain Poems*, reprinted in *What the Trees Said*, by Stephen Diamond (Delacorte, 1971).

SOMETHING ELSE PRESS, INC., *for:* "Olho por olho" by Harold de Campos (on p. 208), from *An Anthology of Concrete Poetry*, ed. by Emmett Williams. Copyright © 1967 by Something Else Press, Inc. All rights reserved. Reprinted by permission of the publisher.

UNIVERSITY OF TORONTO PRESS, *for:* Photograph on p. 38 by Jean Roubier of Rock Fortress of Rocsaliere, West Wall of the Druid Temple, from *The Art of Roman Gaul* by Marcel Pobe. Copyright 1961. Reproduced also by permission of J. M. Dent & Sons Ltd.

ROMAN VISHNIAC, *for:* Photograph of crouching child from *Family of Man*.

WIDE WORLD PHOTOS, INC., *for:* 12 photographs, 1 each of Frederick Douglass (p. 44), Albert Einstein (p. 119), George McGovern (p. 209), W. J. Fulbright (p. 209), Shirley Chisholm (p. 209), Barry Goldwater (p. 209), and Wilbur Mills (p. 209); and 5 of Richard Nixon (p. 205).

WIEN NATURHISTORISCHES MUSEUM, *for:* Photograph of statue, "Venus of Willendorf." Copyright, all rights reserved, by Prahistorische Abteilung Naturhistorisches Museum, Wien.

CONTENTS

Preface xi

Chapter 1   Ideas, Catalysts, Strategies..................................... 1

Choosing and Limiting a Topic 3

Research Ideas

    1. Abortion 4
    2. Optical Illusions 6
    3. Black Hate, White Images 8
    4. Richard Daley: Chicago 10
    5. The Sexual Origins of Religion 12
    6. Victimology 14
    7. Neanderthals Rediscovered 16

Chapter 2   Amazing Library: Quizzes, Puzzles, Dilemmas................. 18

Exploring Resources

    1. Did You Kill Him "in Your God Damned Brooks Brothers Suit"?—
        Biographical Sources 20
    2. "Rend Us Asunder," *Playboy*—Government Publications and
        News Sources 22
    3. Why Are Suicides in Trees?—A Problem in Anthropology and Myth 24
    4. Your Literary I.Q.—Fiction 25
    5. Three Quizzes, Sydney Harris—Wordbooks and Factbooks 27
    6. Rinky Dinky—Rhyming Dictionaries 28
    7. Bottom of the Barrel—Miscellany: You're on Your Own 29

Chapter 3   Fruit of the Tree: Tools of Inquiry............................ 30

Research Steps: A Guide to the Use of Tools Discussed in This Chapter/
Compiling the Preliminary Bibliography 32

How to Evaluate Sources 34

How to Find Material Not in Your Library 35

General Reference Tools 36
   1. Information Desk 37
   2. Encyclopedias 39
   3. Yearbooks 40
   4. Specialized Reference Works (see also pages 70–126) 40
   5. Dictionaries 41
   6. Wordbooks 42
   7. Quotations 43
   8. Factbooks 44
   9. Atlases 47
  10. Bibliographies of Bibliography 48
  11. Guides to Reference Works 49
  12. Bibliographies 49
  13. Card Catalog: The Key to the Library 57
     13.1. Principles of Alphabetizing 59
     13.2. The Dewey Decimal System 60
     13.3. Card Catalog as Subject Bibliography 62
  14. Indexes 64
     14.1. Periodical Indexes 64
     14.2. Pamphlet Indexes 65
     14.3. Essay Index 65
     14.4. Newspaper Indexes 65
     14.5. Book Review Indexes 66
     14.6. Biography Index 67
  15. Government Publications 67
Specialized Reference Works 70
   American Indians 72
   Anthropology 73
   Art 75
   Astronomy 77
   Black Studies
     Afro-American Studies 78
     African Studies 81
   Business 83
   Drug Use 84
   Ecology 86
   Economics 88
   Education 89
   History 91
   Literature
     Genre 93
     British and American 95
     World 97

Chapter 3 *(continued)*

Mass Media 98
Mathematics 100
Music 101
Mythology and Folklore 104
Performing Arts 105
Philosophy 107
Political Science 108
Psychology 110
Recreation and Physical Education 112
Religion 114
Science
   General Science 116
   Biological Science 118
   Physical Science 119
Social Science (General) 120
Sociology 121
Speech 124
Women's Liberation 125

Chapter 4 A Paper before the Paper 128

Pre-Writing Procedures 130
   Scrambled Note Cards 135
   Scrambled Outline 143
Model Outline 145
Model Paper 148

Chapter 5 A Paper of Your Own 170

The Intellectual Process 172
   Conceptualizing from Data: The Emergence of Thesis 172
   The Process of Classification 174
   Fleshing Out the Frame 174
   The Essence of Clarity 176
   Analysis 177
   Unity 178
On the Nature of Plagiarism 179
Documentation: Acknowledging Sources 180
   Numbering and Spacing Footnotes 181
   Abbreviations in Footnoting 181
   Citing Dates 182
   Data Sequence 183
   Short Forms 186
   Differences Between Footnote and Bibliographical Citations .. 187
Documentation Models 188
   Books 188
   Reference Works 197

Chapter 5 *(continued)*

    Periodicals 199
    Newspapers 202
    Government Documents 204
    Miscellaneous Materials 215
Matters of Style 219
    Numerals 219
    Hyphenation 220
    Titles 220
    Italicizing 221
    Plurals 221
    Quotations 222
    The Ten Commandments of Grammar 223
    The Logic of Misspelling 226
    The Necessity for Proofreading 227

Index 229

PREFACE

Every teacher who has ever assigned a research paper—and every student who has ever written one—will probably feel this book is attempting the impossible: vitalizing research processes. For most students, research involves using the card catalog and *Readers' Guide to Periodical Literature*, then finding three or four sources and partially copying from all of them in random sequence. I feel something else is possible: passionate thought, excitement of the quest, creative synthesis, and responsible acknowledgment.

An underlying assumption of this book is that thought precedes writing, and involvement precedes thought. Thus the text opens with "Ideas, Catalysts, Strategies"—clusters of pictures, poems, quotations, and sources designed to attract the eye and stimulate the mind. As I do not think ideas are usually engendered by prescribed assignments, the catalytic materials are suggestive and germinal rather than sharply delimited.

For some students, the germinal ideas may suggest questions to be answered or arguments to be defended or denied. In the research paper, the answers, the defense, or the refutation come from some portion of the accumulated store of human knowledge. The library is the storeroom, and bibliographical tools are the key. This book presents a wide range of tools from bibliographies of bibliography and periodical indexes to specialized reference works in selected fields. The tools are described and illustrated; and running through the collection is a persistent research motif. Instead of illustrating reference works with random entries, whenever possible I have traced one sustained subject: Druids. Why Druids? Why not water pollution or urban decay, student unrest, or the plight of the poor? Perhaps because I feel the mind needs momentary rest from the impact of the present. In part because Druids as a subject seems remote, esoteric, and narrow. This is the kind of subject about which students complain: But I can't find any material. Hopefully, Chapter 3 demonstrates that sophisticated use of the library can yield too much information, not too little; and that in the research quest, numerous possibilities for narrowing a subject emerge. Along with this, Chapter 3 yields the "Fruit of the Tree," the object of the search: the emergent Druid in poetry, history, and art.

When materials are accumulated, they must be systematized and integrated. This Guide provides students with a first-hand experience in these processes: the actual sorting and arranging of note cards. From the groups and subgroups of note cards, outline divisions—the intellectual skeletal structure of the paper—grow. Again, the student has a chance to manipulate components of the paper by arranging scrambled outline segments. Learning here is not purely theoretical; it is involved in doing. The model paper that follows incorporates the note card material and outline structure the student has already worked with. He is able to experience a preliminary paper in all stages of development: research, notetaking, ordering of material, and the ultimate integration of sources into a thematically coherent whole. For some, the model paper may have interest as more than a model because the paper is an account of communal life style and a handbook for entering or founding a commune of one's own. In a time of high unemployment, a guide to survival outside the establishment may have an intrinsic value.

Creative research is at least in part personal synthesis of the knowledge and thoughts of others; responsible research is acknowledgment of indebtedness. Acknowledgment is not only courtesy and honesty but potential power; the documented statement is a weapon while the undocumented may be a lie. This book attempts to provide clear examples of as many documentation patterns as space allows. Although no collection of models can cover every conceivable arrangement of data, the data sequence charts coupled with possible combinations of models will provide for the handling of most documentation situations. Documentation models and format recommendations reflect principles established in the widely accepted second edition of *The MLA Style Sheet*.

Hopefully, this is a book to excite interest, develop skill, and provide a collection of research tools that can be used by all students. If the book fulfills any of these hopes, credit must be shared with my editor, Marie Enders. Her consistent support, untiring attention to detail, and keen eye for ambiguity and inconsistency strengthened the manuscript. For visually implementing my belief that a research guide need not be dull and unappealing, my special thanks to designers Bill O'Donnell and Larry Layton.

Helene D. Hutchinson

THE HUTCHINSON GUIDE TO
WRITING RESEARCH PAPERS

Chapter 1

Ideas, Catalysts, Strategies

CHOOSING AND LIMITING A TOPIC

Here are some research ideas for the student who always asks: What shall I write about? If any interest you, frame a topic of your own and define an angle of approach. The angle of approach is the perspective from which the material is viewed. What you look for and what you see depend entirely upon your angle of vision:

The Ostrich has a longer neck and smaller mouth than his.

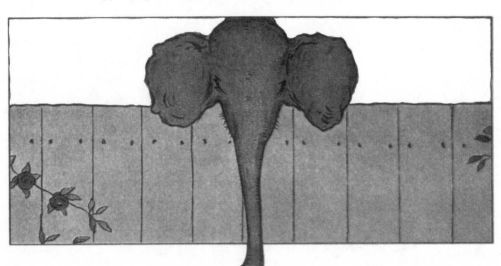

The Elephant leans o'er the fence and wonders why it is

Sometimes you can zero in on a small unit of material, for instance, Mrs. Daley's attempts to ban Mike Royko's critical book about her husband (page 10). You can narrow your range to a study of targets of Black rage in the poetry of Ted Joans (page 8), or study several Black plays looking for Black hatred of white images of goodness: purity, innocence, truth, Santa Claus, even God.

You can approach your material chronologically or thematically, analytically or critically, by genre or by period, by author or by style. You can focus on causes or consequences, problems or solutions, similarities or differences.

Once you have defined your angle of approach, you are ready to begin; and you won't waste time taking notes on superfluous material.

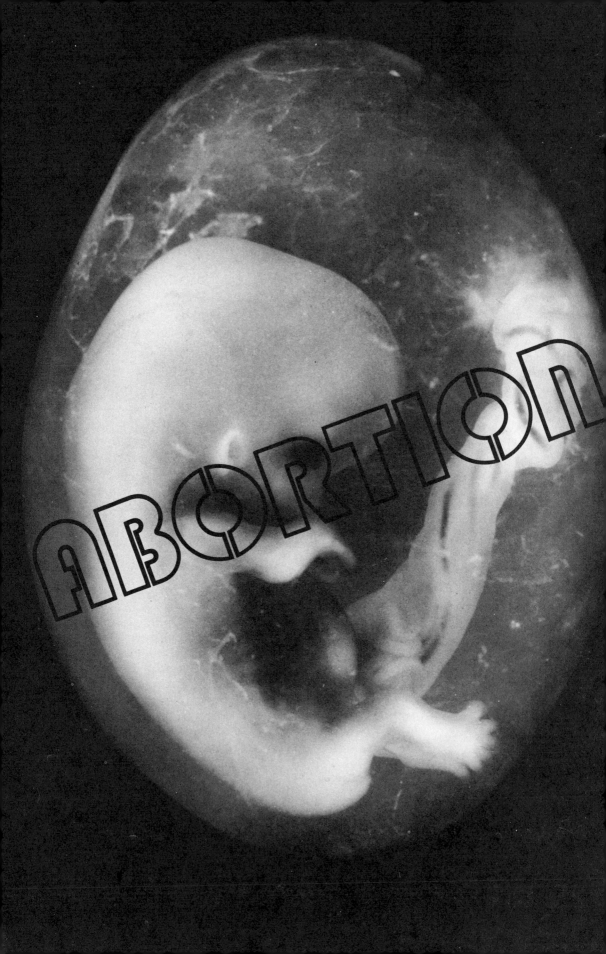

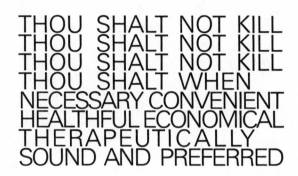

THOU SHALT NOT KILL
THOU SHALT NOT KILL
THOU SHALT NOT KILL
THOU SHALT WHEN
NECESSARY CONVENIENT
HEALTHFUL ECONOMICAL
THERAPEUTICALLY
SOUND AND PREFERRED

Bibliography

Dollen, Charles J., comp. *Abortion in Context: A Select Bibliography*. Metuchen, N.J.: Scarecrow, 1970.

Ebon, Martin, ed. *Every Woman's Guide to Abortion*. New York: Simon & Schuster, 1971.

Ehrlich, Paul R., and John P. Holdren. "Abortion and Morality." *Saturday Review*, 4 Sept., 1971, p. 58.

Granfield, David. *Abortion Decision*. Garden City, N.Y.: Doubleday, 1969.

Grisez, Germain. *Abortion: The Myths, the Realities, and the Arguments*. New York: World, 1970.

Group for the Advancement of Psychiatry. *Right to Abortion: A Psychiatric View*. New York: Scribner's, 1970.

Hall, Robert E., ed. *Abortion in a Changing World*. 2 vols. New York: Columbia University Press, 1970.

Noonan, John T., Jr., ed. *Morality of Abortion: Legal and Historical Perspectives*. Cambridge: Harvard University Press, 1970.

Sloane, Bruce R., ed. *Abortion: Changing Views and Practice*. New York: Grune & Stratton, 1971.

Who Shall Live: Man's Control over Birth and Death. New York: Hill & Wang, 1970.

Williams, Glanville. *Sanctity of Life and the Criminal Law*. New York: Knopf, 1957.

OPTICAL ILLUSIONS

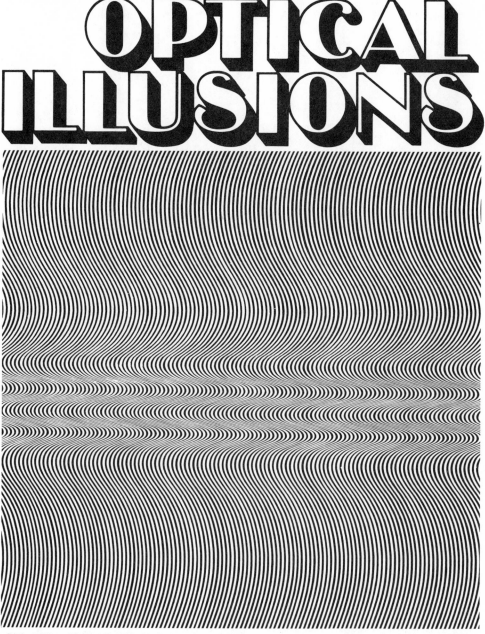

Bridget Riley, "Current." 1964. Synthetic polymer paint on composition board, 58⅜ x 58⅞". Collection, The Museum of Modern Art, New York. Philip Johnson Fund.

THINGS ARE NOT ALWAYS WHAT THEY SEEM TO BE.—W. S. GILBERT

RICKS OF THE EYE/HOW & WHY?

Tom and Ed were angry with each other.
Place your nose on the center circle.
They will embrace each other.

Zollner's illusion of direction
"Long parallel lines appear to diverge in the direction that the crossing lines converge." In this figure, "there are two illusions of direction. The parallel vertical strips appear un-parallel and the right and left portions of the oblique cross-lines appear to be shifted vertically...steady fixation diminishes and even destroys the illusion...hold the figure so that the broad parallel lines are vertical. The illusion is very pronounced in this position; however on tilting the page backward the illusion finally disappears."—Luckiesh[*]

Illustrating fluctuation of attention
This figure "consists of identical patterns in black and white. By gazing upon this steadily it will appear to fluctuate in appearance from a white pattern upon a black background to a black pattern upon a white background. Sometimes fluctuation of attention apparently accounts for the change and... this can be tested by willfully altering the attention from a white pattern to a black one."
—Luckiesh[*]

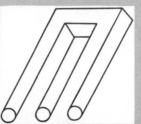

Is this an optical illusion or a trick? How does it work?

[*]From *Visual Illusions* by M. Luckiesh, Dover Publications, Inc., New York, 1965. Reprinted through permission of the publisher.

Bibliography

Brindley, G. S. "Afterimages." *Scientific American*, 209 (Oct. 1963), 84–93.

Compton, Michael. *Optical and Kinetic Art*. London: Tate Gallery, 1967.

Froman, Robert. *Science, Art, and Visual Illusions*. New York: Simon & Schuster, 1970.

Gregory, Richard L. *Eye and Brain: The Psychology of Seeing*. New York: McGraw-Hill, 1966.

Gregory, Richard L. "Visual Illusions." *Scientific American*, 219 (Nov. 1968), 66–76.

Luckiesh, Matthew. *Visual Illusions: Their Causes, Characteristics, and Applications*. New York: Dover, 1965.

Parola, Rene. *Optical Art: Theory and Practice*. New York: Van Nostrand Reinhold, 1969.

Seitz, William C. *The Responsive Eye*. New York: Museum of Modern Art, 1965. (Reproductions of op art.)

Thurston, Jacqueline, and Ronald J. Carraher. *Optical Illusions and the Visual Arts*. New York: Van Nostrand Reinhold, 1966.

BLACK HATE

GOD IS WHITE
SANTA CLAUS IS WHITE
LILIES ARE WHITE
AND THE NEW FALLEN
SNOW IS WHITE
ALONG WITH VIRTUE, PURITY
AND THE ROBES OF ANGELS.

WHITE IMAGES

SANTA CLAWS
Ted Joans

If that white Mother Hubbard comes down my black
    chimney dragging his playful bag
If that red suited faggot starts ho ho hoing on my
    rooftop
If that old fat cracker creeps into my house
If that antique reindeer raper races across my lawn
If that old time nigger knocker fills my wife's stocking
If that haint who thinks he's a saint
Comes sled flying across my home
If that old con man comes on with his toyful jive
If that over stuffed gut busting gangster
    shows up tonight
He and me show gonna have a battling Xmas and it show
    aint gonna be white!

Bibliography

Black Theatre. New York: New Lafayette Theatre, 1969—. (Order from New Lafayette Theatre, Room 103, 200 West 135th St., New York, N.Y. 10030. $2.50 for six issues.)

Chapman, Abraham. *Black Voices: An Anthology of Afro-American Literature*. New York: New American Library, 1968.

Coombs, Orde. *We Speak as Liberators: Young Black Poets*. New York: Dodd, Mead, 1970.

Dover, Cedric. *American Negro Art*. Greenwich, Conn.: New York Graphic Society, 1970.

The Drama Review: Black Theatre, 12 (Summer 1968). (Order from the School of Art, New York University, Publications Office, 32 Washington Place, New York, N.Y. 10003.)

Grier, William H., and Price M. Cobbs. *Black Rage*. New York: Basic Books, 1968.

Joans, Ted. *Black Pow-Wow*. New York: Hill & Wang, 1969.

Jones, LeRoi, and Larry Neal. *Black Fire: An Anthology of Afro-American Writing*. New York: Morrow, 1968.

Journal of Black Poetry. San Francisco, Calif.: Journal of Black Poetry, 1968—. (For subscription, write 922-B Haight St., San Francisco, Calif. 94117. $5.00 per year.)

Nkombo. New Orleans, La.: Nkombo, 1969—. (Poetry, short stories, theatre. For subscription, write P.O. Box 51826, New Orleans, La. 70151. $4.00 yearly.)

Randall, Dudley. *The Black Poets*. New York: Bantam, 1971.

RICHARD DALEY
CHICAGO

R	*YOU'RE RARE*
I	*YOU'RE IMPORTANT*
C	*YOU'RE COURAGEOUS*
H	*YOU'RE HEAVENLY*
A	*YOU'RE ABLE*
R	*YOU'RE RENOWNED*
D	*YOU'RE DILIGENT*
D	*YOU'RE DEMOCRATIC*
A	*YOU'RE ADORABLE*
L	*YOU'RE LOYAL*
E	*YOU'RE ENERGETIC*
Y	*YOU'RE YOUTHFUL*
R	*YOU'RE RARE*
I	*YOU'RE IMPORTANT*
C	*YOU'RE COURAGEOUS*
H	*YOU'RE HEAVENLY*
A	*YOU'RE ABLE*
R	*YOU'RE RENOWNED*
D	*YOU'RE DILIGENT*
D	*YOU'RE DEMOCRATIC*
A	*YOU'RE ADORABLE*
L	*YOU'RE LOYAL*
E	*YOU'RE ENERGETIC*
Y	*YOU'RE YOUTHFUL*

*—A Tribute to His Honor,
by a Ward Committeeman.*

Bibliography

"Daley's Revenge." *Nation*, 7 April 1969, p. 420.

"Democrats Against Daley." *Time*, 21 Feb. 1969, pp. 19–20.

Gleason, William F. *Daley and Chicago: The Man, the Mayor, and the Limits of Power*. New York: Simon & Schuster, 1970.

Gosnell, Harold F. *Machine Politics: Chicago Model*. 2nd ed. Chicago: University of Chicago Press, 1968.

"Mangled Machine." *Time*, 3 April 1972, p. 14.

Royko, Mike. *Boss: Richard J. Daley of Chicago*. New York: Dutton, 1971.

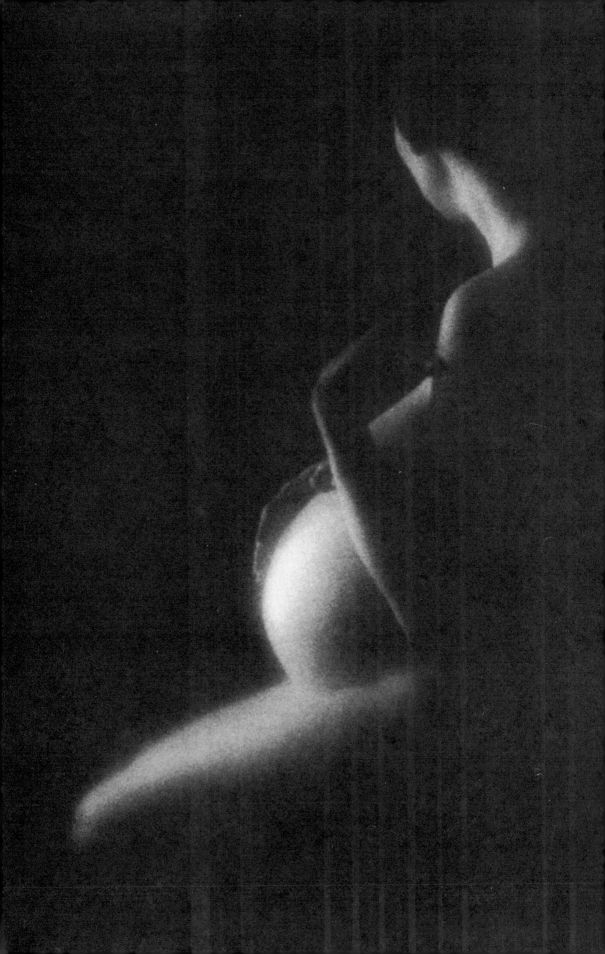

THE
SEXUAL ORIGINS OF RELIGION

EVERY MAJOR RELIGION
SPRINGS FROM SEXUAL
ORIGINS...THERE'S A PAR-
TICULAR SEX FORMATION
THAT UNFOLDS INTO THE
RITUAL AND DOGMA AND
FINALLY THE BELIEF OF
EVERY RELIGION.—NIETZSCHE

Bibliography

Frazer, Sir James. *The Golden Bough*. London: Macmillan, 1955.

Freud, Sigmund. *Moses and Monotheism*. New York: Random House, 1955.

Freud, Sigmund. *Totem and Taboo*. New York: Norton, 1950.

Freud, Sigmund, and Oskar Pfister. *Psychoanalysis and Faith*. New York: Bantam, 1971.

Fromm, Erich. *The Dogma of Christ and Other Essays on Religion, Psychology and Culture*. New York: Holt, Rinehart & Winston, 1963.

Fromm, Erich. *Psychology and Religion*. New Haven: Yale University Press, 1950.

Is the Victim Guilty?
After the slaying of Robert Kennedy, University of Houston Psychologist Richard Evans characterized the Kennedys as "victims in search of assassins." Evans' concept—that victims often invite and help to shape crimes—was not widely held three years ago. Now it is established as a new discipline known as "victimology."
—*Time,* July 5, 1971, p. 42

VICTIMOLOGY

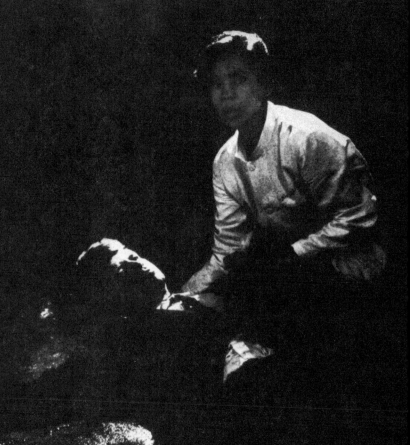

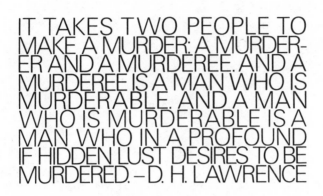

IT TAKES TWO PEOPLE TO MAKE A MURDER: A MURDER-ER AND A MURDEREE. AND A MURDEREE IS A MAN WHO IS MURDERABLE. AND A MAN WHO IS MURDERABLE IS A MAN WHO IN A PROFOUND IF HIDDEN LUST DESIRES TO BE MURDERED. — D. H. LAWRENCE

Bibliography

Fattah, Ezzat Abdel. "Towards a Criminological Classification of Victims." *International Journal of Criminal Police*, 22 (1967), 162–69.

Fattah, Ezzat Abdel. *The Victim—Is He Guilty? The Role of the Victim in Attempted Robbery-Murder Cases*. Montreal: University of Montreal, 1971.

"Is the Victim Guilty?" *Time*, 5 July 1971, p. 42.

Schafer, Stephen. *Victim and His Criminal: A Study in Functional Responsibility*. New York: Random House, 1970.

Von Hentig, Hans. *Criminal and His Victim: Studies in the Sociobiology of Crime*. Hamden, Conn.: Shoe String Press, 1967.

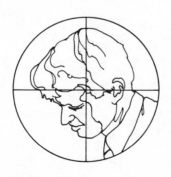

Neanderthals Rediscovered

THE OCCURRENCE
OF FLOWERS WITH
NEANDERTHAL
BURIAL RAISES
THE QUESTION,
WHERE ELSE IN
PRE-HISTORY IS
THERE ANY PARAL-
LEL?–R. S. SOLECKI

Bibliography

Jelinek, Jan. "Neanderthal Man and *Homo Sapiens* in Eastern and Central Europe." *Current Anthropology*, 10, No. 5 (1969), 475–503.

Hooton, Ernest Albert. *Up from the Ape*. New York: Macmillan, 1946.

Solecki, Ralph S. *Shanidar: The First Flower People*. New York: Knopf, 1971.

"Upgrading Neanderthal Man." *Time*, 17 May 1971, pp. 75–76.

Peter Max.

Chapter 2

AMAZING LIBRARY

Quizzes Puzzles Dilemmas

in

out

Peter Max.

Zing along with a colored felt-tip pen to get out of this maze. Swirl around in cosmic thought currents in this cloud head! Feel free in choosing colors—you can't go wrong!

Did you kill him"in your God damned Brooks Brothers su

This is a problem in exploration of the biographical literary resources of your library. Rexroth argues that forces in our civilization either literally kill young, creative people or kill their souls. Dividing the names among the class, support or disprove Rexroth's accusation. How was each artist's work received? Did he pursue it all his life? How did he die? "The sparrow of Cardiff," "the canary of Swansea," by the way, is Dylan Thomas, Welsh poet.

For biographical help, consult Kunitz's books in the Literature section of specialized reference works in Chapter 3 (pages 93–98). See also *Dictionary of American Biography*, *Dictionary of National Biography* (British), *International Who's Who*, *Current Biography*, *Who's Who*, *Who Was Who in America*, and *Who's Who in the World*.

If a particular artist interests you, consider exploring the reasons for his death or disintegration.

THOU SHALT NOT KILL: A MEMORIAL FOR DYLAN THOMAS

Kenneth Rexroth

I.

They are murdering all the young men.
For half a century now, every day.
They have hunted them down and killed
    them.
They are killing them now.
At this minute, all over the world,
They are killing the young men.
They know ten thousand ways to kill them.
Every year they invent new ones.
In the jungles of Africa,
In the marshes of Asia,
In the deserts of Asia . . .
In the slums of Europe,
In the nightclubs of America,
The murderers are at work.

. . . .

You are the murderer.
You are killing the young men.
You are broiling Lawrence on his gridiron.
When you demanded he divulge
The hidden treasures of the spirit,
He showed you the poor.
You set your heart against him.
You seized him and bound him with rage.
You roasted him on a slow fire.

. . . .

You,
The hyena with polished face and bow tie,
In the office of a billion dollar
Corporation devoted to service;
The vulture dripping with carrion,
Carefully and carelessly robed in imported
    tweeds,

Lecturing on the Age of Abundance;

. . . .

You,
The finger man of behemoth,
The murderer of the young men.

II.

What happened to Robinson,
Who used to stagger down Eighth Street,
Dizzy with solitary gin?
Where is Masters, who crouched in
His law office for ruinous decades?
Where is Leonard who thought he was
A locomotive? And Lindsay,
Wise as a dove, innocent
As a serpent, where is he?

. . . .

John Gould Fletcher who could not
Unbreak his powerful heart?
Bodenheim butchered in stinking
Squalor? Edna Millay who had
Her last straight whiskey? Genevieve
Who loved so much; where is she?
    Timor mortis conturbat me.

. . . .

Where is Sol Funaroff?
What happened to Potamkin?
Isidor Schneider? Claude McKay?
Countee Cullen? Lowenfels?
Who animates their corpses today?
    Timor mortis conturbat me.

. . . .

III.

How many stopped writing at thirty?
How many went to work for Time?

. . . .

How many, on the advice of
Their psychoanalysts, decided
A business career was best after all?
How many are hopeless alcoholics?
Rene Crevel!
Jacques Ricgaut!
Antonin Artaud!
Mayakofsky!
Essenin!
Reobert Desnos!
Saint Pol Roux!
Max Jacob!
All over the world
The same disembodied hand
Strikes us down.

. . . .

IV.

He is dead.
The bird of Rhiannon.

He is dead.
In the winter of the heart.

. . . .

He is dead.
The sparrow of Cardiff.
He is dead.
The canary of Swansea.
Who killled him?
Who killed the bright-headed bird?
You did, you son of a bitch.
You drowned him in your cocktail brain.
He fell down and died in your synthetic
    heart.

. . . .

You killed him,
Benign Lady on the postage stamp.
He was found dead at a liberal weekly
    luncheon.
He was found dead on the cutting room
    floor.
He was found dead at a Time policy
    conference.
Henry Luce killed him with a telegram to
    the pope.
Mademoiselle strangled him with a padded
    brassiere.

. . . .

In your lonely crowd you swept over him.
Your custom built brogans and your ballet
    slippers
Pummelled him to death in the gritty street.

. . . .

I want to burn down your editorial offices.
I want to slit the bellies of your frigid
    women.
I want to sink your sailboats and launches.
I want to strangle your children at their
    finger paintings.
I want to poison your Afghans and poodles.
He is dead, the little drunken cherub.
He is dead,
The effulgent tub thumper.

. . . .

There he lies dead,
By the Iceberg of the United Nations.
There he lies sandbagged,
At the foot of the Statue of Liberty.
The Gulf stream smells of blood
As it breaks on the sands of Iona
And the blue rocks of Canarvon.
And all the birds of the deep sea rise up
Over the luxury liners and scream,
"You killed him! You kill him.
In your God damned Brooks Brothers suit,
You son of a bitch."

Using government publications and news sources, find statements of public figures that are as divisive as these. Find statements made by people already appearing in our collection, or add new "offenders" to the list. For government figures, check *Congressional Record*, House and Senate *Journals*, and *Federal Register*. Also check Alan and Jason Pater's *What They Said in 197—: The Yearbook of Spoken Opinion*. See the *New York Times Index, Facts on File, Readers' Guide to Periodical Literature*, and *Vital Speeches*.

If this investigation interests you, think about a paper dealing with politicians' alienation of the young. Some of your data is here.

a sampler of heart-warming sentiments . . .

"You see these bums, you know, blowing up the campuses. Listen, the boys that are on the college campuses today are the luckiest people in the world, going to the greatest universities, and here they are burning up the books, storming around about this issue. You name it. Get rid of the war, there will be another one."

Richard Nixon

"Look at democracy objectively. How does an aspirant for office oust an incumbent? By selling himself and his ideas? To a degree, yes; but that is seldom enough. He must attack the policies of his opponent; as he does, people will side with one candidate or the other. Divisive? Of course—but by dividing, we conquer apathy."

Spiro Agnew

"There is much talk about alienation among our nation's youth, but little discussion of what incites alienation. Here we are discussing what is essentially a psychological state, a decision by the emotions to reject the values of society. This rejection is caused not by events nor by the action of our older generation but by a poisoning of the mood of our youth by constant neurotic attacks on their emotions."

Strom Thurmond

"I'll tell you who's not informed, though. It's these stupid kids. . . . They pick the rhetoric that they want to hear right off the top of an issue and never finish reading to the bottom. . . . And the professors are just as bad if not worse. They don't know anything. Nor do these stupid bastards who are ruining our educational institutions."

John Mitchell

"It is time to rip away the rhetoric and to divide on authentic lines. It is time to discard the fiction that in a country of 200,000,000 people, everyone is qualified to quarterback the Government."

Spiro Agnew

Rend Us Asunder

"[Campus militants are] part and parcel of the revolution. . . . If it takes a blood bath, let's get it over with. No more appeasement."

Ronald Reagan

"Any time you get somebody marching in the streets, it's catering to revolution. My family worked for everything we had. . . . Now these jerks come along and try to give it to the Communists. I want you to crucify Fulbright."

Martha Mitchell

"Some of the radical groups in the country are being led by so-called clergymen. Where many of these men get the 'reverend' in front of their names, I do not know. Certainly, they don't get it from God."

Billy Graham

"We can, however, afford to separate [the student radicals] from our society—with no more regret than we should feel for discarding rotten apples from a barrel."

Spiro Agnew

"If . . . any group was organized on a national basis to subvert our society, then I think Congress should pass laws to suppress that activity. . . . If people demonstrated in a manner to interfere with others, they should be rounded up and put in a detention camp."

Richard Kleindienst

"Make no mistake. This radicalism that infects our Congress *and* poisons our country is at best a bizarre mutation of Democratic liberalism."

Spiro Agnew

"[It] is amazing what [Agnew] has done to help the [news] media—helping it to reform itself. . . . You can't underestimate the power of fear."

Tricia Nixon

On academicians: "It makes me sick at my stomach. They're a bunch of sidewalk diplomats that don't know the score."

Martha Mitchell

"Is this any way to run a country?"

Lawrence O'Brien

Why are suicides in trees? *A problem in anthropology and myth*

Why were suicides put in trees in pre-Renaissance Italy? Why are they, today, put in trees on an island in the Arabian Sea? Is there a link between the two locations? Are there other cultures that associate suicides with trees?

If you unearth enough material and are interested, you might expand this library problem into a research project.

INFERNO
CANTO XIII

CIRCLE SEVEN: *Round Two* | *The Violent Against Themselves*

THE LIVING TOMB OF THE SUICIDES
Sokotra, Arabian Sea

A GAMHEM TREE WHICH STILL FLOURISHES ALTHOUGH ITS TRUNK HAS BEEN HOLLOWED OUT AS A COFFIN **3 TIMES IN 332 YEARS!**

THE ISLAND'S SUICIDES ARE ALWAYS BURIED IN THE TREE - BUT ITS SPONGY WOOD QUICKLY HEALS OVER

Nessus carries the Poets across the river of boiling blood and leaves them in the Second Round of the Seventh Circle, THE WOOD OF THE SUICIDES. Here are punished those who destroyed their own lives and those who destroyed their substance.

The souls of the Suicides are encased in thorny trees whose leaves are eaten by the odious HARPIES, the overseers of these damned. When the Harpies feed upon them, damaging their leaves and limbs, the wound bleeds. Only as long as the blood flows are the souls of the trees able to speak. Thus, they who destroyed their own bodies are denied a human form; and just as the supreme expression of their lives was self-destruction, so they are permitted to speak only through that which tears and destroys them. Only through their own blood do they find a voice. And to add one more dimension to the symbolism, it is the Harpies—defilers of all they touch—who give them their eternally recurring wounds.

I heard cries of lamentation rise and spill
  on every hand, but saw no souls in pain
  in all that waste; and, puzzled, I stood still.

I think perhaps he thought that I was thinking
  those cries rose from among the twisted roots
  through which the spirits of the damned were
    slinking

to hide from us. Therefore my Master said:
  "If you break off a twig, what you will learn
  will drive what you are thinking from your head."

Puzzled, I raised my hand a bit and slowly
  broke off a branchlet from an enormous thorn:
  and the great trunk of it cried: "Why do you break me?"

And after blood had darkened all the bowl
of the wound, it cried again: "Why do you tear me?
Is there no pity left in any soul?

Men we were, and now we are changed to sticks;
well might your hand have been more merciful
were we no more than souls of lice and ticks."

—Dante Alighieri,
The Divine Comedy

YOUR LITERARY I.Q.

To make headway with these, you need indexes of fictional characters, dictionaries of proper names, such as the *New Century Cyclopedia of Names*, and either a good reading background or *Masterplots*.

YOUR LITERARY I.Q.
Conducted by David M. Glixon
THEIR MAJESTIES

You are requested by Anne McCaughey of Philadelphia to figure out to which sovereign each of these characters owed allegiance, and according to which author.

1. Constance Baynes ( )	A. Alexander I	a. Bennett
2. Eugene Bazarov ( )	B. Alexander II	b. Cervantes
3. Pierre Bezuhov ( )	C. Charles I	c. Dickens
4. Hans Castorp ( )	D. Charles X	d. Dumas
5. D'Artagnan ( )	E. George II	e. Hugo
6. Quasimodo ( )	F. George III	f. Mann
7. Rowena ( )	G. George IV	g. Scott
8. Becky Sharp ( )	H. Louis XI	h. Stendhal
9. Julien Sorel ( )	I. Louis XIII	i. Sterne
10. Dulcinea del Toboso ( )	J. Richard I	j. Thackeray
11. Uncle Toby ( )	K. Victoria	k. Tolstoy
12. Tracy Tupman ( )	L. William II	l. Turgenev

HOME MADE HINTS ABOUT BOOKS OR PLAYS
Name the book or play.

1. Emma Rouault marries a dull doctor.

2. Can Carol Kennicott bring culture to Gopher Prairie, Minnesota?

3. He and Mattie decide on suicide and they crash their sled into a tree.

4. Lieutenant Frederic Henry is in the Italian Army Ambulance Corps in World War I when he meets a nurse.

5. The dreams of Humphrey Chimpden Earwicker who runs a Dublin public house.

6. Robert Jordan is an American fighting for the Spanish Loyalists.

7. The reporter Hildy Johnson conceals the murderer in a desk.

8. Raskolnikov plans to murder an old female pawnbroker.

9. Uriah Heep is outsmarted by Mr. Micawber.

10. He leaves Linda, Happy and Biff just after the last payment on the house.

11. A Norwegian settler, Per Hansa, toils the earth of South Dakota.

12. Laura collects old phonograph records and glass animals.

13. Eighty years old, he lives at Mrs. Wickett's across from Brookfield school in England.

14. Wang Lung takes Lotus, a former prostitute, as his second wife.

15. Tom Joad travels west.

16. Pip is influenced by Miss Havisham who was jilted on her wedding night.

17. Daisy drives Jay's car and kills her husband's mistress.

18. "He" becomes a clown.

19. A shop foreman from Bridgeport goes back in time to the Round Table.

20. Mrs. Rochester is locked up in the upper part of the house.

21. The immigrant Rudkus works in the slaughterhouses of Chicago.

22. "Captain" Jack and Joxer are regulars in the Dublin pubs.

23. Wolf Larson is captain of the "Ghost."

24. After an illegitimate child with Vronsky she throws herself in front of a train.

25. Fix follows Fogg.

26. An American expatriate in Paris writes the autobiography of her secretary and companion.

27. The high-powered go-getter realtor salesman from Zenith and his Good Citizens' League.

28. Polly Peachum and Lucy Lockit love the highwayman Macheath.

29. Tyltyl and Mytyl start searching and are joined by Fire, Bread and Milk.

30. July, 1714. Brother Juniper sees the bridge collapse in Peru.

Three Quizzes by Sydney Harris

Wordbooks and factbooks will get you through these. See if your library has *Brewer's Dictionary of Phrase and Fable* or Ackerman's *Popular Fallacies* which might help with Harris's "simpler quiz."

TIMEWORN PHRASES FOR QUIZ FANS

Today's subject is going to be popular phrases and sayings. If you can answer half the questions, you're entitled to preen.

1. Was anyone actually reputed to have been "killed by kindness"?
2. What is meant by someone "of the same kidney"?
3. Why do we speak of "the acid test" for something?
4. What, in actual terms, is a "battle royal"?
5. How did a "moot point" get its name?
6. What is the origin of the phrases, "Let the cat out of the bag" and "buy a pig in a poke"?
7. What did it originally mean to get off "scot free"?
8. Why do we refer to something as done "in the nick of time"?
9. Can even an experienced sailor explain why a temporary rigging on a ship is called a "jury-rig"?
10. What is the historical incident behind the phrase, "to leave no stone unturned"?

A CHALLENGE TO TRUE DOG LOVERS

Here is a quiz, more or less literary, all about dogs and canine expressions. You must get half the questions right to become a Certified Dog Lover.

1. What is "a dog in a doublet"?
2. Where is the expression to be found "A living dog is better than a dead lion"?
3. Identify the lines: "I am His Highness' dog at Kew; pray, tell me, sir, whose dog are you"?
4. Who was Aubry's dog?
5. What dog do the Moslems admit to heaven?
6. Give the names of the famous dogs who belonged to (a) Lord Byron, (b) Ulysses, (c) Prince Rupert, (d) Isaac Newton, (e) Punch.
7. What philosopher surnamed himself "the dog"?
8. Why are days of intense heat called "dog days"?
9. What do the British mean by a "dogsbody"?
10. Why are the evening watches aboard ship called "dogwatches"?
11. What do the Canary Islands have to do with dogs?
12. Why is the common wild rose also called "dog rose"?

Don't just answer "true" or "false"! Verify your answer.

A "SIMPLER" HARRIS QUIZ

1. Canute, the Danish king of England, once commanded the tides to stand still as evidence of his unlimited power.
2. Delilah, in the Biblical story, cut off Samson's hair while he was sleeping.
3. Lincoln was elected President in 1860, and re-elected in 1864, on the Republican Party ticket.
4. "The Midas touch" is a lucky thing to possess.
5. "Do not let your right hand know what your left hand is doing" is cited in the Bible as an example of confusion.
6. A "leading question" is an especially pointed one that a lawyer asks of a hostile witness.
7. Billy the Kid, the famous Western outlaw, was born in New York City.
8. A "dead reckoning" in marine navigation is a dead right calculation of one's position.
9. A person who is "intoxicated" is drunk.
10. The Pilgrim Fathers who came to America on the Mayflower began the trip from England.

If you're not facile with rhymes, get help from a rhyming dictionary.

RHYMES

Rinky Dinky is an old game of giving clues and figuring out a two word answer that rhymes. Example: A lazy driver might be a "loafer chauffeur." Or a Tucker award is a "Sophie trophy."

1. Crazy candy
2. Hare regularity
3. Phony pastry shop
4. Museum payday
5. Madame Curie's playground
6. Alps crosser man eater
7. A baluster tobacco container
8. Skull flower
9. Yearly handbook
10. Balkan sickness
11. Budapest non-meater eater
12. Give away fun
13. The width of a trite remark
14. Insincere praise of a pitcher and catcher
15. Oslo university student
16. Pornographic tranquility
17. A raving clerk
18. A mediocre rear end
19. Walking cowboy
20. Nixon at home
21. Sneaky clergyman
22. Cannon booze maker
23. Songlike supernatural event
24. Two wheel glacier
25. A recorded past enigma
26. Often right
27. La Paz trifles
28. Kitchen covering gas
29. Boom boom convent
30. Mothers' Greek club
31. Tennis coat
32. Starling fishing gear
33. Lettuce song
34. Texas city mansion
35. Painter's butler

BOTTOM OF THE BARREL

MISCELLANY: YOU'RE ON YOUR OWN

1. Who was Jackson Haines?
2. Who founded the communistic colony called Helicon Hall in Englewood, New Jersey and it burned down. Who was that guy?
3. Who coined the words "birth control"?
4. Who wrote the play *The Life and Death of Tom Thumb the Great* in the year 1730?
5. The word "malapropism" came from what play?
6. Who coined the words "the Bible Belt" and "the Booboisie"?
7. Who created the term "Lost Generation"?
8. Who wrote a book in 1954 called *Black Power*?
9. DuBose Heyward wrote a novel that was later a play and an American opera. The novel?
10. A poem by Stéphane Mallarmé inspired what musical prelude by Debussy?
11. A novel by Prosper Mérimée inspired what musical work by Bizet?
12. *Liliom* by Ferenc Molnar was the source for what Rodgers and Hammerstein musical?
13. Another book to music. Henri Murger's *The Bohemians of the Latin Quarter* was put to music by what composer and what opera?
14. What was the dog's name in Jack London's *Call of the Wild*?
15. What was the dog's name in *Peter Pan*?
16. How about Elizabeth Barrett Browning's pooch. What was that dog's name?
17. Mary Roberts Rinehart wrote a number of humorous novels about an eccentric spinster whose name was?
18. Who wrote *Portrait of the Artist as a Young Dog*?
19. During World War II, William Joyce was known by what name?
20. What did Maxwell Anderson and Laurence Stallings write in 1924?
21. William Saroyan and Honoré de Balzac both wrote novels that had the same title . . . so what? So what's the title? (Yes but Balzac was first and in French.)
22. Who invented the safety pin?
23. What do you suppose Dr. Alphonse David Rockwell invented that was used for the first time on August 6, 1890 at Auburn Prison in New York?
24. Here's a real good one. Sir John Suckling 1609-1642 was a poet and dramatist and he had the gambling bug and he invented a game that uses cards. Not poker. What?
25. Speaking of games, in tennis "love" is nothing; in what game is 19 nothing?

Chapter 3

FRUIT of the TREE
tools of inquiry

AND THE LORD GOD COMMANDED THE MAN, SAYING, OF EVERY TREE OF THE GARDEN THOU MAYEST FREELY EAT: BUT OF THE FRUIT OF THE TREE OF KNOWLEDGE OF GOOD AND EVIL, THOU SHALT NOT EAT OF IT: FOR IN THE DAY THAT THOU EATEST THEREOF THOU SHALT SURELY DIE. —GENESIS 2:16, 17

The Tree of Knowledge

Research Steps
A Guide to the Use of Tools Discussed in this Chapter

After you have selected a topic and tentatively determined the angle of approach, you will need to find out what kinds of information are available.

Read one or two articles on your subject in good general encyclopedias. This will give you an overview and help you limit your subject, thus saving you the pointless labor of accumulating material you won't need.

Consult SPECIALIZED REFERENCE WORKS in your field: encyclopedias, dictionaries, handbooks, histories, and so on. For aid in finding additional specialized reference works, consult GUIDES TO REFERENCE WORKS.

If your subject is contemporary, go to YEARBOOKS, general and specialized (See pages 75–125 of this text for lists of specialized yearbooks).

Consult BIBLIOGRAPHIES OF BIBLIOGRAPHY for lists of books that contain sources in your field. If you're fortunate, you'll find a whole book that lists available material in your field.

Consult BIBLIOGRAPHIES which are simply lists of books arranged or indexed by subject.

Now you are ready to use your library's CARD CATALOG. First see which of your sources your library holds. Then proceed to use the card catalog as a subject bibliography; that is, look under your subject and related subjects to see what is available.

Consult INDEXES for periodical articles, pamphlets, essays, newspaper coverage, book reviews, and bibliographical sources.

Explore the wide range of material available in GOVERNMENT DOCUMENTS.

Compiling the Preliminary Bibliography

Compiling accurate 4 x 6-inch bibliographical cards NOW will simplify the final stage of your work (listing all sources alphabetically at the end of your paper). See page 187 for correct bibliographical form. After you have evaluated your sources, simply destroy any inappropriate cards.

Encyclopedia articles often include lists of sources you might want to consider. Copy these on separate cards.

Many of the books and articles you consult will contain bibliographies. Often the author's footnotes will lead you to additional valuable sources.

Often there is a bibliography heading in a subject category: "Drama—Bibliography," for instance. This means your library holds specialized bibliographies in your field. From the card catalog, also get Dewey Decimal numbers for works in your field. Go to the stacks and browse. This is a good way to select sources. Make a bibliography card for each source you select, referring to appropriate models, pages 187–218.

Often periodical articles indexed in *Social Sciences and Humanities Index* as well as in specialized indexes contain extensive bibliographies.

Definitions of unfamiliar terms will be found in DICTIONARIES and WORDBOOKS. Remember that many specialized dictionaries will be listed under subject headings. (See pages 41–42 of this chapter.)

If you plan to quote a definition in your paper, prepare a bibliography card.

Go to appropriate FACTBOOKS for dates and other factual detail.

Prepare a bibliography card if you plan to incorporate any of this factual material into your paper.

If geographical locale is significant, refer to a good ATLAS.

When your subject is well narrowed, you might check collections of QUOTATIONS for famous passages about your topic. These may provide an angle of approach, an epigraph for your paper, an opener for your introductory paragraph, an authoritative substantiation of a point, or even a unifying thesis.

If a collection of quotations contains sufficient bibliographical data, make a bibliography card. Otherwise copy the data provided after the quotation itself and ultimately incorporate this information into the *body* of your paper; e.g., "Nietzsche wrote in *Thus Spake Zarathustra*. . . ."

Bibliography Index

DRUIDS and DRUIDISM
    Piggott, Stuart. Druids. (Ancient peoples and
    places, v 63) Praeger '68 p 197-203

Bibliography Card See Model, pages 193–94 for series with Roman numerals.

Piggott, Stuart. Druids. Ancient Peoples and Places, LXIII. New York: Praeger, 1968.

Bibliography, pp. 197–203.

Often place of publication is not included in index entries. Find publishers' locations in *Books in Print*, Volume 2, available in all libraries.

HOW TO EVALUATE SOURCES

By now you have accumulated an extensive list of articles and books. Probably many angles of approach have emerged. In order to narrow your topic, select *one* angle and discard all sources that are not related to it.

Next reexamine the sources you have kept:

1. Are statements or arguments substantiated? If no footnotes or other documentation support them, you may be dealing with hot air.

2. Is the author objective? Examine the language. For example, LBJ probably won't get unbiased treatment in this book:

> The first thing we must do—and this is absolutely prerequisite to a better appreciation of Johnson—is admit the man is not likeable and that he is, in fact, treacherous, dishonest, manic-aggressive, petty, spoiled, and above all accidental.*

Even a title or cover may provide a tip-off:

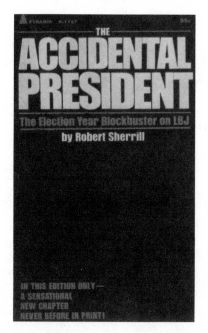

3. Is the author competent? Investigate his background in a general and/or specialized biography. Determine whether or not he is an authority in his particular field.

4. If your topic is contemporary, are your sources current? Check the copyright (not reprint) date and see if there are references to recent findings, statistics, and so on.

*Robert Sherrill, *The Accidental President* (New York: Pyramid, 1967), p. 9.

Finally, for an informed general evaluation of the article or book, check an appropriate index for the source of at least one review. (In addition to providing sources, *Book Review Digest* includes actual summaries of reviews.)

HOW TO FIND MATERIAL NOT IN YOUR LIBRARY

Q. What if my library doesn't have the material I need?

A. Get it elsewhere.

Q. How?

A. Go to other nearby libraries. Buy. Borrow.

Q. How can I find out if other libraries have the material I need?

A. If a call or visit isn't feasible, check books in the *National Union Catalog* and *The National Union Catalog Register of Additional Locations*. These list libraries holding books cataloged by the Library of Congress. Check periodicals in the *Union List of Serials in Libraries of the United States and Canada*. This source provides the names of libraries that have the periodicals and tells if they are available on microfilm. If the library holding your source is too far away to visit, ask your librarian if an inter-library loan can be arranged.

Q. How can I find prices and ordering information for material I might be able to buy?

A. *Books in Print* and *Paperbound Books in Print* provide prices and publishers' addresses. *Vertical File Index* and *Public Affairs Information Service Bulletin* provide a list of inexpensive materials with publishers' addresses. (Don't forget to check your library's Vertical File—a set of cabinets containing pamphlets classified by subject.) *The Monthly Catalog of United States Government Publications*, which is indexed by subject, includes prices where applicable. Many of the materials listed cost as little as $.10. If no price is listed, the item is free. Often back issues of periodicals can be ordered from the publisher. Addresses can be found in *Ulrich's Guide to Periodicals*. Back issues can also be ordered from many back-issue magazine establishments. (See city telephone directories.)

Q. How can books be obtained on microfilm?

A. Refer to *Books on Demand: A Catalog of Titles*. (University Microfilm, Ann Arbor, Mich.) This source contains a list of books currently available on microfilm.

Q. How can out-of-print books be obtained?

A. These may be ordered from companies that specialize in procurement of out-of-print books. Check classified advertisements in *Saturday Review*. Almost any out-of-print book may also be obtained on microfilm. University Microfilm charges a minimum of $3.00.

GENERAL REFERENCE TOOLS

Salvador Dali, "Dali at the Age of Six..."

I do not know what I may appear to the world; but to myself I seem to have been only like a boy playing on the seashore, and diverting myself in now and then finding a smoother pebble or a prettier shell than ordinary, whilst the great ocean of truth lay all undiscovered before me. — Sir Isaac Newton

1. INFORMATION DESK

In large libraries you will be able to get a list of services, a floor plan, a directory, a map. In smaller libraries you will get miscellaneous information, friendly help, and a good start. Northwestern University Library distributes these:

trust in god
there are no druids

—Meugant

Druids come after drugs in many directories. They are remote, esoteric, improbable, vaguely associated with evil and magic, hidden in the distance of antiquity. One wouldn't expect to find much about Druids anywhere; so I looked for them in mundane sources and found legends, rock circles, incantations, fear, and the west wall of the temple of Rocsaliere. Why bother? Well, even *you* couldn't pick a more unlikely topic. Read on.

Rock Fortress of Rocsaliere. West Wall of the Druid Temple.

2. ENCYCLOPEDIAS

Chambers Encyclopedia. New rev. ed. 15 vols. New York: Pergamon, 1967.

DRUID (Irish *drui*, pl. *drúid*), was the term applied by the Celts to a class of learned men, famous in Gaul as early as 200 B.C.... The Romans disliked the druids as an influence hostile to the conquest and took steps to deprive them of power and prestige. Under Claudius the druidic order was suppressed on the ground that its religion was 'barbarous and inhuman'.

An ancient survival which would justify these epithets was the practice of human sacrifice. Caesar suggests that such events took place only in time of war or intense stress and that the victims were mostly criminals. Divination (from the convulsions of the dying) and expiation were the underlying ideas.

When Pliny wrote his *Natural History* (c. A.D. 77) the druids in Gaul had degenerated to the status of magicians. To this author we owe our knowledge of their connexion with the mistletoe. It was to them the most sacred of plants, at least when growing upon the oak. The ceremony of gathering took place on the sixth day of the moon. 'Having made preparation for sacrifice and a banquet beneath the trees, they bring there two white bulls, whose horns are then bound for the first time. The priest, clad in a white robe, mounts the tree and cuts the mistletoe with a golden sickle, and it is received into a white cloak by others. Then they kill the victims, praying that god may render this his gift propitious to those to whom he has granted it.'...

Topics: Druidic Cult of Sacrifice; Pagan Origins of Christmas Symbols

Collier's Encyclopedia. Ed. William D. Halsey et al. 24 vols. New York: Macmillan, 1971.

Columbia Encyclopedia. Ed. William Bridgwater and Seymour Kurtz. 3rd ed. New York: Columbia University Press, 1963.

Encyclopedia Americana. International ed. Ed. George A. Cornish. 30 vols. New York: Americana, 1970.

Encyclopaedia Britannica. Ed. Warren E. Prece et al. 24 vols. Chicago: Encyclopaedia Britannica, 1970.

Encyclopedia International. Ed. Stanley Schindler et al. 20 vols. New York: Grolier, 1970.

The New Caxton Encyclopedia. 20 vols. London: Thames, 1969.
(A beautiful set with brilliant, full color illustrations.)

3. YEARBOOKS

Go to yearbooks when your subject is current.

Americana Annual. New York: Americana Corp. 1910—.
The Annual Register of World Events. New York: Longmans, 1758—.
Britannica Book of the Year. Chicago: Britannica, 1958—.
Chamber's World Survey. London: Newnes, 1960—.
Collier's Year Book. New York: Collier, 1938—.
The Year Book of World Affairs. New York: Praeger, 1970—.

4. SPECIALIZED REFERENCE WORKS

Here is an illustration of how specialized reference works in the last section of this chapter can be helpful in the early stages of research.

> *Mythology of All Races.* Ed. Canon J. A. MacCulloch et al. 12 vols.
> Boston: Marshall Jones, 1932.

The index volume yielded this:

> Druids, iii. 14, 20, 29, 30, 32, 36, 40,
> 42, 43, 52, 54, 60, 65, 67, 72, 79, 81,
> 84, 88, 140, 147, 157, 164, 167, 168,
> 175
> —religion of, assimilated to that of
> Rome, iii. 8
> —sacred verse of, iii. 8, 9

One page this:

> A legend reported by Pliny concerns some natural product, perhaps a fossil *echinus*, in explanation of the origin of which this myth was current, or to it an existing serpent-myth had been attached. Numerous serpents collected on a day in summer and, intertwining, formed a ball with the foam from their bodies, after which their united hissings threw it into the air. According to the Druids, he who would obtain it must catch it on a mantle before it touched the ground and must escape hastily, putting running water between himself and the pursuing serpents. The ball was used magically.

I AM A SKILLFUL COMPOSER: I AM A CLEAR SINGER: I AM A TOWER: I AM A DRUID. I AM AN ARCHITECT: I AM A PROPHET: I AM A SERPENT...—TALIESIN

Possible topic: Druidic Serpent Cults

5. DICTIONARIES

DICTIONARIES ARE LIKE WATCHES: THE WORST IS BET-
TER THAN NONE, AND THE BEST CANNOT BE EXPECTED
TO GO QUITE TRUE.—PIOZZI

The American Heritage Dictionary of the English Language. New York: American
Heritage, 1969.

---

dru·id (drōō′ĭd) *n.* Also **Dru·id.** A member of an order of priests
in ancient Gaul and Britain, who appear in Welsh and Irish
legend as prophets and sorcerers. [Latin *druides,* druids, from
Gaulish. See **deru-** in Appendix.*] —**dru·id′ic, dru·id′i·cal** *adj.*
—**dru′id·ism′** *n.*

The Concise Dictionary of Twenty-Six Languages in Simultaneous Translations. New
York: Polyglot, 1968.

A Dictionary of American English. Ed. W.A. Craigie. 4 vols. Chicago: University of Chicago Press, 1938.

A Dictionary of Americanisms on Historical Principles. Ed. Mitford Matthews.
Chicago: University of Chicago Press, 1951.

A Dictionary of Symbols. By Juan Eduardo Cirlot. New York: Philosophical
Library, 1962.

The Oxford English Dictionary. Ed. James A. H. Murray et al. 13 vols. New
York: Oxford University Press, 1933.

(A re-issue of *A New English Dictionary on Historical Principles.* Provides historical development of meaning. Dates provided for shifting definitions.)

Webster's Third New International Dictionary of the English Language, Unabridged.
Springfield, Mass.: Merriam, 1966.

---

dru·id \′drüɔd\ *n* -s [L *druides, druidae,* pl., fr. Gaulish
druides; akin to OIr *druī* (pl. *druid*) wizard, *daur* oak tree, W
derwen oak tree, OE *trēow* tree — more at TREE] **1 a** *often cap*
: a member of a priesthood in ancient Gaul, Britain, and Ireland who are said to have studied the natural sciences, proph-
esied through priestly sacrifices, and acted as judges and
teachers but who later appeared in Irish and Welsh sagas and
Christian legends as magicians and wizards **b :** BARD, PROPHET
2 : an officer of the Welsh bardic assembly — compare GORSEDD

By permission. From *Webster's Third New International
Dictionary* © 1971 by G. & C. Merriam Co., Publishers
of the Merriam-Webster Dictionaries.

6. WORDBOOKS

Adam, Ramon F. *Western Words: A Dictionary of the American West*. Rev. ed. Norman: University of Oklahoma Press, 1968.

Bliss, Alan Joseph. *A Dictionary of Foreign Words and Phrases in Current English*. New York: Dutton, 1966.

Franklyn, Julien. *A Dictionary of Rhyming Slang*. 2nd ed. London: Fernhill, 1961.

"BLADDER OF FAT" = A HAT (Probably an old, greasy one.)

"BIT OF BLINK" MEANS A DRINK   "JOHN HOP" IS A COP

"BEES AND HONEY" STAND FOR MONEY

Hill, Robert H. *Dictionary of Difficult Words*. New York: John Day, 1971. (A must for crossword puzzle fans.)

Marks, Joseph. *New French-English Dictionary of Slang and Colloquialisms*. New York: Dutton, 1971.
("an invaluable aid and comfort to any American trying to read a modern French novel or play. Argot and slang terms are classified under some 7,000 entries . . ."—David Glixon)

Mawson, Sylvester C. *New Roget's Thesaurus in Dictionary Form*. Ed. Norman Lewis. Rev. and enl. ed. New York: Putnam's, 1969.

Morris, William, and Mary Morris. *Dictionary of Word and Phrase Origins*. 3 vols. New York: Harper & Row, 1971.

Partridge, Eric. *Dictionary of the Underworld*. Rev. ed. New York: Macmillan, 1961.

Pugh, Eric. *A Dictionary of Acronyms and Abbreviations*. 2nd rev. and enl. ed. Hamden, Conn.: Archon, 1970.
(Good subject index.)

The Stanford Dictionary of Anglicised Words and Phrases. By Charles A. M. Fennell. New York: Cambridge University Press, 1964.

Webster's Dictionary of Proper Names. Springfield, Mass.: Merriam, 1971.

Wilstach, F. L. *Dictionary of Similes*, 1924. Rpt. New York: Adler, 1969.

A mouth like the whale that swallowed a whole fleet. —THOMAS LODGE.

Mouth that looked like a red gash from a sabre cut. — GUY DE MAUPASSANT.

Wood's Unabridged Rhyming Dictionary. New York: World, 1943.

bantam—phantom

	knee deep	urgent	lantern
tantrum	sea deep	emergent	can turn
scant rum	tree deep	detergent	can't earn

7. QUOTATIONS

THE WISDOM OF THE WISE AND THE EXPERIENCE OF THE AGES MAY BE PRESERVED BY QUOTATIONS.
—ISAAC D'ISRAELI

NEXT TO THE ORIGINATOR OF A GOOD SENTENCE IS THE FIRST QUOTER OF IT.—RALPH WALDO EMERSON

QUOTATION CONFESSES INFERIORITY.
—RALPH WALDO EMERSON

ONE MUST BE A WISE READER TO QUOTE WISELY AND WELL.—A. B. ALCOTT

Adams, Joey. *Son of Encyclopedia Humor*. New York: Bobbs-Merrill, 1970.

Baron, Joseph L. *A Treasury of Jewish Quotations*. Rev. ed. Cranbury, N. J.: A. S. Barnes, 1965.

Bartlett, John. *Familiar Quotations: A Collection of Passages, Phrases, and Proverbs Traced to Their Sources in Ancient and Modern Literature*. 14th ed. Boston: Little, Brown, 1968.

Brown, Raymond Lamont, comp. *A Book of Proverbs*. New York: Taplinger, 1970.
(1500 proverbs. Subject classification.)

Field, Claud. *A Dictionary of Oriental Quotations*. New York: Macmillan, 1911. Rpt. Detroit: Gale, 1969.
(Drawn from Arabic and Persian cultures.)

Le Comte, Edward Semple. *A Dictionary of Last Words*. New York: Philosophical Library, 1955.

Franklin D. Roosevelt:
"I have a terrific headache."

Theodore Roosevelt:
"Please put out the light."

Frederick Douglass, c 1817-1895.

Frederick Douglass:
"Why, what does this mean?"

Amelia Earhart:
"Please know that I am quite aware of the hazards. I want to do it. Women must try to do things as men have tried."

George Bernard Shaw:
"Sister, you're trying to keep me alive as an old curiosity, but I'm done, I'm finished. I'm going to die."

Jesus Christ:
"My God! Why hast thou forsaken me?"

Pater, Alan F., and Jason R. Pater, eds. *What They Said in 197—: The Yearbook of Spoken Opinion*. Beverly Hills: Monitor, 197—.
(A range that includes figures as diverse as Richard M. Nixon and Muhammed Ali.)

Stevenson, Burton, ed. *Home Book of Shakespeare Quotations*. New York: Scribner's, 1966.

Stevenson, Burton. *Macmillan Book of Proverbs*. New York: Macmillan, 1965.

Tripp, Rhoda Thomas, ed. *The International Thesaurus of Quotations*. New York: Crowell, 1970.

8. FACTBOOKS

Ackermann, Alfred Seabold. *Popular Fallacies, a Book of Common Errors: Explained and Corrected with Copious Reference to Authorities*. London: Old Westminster Press, 1950. Rpt. Detroit: Gale, 1970.
(Some of the subject heads: domestic fallacies, weather, religion.)

DID YOU KNOW THE FOLLOWING ARE FALLACIES?

That "snakes love music and are charmed by it"?

That "mahogany is wood obtained from one particular kind of tree"?

That "we have only five senses"?

That "the earliest extant mss. of the New Testament date from the time of Jesus Christ"?

That "a pound of feathers is lighter than a pound of lead"?

That "when Jesus was crucified His feet as well as His hands were nailed to the cross"?

Brewer, Ebenezer Cobham. *Brewer's Dictionary of Phrase and Fable.* 10th rev. ed. New York: Harper & Row, 1964.
(Myth, superstition, slang, national legend, fiction, terminology.)

DID YOU KNOW?

That Jim Crow was a popular Afro-American "song and dance of the last century....A renegade or turn coat was called a Jim Crow from the burden of the song:

> Wheel about and turn about
> and do jis so,
> Ebry time I wheel about
> I jump Jim Crow"?

DID YOU KNOW?

That the term "'ham actor' derives probably from the fact that in the 19th century theatrical make-up was removed with the fat of hamchops"?

Carruth, Gorton. *The Encyclopedia of American Facts and Dates.* 5th ed. New York: Crowell, 1970.
("Did you know that the first marriage in the American colonies was performed in 1609? Or that the first doctor arrived the following year, increasing the population to 210? Another wedding, Tiny Tim's, made the book's last column."—David Glixon)

Chambers, Robert, ed. *The Book of Days: A Miscellany of Popular Antiquities in Connection with the Calendar, Including Anecdote, Biography, and History, Curiosities of Literature and Oddities of Human Life and Character.* 2 vols. 1886. Rpt. Detroit: Gale, 1967.

Chaundler, Christine. *Every Man's Book of Superstitions.* New York: Philosophical Library, 1971.

(A compendium of superstitions, well indexed, highly readable.)

Douglas, George W. *The American Book of Days.* 2nd ed. New York: Wilson, 1948.

(Facts about religious and secular holidays, festivals, and other memorable days.)

Facts on File: Weekly World News Digest with a Cumulative Index. New York: Facts on File, 1938—.

(Current. Subject index provides easy access to digests of current events. Excellent cross referencing.)

Garrison, Webb. *The Ignorance Book.* New York: Morrow, 1971.

(Identifies itself as a "Compendium of Useless Information on Matters of Concern to Everyone.")

Kane, Joseph. *Pocket Book of Famous First Facts.* Englewood Cliffs, N.J.: Prentice-Hall, 1970.

Macadam, Ivison, ed. *Annual Register of World Events.* New York: St. Martin's, 1971—.

Mason, Francis K., and Martin C. Windrow, comps. *Air Facts and Feats.* Garden City, N.Y.: Doubleday, 1971.

("The editors . . . answer practically any . . . non-scientific question you might have about human flight."—David Glixon)

McWhirter, Norris, and Ross McWhirter. *Guiness Book of World Records.* 9th ed. New York: Sterling, 1971.

("Information on such superlatives as highest, lowest, biggest, fastest, oldest, greatest, strongest, etc., in the areas of man, animals, nature, the universe . . ."—ARBA, 1971)

New Century Cyclopedia of Names. Ed. Clarence L. Barnhart and William D. Halsey. 3 vols. New York: Appleton, 1954.

Statesman's Yearbook. Ed. S. H. Steinberg. New York: St. Martin's, 1864—.

(Contains information about world organizations as well as a wide range of international factual data.)

United Nations Statistical Yearbook. New York: The United Nations, 1948—.

U. S. Bureau of the Census. *Statistical Abstracts of the United States.* Washington, D.C.: U.S. Government Printing Office, 1878—.

U. S. Department of State. *Fact Book of the Countries of the World.* New York: Crown, 1970.

World Almanac and Book of Facts. Ed. H. Lumen Long. New York: World Almanac, 1868—.

That of the 2,146,000 persons who married in 1969, 660,000 were divorced?

That in 1969 27.9 out of each 100,000 deaths in the U.S. were in motor vehicles?

That 55,835 burglaries occurred in Chicago in 1969 and 196,432 in New York?

That 1,000,000 persons speak Wolof; 4,000,000 speak Xhosa; 13,000,000 speak Swahili; 187,000,000 speak Spanish; and 326,000,000 speak English?

That in April 1970 the population of Nevada (109,889 sq. mi.) was 481,893 and the population of New York (47,869 sq. mi.) was 17,979,712?

9. ATLASES

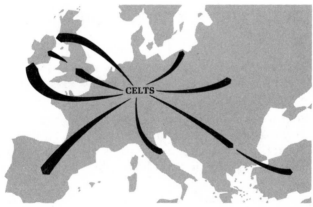

Map of Celtic Europe circa 300 B.C.

The Atlas of the Universe. By Patrick Moore. Chicago: Rand McNally, 1970.

Bjorklund, Oddvar, et al. *Historical Atlas of the World.* New York: Barnes & Noble, 1970.

Boyd, Andrew. *Atlas of World Affairs.* New York: Praeger, 1970.
   ("In seventy-six sections, each with a clear black and white regional map . . . Boyd deftly outlines the sources, extent, and course of man's territorial quarrels."—David Glixon)

Fitzgerald, Ken. *Space-Age Photographic Atlas.* New York: Crown, 1970.
   ("A collection of 200 black and white photos taken from planes, spacecraft, and man-made satellites."—David Glixon)

Hammond World Atlas. 2 vols. New Perspective ed. Maplewood, N.J.: Hammond, 1966.

Lord, Clifford L., and Elizabeth H. Lord, eds. *Historical Atlas of the United States*. Rev. ed. New York: Johnson Reprint Co., 1969.

National Geographic Atlas of the World. 3rd rev. ed. Washington, D.C.: National Geographic, 1971.

("One of the most up-to-date as well as one of the best . . . of all international atlases."—David Glixon)

Palmer, R. R., ed. *Atlas of World History*. Chicago: Rand McNally, 1969.

U. S. Department of the Interior. Geological Survey. *The National Atlas of the United States of America*. Washington, D.C.: U. S. Government Printing Office, 1970.

Van der Heyden, A. A. M., and H. H. Scullard, eds. *Atlas of the Classical World*. New York: Nelson, 1960.

Van Royen, William, ed. *Atlas of the World's Resources*. Vol. I: *The Agricultural Resources of the World*. Vol. II: *The Mineral Resources of the World*. Englewood Cliffs, N.J.: Prentice-Hall, 1952–54.

10. BIBLIOGRAPHIES OF BIBLIOGRAPHY

Besterman, Theodore. *A World Bibliography of Bibliographies and of Catalogs, Abstracts, Digests, Indexes, and the Like*. 4th ed. 4 vols. Lausanne, Switzerland: Societas Bibliographica, 1965.

(As this bibliography is international, descriptive entries are in the language of the original publication. Arrangement is by subject with an author index. Within each subject category, entries are chronologically ordered. Remember that each source is a bibliography, or list of books, in itself.)

Drugs, drug addiction.

BRIEF list of references on stimulants (exclusive of alcohol). Library of Congress: [Washington] 1920. ff.5. [46.]★
· ·
NARCOTIC addiction. A selected list of references in English. National library of medicine: Reference division: Washington [1959]. pp.14. [99.]★
· ·
Druids.
GEORGE F[RASER] BLACK, Druids and Druidism. A list of references. Public library: New York 1920. pp.16. [350.]
Drukarnia narodowa.
DRUKARNIA narodowa w Krakowie 1895-1935. Krakowie [1935]. pp.282.cxxviii. [3500.]

Bibliographic Index: A Cumulative Bibliography of Bibliographies. New York: Wilson, 1938—.

(This source is kept current with April and August issues followed by annual cumulations each December. Arrangement is by subject. All sources are either bibliographies in their entirety or contain bibliographies.)

Bulletin of Bibliography and Magazine Notes. Boston: Faxon, 1897—.

(Kept current. Four issues annually. Index at the end of each bound volume. Each issue contains specialized bibliographies. If you find your subject in one of the issues, your bibliographical work is done!)

11. GUIDES TO REFERENCE WORKS

American Reference Books Annual. Ed. Bohdan S. Wynar. Littleton, Colo.: Libraries Unlimited, 1970, 1971.

(An important and valuable tool. Arranged by subject. Indexed by author, title, and subject. Contains full evaluative descriptions of current reference works. When you *begin* research, check ARBA for reference works in your field.)

Booklist and Subscription Books Bulletin. Chicago: American Library Association, 1905—.

(Excellent reviews of reference works. See Bibliographies, page 51, for description.)

Winchell, Constance. *Guide to Reference Books.* 8th ed. Chicago: American Library Association, 1967. Supplements: 1968, 1970.

(Additional supplements will be issued. Like ARBA, arranged by subject; indexed by author, title, and subject. Full evaluative descriptions of all varieties of reference tools. Use current volume for expert commentary on new tools. Freely refer to earlier volumes for evaluation of older materials. The 1968 and later supplements were edited by Eugene P. Sheehy.)

12. BIBLIOGRAPHIES

American Book Publishing Record. Annual Cumulations. Ed. Phyllis B. Steckler. New York: Bowker, 1960—.

(Current. Cumulations of *Publishers' Weekly.* Arranged by subject, according to Dewey Decimal classification, and indexed by author and title. To use profitably as a subject guide, see breakdown of Dewey Decimal system, pages 60–61. For example, in looking for material about Druids I went to the 290's: "Other religions and comparative religions," under the 200 heading, Religion. It was also profitable to look in the 390's "Customs and Folklore," under the 300 heading, Social Science. As a further aid, check your subject in the card catalog for a 10's breakdown or ask your librarian for a copy of the *Dewey Decimal System*. Then you will know exactly which range of numbers is devoted to your subject.)

---

299   Other Religions

ANGUS, Samuel, 1881-1943   299
The mystery-religions and Christianity; a study in the religious background of early Christianity. Introd. by Theodore H. Gaster. New Hyde Park, N. Y., University Bks. [1967c.1966] xxiv, 359p. 24cm. (Univ. lib. of comp. relig.) Bibl. [BL610.A6 1966] 66-27423 10.00
1. Mysteries, Religious. 2. Christianity and other religions. I. Title.
Originally published by Scribners in 1925. New introduction.

CHADWICK, Nora (Kershaw) 1891-   299.16
The druids. Cardiff, Wales Univ. Pr. [Mystic, Conn., Verry] 1966. xii,119p. 23 cm. Bibl. [BL910.C5] 66-70314 3.50
I. Druids and Druidism.
A reevaluation of the spiritual and cultural contributions of the early Celtic peoples of Gaul. Emphasis is on contemplation of the natural universe as well as philosophical and educational duties.

KENDRICK, Sir Thomas Downing   299.16
The Druids; a study in Keltic prehistory [by] T. D. Kendrick. New York, Barnes & Noble [1966] xiv, 227p. illus., maps, plans, plates, port. 23cm. Reprint of a work first pub. in 1927. [BL910.K4 1966] 66-7817 8.50.
1. Druids and Druidism. 2. Celts — Religion. 3. Temples, Druid. I. Title.
Originally published in Great Britain.

PIGGOTT, Stuart   299'.1'6
The Druids. New York, Praeger [1968] 236p. illus., facsims., maps, plans, ports. 22cm. (Ancient peoples & places, v.63) Bibl. [BL910.P5 1968] 68-8971 7.50
1. Druids and Druidism. I. Title.

ROSS, Anne, PH. D.   299'.16
Pagan Celtic Britain: studies in iconography and tradition. London, Routledge & K. Paul; New York, Columbia, 1967. xxxiii, 433p. illus., 96 plates, maps, plan. 25½cm. Bibl. [BL900.R6] 67-16099 25.00
1. Celts—Religion. 2. Celts—Antiq. I. Title.

"Repousse silver plate, 25 x 40 cm., one of five decorating the interior of a ceremonial cauldron found in a peat bog at Gundestrup, Himmerland, Denmark....The scene shows a deity of heroic proportions apparently drowning a victim in a tub....The remainder of the panel should probably be read as a continuous procession of warriors....It has alternatively been suggested that the victim is being committed to a ritual sacrificial shaft."—Stuart Piggott

Booklist and Subscription Books Bulletin. Chicago: American Library Association, 1905—.

(Current. Published twice a month with bound annual cumulations. Excellent concise evaluative descriptions of current books. One section is classified according to the Dewey Decimal system. The author, title, subject index at the end of each issue and bound annual cumulation makes *Booklist* a valuable subject bibliography.)

100-200 PHILOSOPHY—RELIGION
Piggott, Stuart. The Druids. (Ancient peoples and places) 1968. 236p. illus., facsims., maps, plans, ports. Praeger, $7.50.
Identifying two types of Druids—Druids-as-known, those from history who served as priests in the pre-Roman Celtic religion, and Druids-as-wished-for, those created by imaginative writers—a British professor describes the Celtic society in which the first type lived in the second century B.C., the sources of information about Druids in classical and vernacular writings, and the creation of the Druid myths. Photographs and line drawings illustrate the scholarly, synoptic text for students of ancient history or classical literature and the inquiring general reader.
299'.1'6 Druids and Druidism   68-8971

WHAT INTEREST HAS THE PRESENT AGE IN A VIEW OF THE ERRORS AND PREJUDICES OF THE PAGAN BRITONS?—EDWARD DAVIES

WHAT INTEREST HAS THE FUTURE IN THE ERRORS AND PREJUDICES OF THE AMERICAN 1970'S?

Books in Print: An Author, Title, Series Index. . . . New York: Bowker, 1948—. (Current. Not only tells you if your book is in print and easily available, but provides publisher and date of publication. *Books in Print* has author and title volumes, but annoyingly provides dates only in the author volume. Publishers' addresses appear at the end of Volume 2: Titles. These are useful for direct ordering of books and completion of bibliographical data.)

Translate entries into correct bibliographical form. Do not copy verbatim.

Druid Stone. Simon Majors. pap. 0.60. Paperback Lib.

Druids. Nora K. Chadwick. 3.50. Verry.

Druids. Stuart Piggott. 8.50x. Praeger.

▶ Druids. 2nd ed. Thomas D. Kendrick. 8.00. B&N.

Kendrick, Thomas D. *Druids*, 2nd ed.
New York: Barnes & Noble, 1968.

British National Bibliography. London: Council of the British National Bibliography, 1950—.
(Current. Weekly lists with annual cumulations. Two part issues: subject arrangement, Dewey Decimal classification and alphabetical author-title index. Fullest information in subject index. An annotated list of all books published in Great Britain. To use as a subject bibliography, find Dewey Decimal classification of your subject and check appropriate numbers in each volume.)

299.16—CELTIC RELIGIONS
299.16s—Druids

CHADWICK, Nora Kershaw
The druids. Cardiff, Wales U.P., 12/6. [d Jan]
1966. *xxii,119p. 22½cm.*

(B66-2285)

KENDRICK, Sir Thomas Downing
The Druids: a study in Keltic prehistory. 2nd ed.,
new impression. London, Cass, 45/-. Aug 1966.
*xv,227p. front.(port.), illus., 7 plates, maps, plans,
diagrs. 22½cm.*
Originally published, London, Methuen, 1927.

(B66-17611)

STEINER, Rudolf
Man in the past, the present and the future: the
evolution of consciousness: three lectures given in
Stuttgart, 14th, 15th, 16th September, 1923; translated [from the German] by E. Goddard, [and] The
sun-initiation of the Druid priest and his moon-
science: lecture given in Dornach, 10th September,
1923; [translated from the German]. London,
Rudolf Steiner P., 10/6. Apr 1966. *80p. 20½cm.
P bk.*

(B66-8861)

299.16sab—*Periodicals*
The DRUID. No. 1. 77 Carlton Ave., London, S.E.21,
The Druid Order, 2/6 (9/-per annum). 1965.
20½cm. Sd.
Approx. 3 issues per annum.

(B66-11835)

The Heroic Gaul: a late nineteenth-century statue of Ambiorix,
chief of the tribe of the Eburones in the first century B.C. at
Tongres in Belgium. From *The Druids*, by Stuart Piggott (New
York: Praeger, 1968).

Cumulative Book Index: A World List of Books in the English Language. New York: Wilson, 1898—.

(Current. A single alphabetical, author, title, subject index. Each volume contains only titles published during the specified years. For earlier publications, see preceding volumes. A directory of publishers at the end of the second volume of each cumulation. Highly accessible subject bibliography.)

Druids and Druidism
    Owen, A. L. The famous Druids. $4.80 (30s)
    '62 Oxford
	.1961–62
	Volumes

Druids and druidism
    Chadwick. N. K. The Druids. 12s 6d '66 Univ.
    of Wales press
    Kendrick, T. D. The Druids: a study in
    Keltic prehistory. $8.50 '66 Barnes & Noble:
    45s Cass
        See also
    Mythology, Celtic
	1965–66
	Volumes

Forthcoming Books Now Including New Books in Print: A Forecast of Books to Come. . . . New York: Bowker.

(Current. Indexed by author and title. As subject areas are frequently evident in wording of titles, this serves as a guide to current publications.)

> For further information about titles in *Books in Print, Forth-Coming Books,* and *Subject Guide to Books in Print,* check *Publishers Trade List Annual, Booklist, National Union Catalog, Book Review Digest.*

See also Celt

Celtic Fairy Tales. Ed. by Joseph Jacobs. 7.95. World Pub.
Celtic Fairy Tales. Ed. by Joseph Jacobs. Repr. of 1892 ed. pap. 1.75. Dover.
Celtic Folk & Fairy Tales. Joseph Jacobs. 3.50. Putnam.
Celtic Literatures: Classification Schedule, Classified Listing by Call Number, Chronological Listing, Author & Title Listing. 25.00x. Harvard U Pr.
Celtic Myth & Arthurian Romance. Roger S. Loomis. Repr. of 1927 ed. lib. bdg. 13.95. Haskell.

Druids, so esoteric, narrow, improbable and remote a subject, is too vast to be covered in its totality even in a doctoral dissertation. So narrow your subject, and narrow it again.

Druidic Fairytales? Druidic Lore in Arthurian Romance?

Hale, Barbara M. *The Subject Bibliography of the Social Sciences and Humanities.* New York: Pergamon, 1970.

Koltay, Emery, ed. *Irregular Serials and Annuals: An International Directory.* 2nd ed. New York: Bowker, 1971.

(This is a subject guide to annual and irregularly published materials. Indexed by title and subject. A good route to current materials in your field.)

Library of Congress. *Library of Congress Catalog, Books: Subjects.* Totowa, N.J.: Rowman & Littlefield, 1955—.

(Current. An invaluable aid in research providing a subject guide to all books held by the Library of Congress and other libraries using Library of Congress catalog cards.)

Library of Congress. *National Union Catalog: A Cumulative Author List.* Washington, D.C.: Library of Congress, 1948—.

(Current. A list representing Library of Congress printed cards and titles reprinted by other American libraries. Use this valuable source to find bibliographical data and card catalog information. This catalog is the equivalent of access to the author file in the Library of Congress card catalog.)

DRUID TEMPLES see Temples, Druid
DRUIDS AND DRUIDISM
     see also Bards and bardism; Folk-lore
     of trees; Mythology, Celtic
Bouchet, Paul.
    Science et philosophie des druides. Drancy, l'auteur, 40, rue du Colonel-Fabien; Blainville-sur-mer, l'Amitié par le livre, 1968.
     192 p. 22 cm. 12 F
    BL910.B68   68–132838

Chadwick, Nora (Kershaw) 1891–
    The druids, by Nora K. Chadwick. Cardiff, Wales U. P., 1966.
     xxii, 119 p. 22½ cm. 12/6
    BL910.C5   299.16   66–70314

Kendrick, *Sir* Thomas Downing.
    The Druids: a study in Keltic prehistory [by] T. D. Kendrick. 2nd ed., new impression. London, Cass, 1966.
     xv, 227 p. front. (port.), Illus., 7 plates, maps, plans, diagrs. 22½ cm. 45/–
    BL910.K4 1966a   299'.16   67–80756

Kendrick, *Sir* Thomas Downing.
    The Druids; a study in Keltic prehistory [by] T. D. Kendrick. New York, Barnes & Noble [1966].
     xiv, 227 p. Illus., maps, plans, plates, port. 23 cm.
    BL910.K4 1966   299.16   66–7817

Piggott, Stuart.
    The druids. London, Thames & Hudson, 1968.
     239 p. Illus., facsims., 4 maps, plans. 21 cm. (Ancient peoples and places, v. 63) 42/–
    BL910.P5 1968b   299'.16   72–353222

Piggott, Stuart.
    The Druids. New York, Praeger [1968]
     236 p. Illus., facsims., maps, plans, ports. 22 cm. (Ancient peoples and places, v. 63) $7.50
    BL910.P5 1968   299'.1'6   68–8971

Library of Congress. *National Union Catalog . . . Register of Additional Locations.* Washington, D.C.: Library of Congress, 1965—.

("Provides additional locations of titles which have been reported since the original listing of these titles in the *Catalog*." There are two lists: "one numerical by card number, the other alphabetical by main entry." To use numerical list, simply copy Library of Congress number of book you are seeking, find number in this Register, and translate abbreviations of libraries holding your book. The key to "symbols indicating location" is in the front of each volume.)

Paperbound Books in Print: A Title, Author, and Subject Index. New York: Bowker.

(Current. Publishers' addresses are at the back of each volume. Listed here are books you can order easily and inexpensively.)

Subject Guide to Books in Print. New York: Bowker.

(Current. An excellent reference tool that enables you to find books in print in your field.)

DRUIDS AND DRUIDISM
see also Folk Lore of Trees; Mythology, Celtic
Chadwick, Nora K. Druids. 1966. 3.50. Verry.
Daniel, Jon. Philosophy of Ancient Britain. 1970.
   10.75. (ISBN 0-8046-0726-5). Kennikat.
Kendrick, Thomas D. Druids. (II). 2nd ed. 1928. 8.00.
   B&N.
Piggott, Stuart. Druids. (Ancient Peoples & Places
   Ser). (II) 1968. 8.50. Praeger
DRUIDISM AND CHRISTIANITY
see Christianity and Other Religions. Druidism

Union List of Serials in Libraries of the United States and Canada. 3rd ed. 5 vols. New York: Wilson, 1965.

(This source lists libraries holding serials—periodicals and other recurring publications. Entries arranged by title. Names of holding libraries abbreviated. Key to abbreviations in front of each volume. "The symbols L, L*, P, and M following the name of the library refer to the libraries' facilities for lending serials and for furnishing photocopies and microfilm." If your school library does not carry a periodical you need, go to *Union List of Serials*.)

13. CARD CATALOG: THE KEY TO THE LIBRARY

The card catalog is the key to the use of the library. It is also the most immediately accessible SUBJECT BIBLIOGRAPHY you have. Cards are filed under three main heads: author, title, and subject.

299.16

Piggott, Stuart.
　　The druids. London, Thames and Hudson [1968]

　　236 p. illus., facsims., maps, plans. 22cm (Ancient peoples and places, v. 63) $7.50.

　　Bibliography: p. 197-203

　　1. Druids and druidism. I. Title (Series)

BL910.P5 1968　　　　　　299^1.1′6　　　　　68-8971

Library of Congress　　　　　　　[3]

The Druids

Piggott, Stuart.
　　The druids. London, Thames and Hudson [1968]

　　236 p. illus., facsims., maps, plans. 22cm (Ancient peoples and places, v. 63) $7.50.

　　Bibliography: p. 197-203

　　1. Druids and druidism. I. Title (Series)

BL910.P5 1968　　　　　　299^1.1′6　　　　　68-8971

Library of Congress　　　　　　　[3]

DRUIDS AND DRUIDISM

Piggott, Stuart.
　　The druids. London, Thames and Hudson [1968]

　　236 p. illus., facsims., maps, plans. 22cm (Ancient peoples and places, v. 63) $7.50.

　　Bibliography: p. 197-203

　　1. Druids and druidism. I. Title (Series)

BL910.P5 1968　　　　　　299^1.1′6　　　　　68-8971

Library of Congress　　　　　　　[3]

```
    299.16
 1  P631dr
       2 Piggott, Stuart.
           3 The druids.  London, Thames and Hudson [1968]

           4 236 p. illus., facsims., maps, plans.  22cm (Ancient peoples and
              places, v. 63) $7.50.

           5 Bibliography: p. 197-203


           6 1. Druids and druidism.   I. Title (Series)

       7 BL910.P5        1968              299¹.1′6              68-8971


              Library of Congress                    [3]
```

1. $\dfrac{299.16}{P631dr}$ is the call number of the book, Dewey Decimal number over author number.

2. "Piggott, Stuart" is the author's name. On many cards, author's dates of birth and death follow his name. If he is living, an open ended date often follows his name: Jones, Edward, 1920—.

3. "The druids" is the title of the book. London is the place of publication, Thames and Hudson the publisher. Date of publication is 1968.

4. There are 236 pages in this book. It contains illustrations, facsimilies, maps, and plans. The book is 22 cm. in size. It is volume 63 in a series entitled "Ancient People and Places."

5. The book contains bibliographical listings on pages 197–203.

6. The book is listed, not only under author, but under the subject heading "Druids and druidism" and under the title mentioned above.

7. BL910.P5 is the Library of Congress catalog number. 299¹.1'6 is the Dewey Decimal number. 68–8971 is the number librarians use in re-order the card.

Subject and title cards are duplications of the author card. However, on the subject card, the subject is typed in above the author's name. The title is typed above the author's name on the title card.

13.1. Principles of Alphabetizing

Although alphabetizing procedures may vary from library to library, the following principles frequently apply:

(a) *The*, *A*, and *An* are ignored in alphabetizing. A book entitled *The History of Western Man* would be alphabetized in the *H's*.

(b) Word by word alphabetizing takes precedence over letter by letter.

WORD BY WORD	LETTER BY LETTER
South America	South America
South Orange	Southbridge
Southbridge	Southern Hemisphere
Southern Hemisphere	South Orange
Southport	Southport

(c) Acronyms, abbreviations, arbitrary letter combinations occur at the beginning of the alphabetical listing:

NAACP
NCRA
NEWZ
New England
Newark

(d) Names beginning with *Mc* are alphabetized with the *Mac's*.

Mabby, Jules
Macbeth
McCracken, Flora
MacCullough, Abraham

(e) Names beginning with *St.* are alphabetized with the *Saint's*.

St. Barton, Jerome
Saint Clement, Arthur

(f) Names of lakes, mountains, seas, and so on are alphabetized by base word following geographic identification.

Gibralter, Straits of
Marmara, Sea of
Mendocino, Cape

13.2. The Dewey Decimal System

In the upper left-hand corner of each card is the call number. The top number is the Dewey Decimal classification. The Dewey Decimal system relies on a process of division and subdivision. Initially, all works are classified under one of ten headings.

<table>
<tr><td colspan="2">First Summary
The 10 Classes</td></tr>
<tr><td>000</td><td>Generalities</td></tr>
<tr><td>100</td><td>Philosophy & related disciplines</td></tr>
<tr><td>200</td><td>Religion</td></tr>
<tr><td>300</td><td>The social sciences</td></tr>
<tr><td>400</td><td>Language</td></tr>
<tr><td>500</td><td>Pure sciences</td></tr>
<tr><td>600</td><td>Technology (Applied sciences)</td></tr>
<tr><td>700</td><td>The arts</td></tr>
<tr><td>800</td><td>Literature & rhetoric</td></tr>
<tr><td>900</td><td>General geography, history, etc.</td></tr>
</table>

The ten main divisions are further divided in units of ten, providing greater precision in classification.

Second Summary
The 100 Divisions

000	Generalities	500	Pure sciences
010	Bibliographies & catalogs	510	Mathematics
020	Library science	520	Astronomy & allied sciences
030	General encyclopedic works	530	Physics
040		540	Chemistry & allied sciences
050	General periodicals	550	Earth sciences
060	General organizations	560	Paleontology
070	Newspapers & journalism	570	Anthropolog. & biol. sciences
080	General collections	580	Botanical sciences
090	Manuscripts & book rarities	590	Zoological sciences
100	Philosophy & related	600	Technology (Applied sci.)
110	Ontology & methodology	610	Medical sciences
120	Knowledge, cause, purpose, man	620	Engineering & allied operations
130	Pseudo- & parapsychology	630	Agriculture & agric. industries
140	Specific philosophic viewpoints,	640	Domestic arts & sciences
150	Psychology	650	Business & related enterprises
160	Logic	660	Chemical technology etc.
170	Ethics (Moral philosophy)	670	Manufactures processible
180	Ancient, med., Oriental philos.	680	Assembled & final products
190	Modern Western philosophy	690	Buildings
200	Religion	700	The arts
210	Natural religion	710	Civic & landscape art
220	Bible	720	Architecture
230	Christian doctrinal theology	730	Sculpture & the plastic arts
240	Christ. moral & devotional theol.	740	Drawing & decorative arts
250	Christ. pastoral, parochial, etc.	750	Painting & paintings
260	Christ. social & eccles. theol.	760	Graphic arts
270	Hist. & geog. of Chr. church	770	Photography & photographs
280	Christ. denominations & sects	780	Music
290	Other religions & compar. rel.	790	Recreation (Recreational arts)
300	The social sciences	800	Literature & rhetoric
310	Statistical method & statistics	810	American literature in English
320	Political science	820	Engl. & Anglo-Saxon literature
330	Economics	830	Germanic languages literature
340	Law	840	French, Provencal, Catalan lit.
350	Public administration	850	Italian, Romanian etc. literature
360	Welfare & association	860	Spanish & Portuguese literature
370	Education	870	Italic languages literature
380	Commerce	880	Classical & Greek literature
390	Customs & folklore	890	Lits. of other languages
400	Language	900	General geog. & history etc.
410	Linguistics & nonverbal lang.	910	General geography
420	English & Anglo-Saxon	920	General biog., geneal., etc.
430	Germanic languages	930	Gen. hist. of ancient world
440	French, Provencal, Catalan	940	Gen. hist. of modern Europe
450	Italian, Romanian, etc.	950	Gen. hist. of modern Asia
460	Spanish & Portuguese	960	Gen. hist. of modern Africa
470	Italic languages	970	Gen. hist. of North America
480	Classical & Greek	980	Gen. hist. of South America
490	Other languages	990	Gen. hist. of rest of world

Each subdivision is further divided in units of ten, providing even greater precision in classification.

		Summaries	
		Religion	
200	Religion	250	Christ. pastoral & parochial
201	Philosophy of Christianity	251	Preaching (Homiletics)
202	Miscellany of Christianity	252	Sermons
203	Dictionaries of Christianity	253	Pastor
204		254	Parish govt. & administration
205	Serial publs. on Christianity	255	Religious congregations & orders
206	Organizations on Christianity	256	
207	Study of Christianity	257	
208	Collections on Christianity	258	Parochial welfare work
209	Hist. & geography of Christianity	259	Other parochial activities
210	Natural religion	260	Chr. social & eccles. theol.
211	Knowledge of God	261	Social theology
212	Nature of God	262	Church govt., org., nature
213	Creation	263	Times of religious observance
214	Theodicy	264	Public worship
215	Science & religion	265	Other rites & ceremonies
216	Good & evil	266	Missions
217	Worship & prayer	267	Associations for religious work
218	Immortality & eternity	268	Religious training & instruction
219	Analogy	269	Organized spiritual renewal
220	Bible	270	Hist. & geog. of Chr. church
221	Old Testament	271	Religious congregations & orders
222	Historical books	272	Persecutions
223	Poetic books	273	Heresies
224	Prophetic books	274	Christian church in Europe
225	New Testament	275	Christian church in Asia
226	Gospels & Acts	276	Christian church in Africa
227	Epistles	277	Christian church in No. America
228	Revelation (Apocalypse)	278	Christian church in So. America
229	Apocrypha, pseudepigrapha, etc.	279	Christian church elsewhere
230	Christian doctrinal theology	280	Christ. denominations & sects
231	God, Trinity, Godhead	281	Primitive & Oriental churches
232	Jesus Christ & his family	282	Roman Catholic Church
233	Man	283	Anglican churches
234	Salvation (Soteriology)	284	Protestants of Continental origin
235	Invisible world	285	Presb., Amer. Ref., Congr. chs.
236	Eschatology	286	Bapt., Disc. of Christ, Adventists
237		287	Methodist churches
238	Creeds & confessions of faith	288	Unitarianism
239	Apologetics & polemics	289	Other denominations & sects
240	Christ. moral & devotional	290	Other religions etc.
241	Moral theology	291	Comparative religion
242	Prayers & meditations	292	Classical (Gr. & Rom.) religion
243	Evangelistic writings	293	Germanic religion
244		294	Brahmanism & related religions
245	Hymns	295	Zoroastrianism
246	Symbolism etc.	296	Judaism
247	Sacred furniture etc.	297	Islam & its derivatives
248	Personal religion	298	
249	Worship in family life	299	Other religions

Further subdivisions occur decimally until a precise number is provided for each book. For example, Stuart Piggott's *The Druids*, falling in the 299 division, is numbered 299.16. Alex MacBain's *Celtic Anthology and Religion* is also numbered 299.16. The two books in the same category are separated by the author number appearing below the Dewey Decimal number in the upper left-hand corner of the card. *The Druids* is designated 299.16 and P631dr

MacBain's book 299.16. M118c The opening capital letters stand for the authors'

last names, Piggott and MacBain; the lower case letters for the key words in the titles, *Druids* and *Celtic*.

Not only does the Dewey Decimal system enable you to find books in your library, it is also the key to all sources similarly classified: Of these, we have examined *American Book Publishing Record*, page 49; *Booklist*, page 51; and *British National Bibliography*, page 52. Familiarity with the Dewey Decimal system tells you exactly where to look in classified sources. Additionally, once you know the Dewey Decimal numbers of your subject, you can browse in the stacks yourself. You are not confined to using the catalog to find numbers of books you have already discovered.

13.3. Card Catalog as Subject Bibliography

To use the card catalog as a subject bibliography, check not only your subject but all leads provided on *See also* cards which suggest alternative headings. Observe subtitles in books you find, chapter headings, and footnotes. Figure out the categories your subject falls under, related fields, alternative wordings. Then let your mind range freely over possibilities and the catalog offerings.

DRUIDS   MAGIC   WITCHCRAFT
ARCHAEOLOGY   HISTORY, CELTIC
STONEHENGE   ARCHAEOLOGY, CELTS
ANTHROPOLOGY
FAIRYTALES
GAULS   HISTORY,   SORCERY
ANCIENT BRITISH

At the end of the search is treasure, like this: the voice of the Druidic Bard, Taliesin, calling across the centuries.

...I WAS FORMED BY THE EARTH BY THE FLOWERS OF THE NETTLE BY THE WATER OF THE NINTH WAVE....I WAS IN THE BARK WITH DYLAN WHEN THE WATER FELL LIKE THE LANCES OF THE ENEMY FELL INTO THE ABYSS. I HAVE BEEN A SPOTTED SERPENT ON THE MOUNTAIN. I HAVE BEEN A VIPER IN THE LAKE. I HAVE BEEN A STAR AMONG CHIEFTAINS....I HAVE SLEPT IN A HUNDRED CIRCLES.—ENCYCLOPEDIA OF SUPERSTITIONS, FOLKLORE AND THE OCCULT SCIENCES OF THE WORLD.

A vision and a mystery:

The circles of rude, undressed stone found in various parts of the British Isles have been for the last two centuries alike the puzzle and the contention ground of archaeologists.

—Alex McBain

What is the origin and history of these stone circles? We may apply to history, to etymology, and to tradition in vain. The historians of the ancient world took practically no notice of them. Caesar may have stood among the pillared stones of Carnac...but as these monuments did not interfere with his martial or political designs, he...makes no reference to them.—Alex MacBain

An interpretation and a topic:

I rather suspect that these stones were either the very images of the gods, to whom the temples were dedicated, or that they were esteemed particularly sacred to them, and viewed as emblems of their presence.—Edward Davies

14. INDEXES

14.1. Periodical Indexes

N. W. Ayer & Son's Directory of Newspapers and Periodicals. Philadelphia: N. W. Ayer & Son, 1880—.

(A guide to newspapers and periodicals, not articles.)

British Humanities Index. Old Woking, Surrey: Unwin, 1962—.

Canadian Periodical Index. Ottawa: Canadian Library Association, 1931—.

(Current. An author and subject index to articles in Canadian periodicals.)

Index to Little Magazines. Chicago: Swallow, 1943—.

(Kept current with annual volumes. Indexed by author only.)

Readers' Guide to Periodical Literature. New York: Wilson, 1905—.

(Current. An author, subject index to such popular periodicals as *Life, Time, Saturday Review, Vital Speeches*, rather than journals or little magazines indexed in *Social Science and Humanities Index*.)

Social Science and Humanities Index: A Guide to Periodical Literature in the Social Sciences and Humanities. New York: Wilson, 1907—.

(Current. Formerly *International Index*. Subject and author index. Addresses of publishers in front.)

Basic Form of Entry in the Periodical Index

DRUIDS
  Annandale druids: a Blake crux. J. Adlard. Notes & Quer 14:19-20 Ja '67

DRUIDS
  William Stukeley: an eighteenth century antiquary, by S. Piggott. Review
    New Statesm & Nation 39:660 Je 10 '50. G. Grigson

DRUIDS
  Blake and the druids. P. F. Fisher. bibliog f J Engl & Germ Philol 58:589-612 O '59

14: 19-20 Ja '67 means the article is in volume 14, pages 19-20, in the issue dated January 1967

A Topic:
Druids in the poetry
of William Blake

The Serpent Temple. Engraving forming the final page of William Blake's *Jerusalem* (1804-20)....The giant allegorical figures are those of Los with hammer and tongs, and Vala with a distaff.

Subject Guide to Periodical Indexes and Review Indexes. By Jean Spealman Kujoth. Metuchen, N.J.: Scarecrow, 1969.

(This useful tool does not list articles but specialized indexes of articles.)

Ulrich's International Periodicals Directory. By Merle Rohinsky. 2 vols. 14th ed. New York: Bowker, 1971.

(Annual. A subject guide to periodicals, not articles. An excellent tool for identifying periodicals in your field. Title index in the back of volume II directs you to annotated main entry, providing description of scope, ordering information, prices, and publisher's address.)

14.2. Pamphlet Indexes

Public Affairs Information Service Bulletin. New York: Public Affairs Information Service, 1915—.

(Current. Weekly. "A selective subject list of the latest books, pamphlets, government publications, reports of public and private agencies and periodical articles relating to economic and social conditions, public administration and international relations, published in English throughout the world." Directory of publishers and organizations in the front of each issue.)

Vertical File Index of Pamphlets. New York: Wilson, 1935—.

(Current. An annotated subject, title index to pamphlets, leaflets, posters, booklets, and so on. As most of the items are inexpensive, this is an excellent source for current materials probably not available in your library.)

14.3. Essay Index

Essay and General Literature Index. New York: Wilson, 1900—.

(Current. Annual cumulations. "An index to about 40,000 essays and articles in 2,144 volumes of collections of essays and miscellaneous works." Subject, author, title indexing.)

14.4. Newspaper Indexes

N. W. Ayer & Son's Directory of Newspapers and Periodicals. Philadelphia: N. W. Ayer & Son, 1880—.

Christian Science Monitor Index. Boston: Christian Science Publishing Society, 1960—.

(Current. Subject index.)

New York Times Index. New York: New York Times, 1913—.

(Current. Twice monthly. Annotated author, subject index to the *New York Times*. As dates are fixed, this can serve as an index to all U.S. newspapers.)

Times. London. *Index to the Times*. London: Times Office, 1907—.

(Current. Alphabetically arranged by subject, author index to all news reported in the London *Times*. Unannotated.)

Wall Street Journal Index. New York: Dow Jones.

(Current. Classified index. News items located by month, date, page and column. Thus "7/24—15:1" means July 24, p. 15, col. 1.)

14.5. Book Review Indexes

Book Review Digest. New York: Wilson, 1905—.

(Current. "An index to reviews of current fiction and non-fiction appearing in selected periodicals and journals." Subject and title index follows author index in each volume. Each entry includes a digest of the review indexed. Use this tool as an aid in evaluating sources and a guide in ordering books for your personal library.)

Book Review Index. Ed. Mildred Schlientz. Detroit: Gale, 1965—.

(Current. Indexing by author and title of book reviewed.)

Index to Book Reviews in the Humanities. By Phillip Thomson. Detroit: Thomson, 1960—.

(An author index. The entry uses the following sequence: author, title, reviewer, periodical code number translated in front matter, date, and page.)

Masterplots Annual. New York: Salem, 1954—.

(Detailed plot summaries of novels and plays.)

Saturday Review Index, 1924–1944. Ann Arbor, Mich.: Bowker, 1971.

(Indexes all reviews, poems, essays, editorials that appeared in *Saturday Review* during the 20-year period covered.)

A Druid. Engraving from Aylett Sammes, *Bitannia Antique Illustrata*, London, 1676.

The Unheroic Druid. The Druid Panoramix from the modern French comic strip series by Goscinny and Uderzo, Asterix le Gaulois.

14.6. Biography Index

Biography Index: A Cumulative Index to Biographical Materials in Books and Magazines. New York: Wilson, 1947—.

15. GOVERNMENT PUBLICATIONS

Body, Alexander C. *Annotated Bibliography of Bibliographies on Government Publications and Supplementary Guides to the Superintendent of Documents Classification System: Second Supplement.* Kalamazoo: Western Michigan University, 1970.

(This source will lead you to bibliographies of government publications. Author, title, subject index. $2.00. For sale by author: Alexander C. Body, 925 Westfall, Kalamazoo, Mich. 49007.)

Government Reference Books: A Comprehensive Guide to U.S. Publications. Comp. Sally Wynkoop. Littleton, Colo.: Libraries Limited, 1970.

(604 titles. Author, title, subject index; prices; ordering information. Current coverage of bibliographies of government materials in all fields.)

National Council for Social Studies. *How to Locate Useful Government Publications.* Washington, D.C.: National Council for Social Studies, 1968.

(Available for $ .25 from National Education Association, 1201 16th St. N.W., Washington, D.C. 20036.)

Public Information Service Bulletin. New York: Public Affairs Information Service, 1915—.

(Subtitle: "A selective list of the latest books, pamphlets, government publications, reports of public and private agencies and periodical articles, relating to economic and social conditions, public administration and international relations, published in English throughout the world.")

Schmeckebier, Laurence F., and Roy B. Eastin. *Government Publications and Their Use.* Rev. ed. Washington, D.C.: Brookings Institution, 1969.

(An excellent guide to bibliography of government documents. Contains annotated lists of catalogs and indexes of government documents, bibliographies, congressional publications, presidential papers, government periodicals, microfilm editions of federal documents. Thorough and clear.)

United Nations Documents Index. New York: United Nations Publications, 1950—.

(Subject indexing of all United Nations publications. Monthly. If a U. N. publication is not available in your bookstore, write to United Nations, Sales Section, New York, N.Y. Be sure to provide document number.)

U. S. Department of Health, Education, and Welfare. Library. *Author-Title Catalog of the Department Library.* 29 vols. Boston: Hall, 1966.

U. S. Department of Health, Education, and Welfare. *Subject Catalog of the Department Library*. 20 vols. Boston: Hall, 1965.

(500,000 volumes indexed by subject. Important list of departmental publications, many of which can be purchased inexpensively.)

U. S. Library of Congress. *Checklist of State Publications*. Washington, D.C.: U. S. Government Printing Office, 1895—.

(Current. Materials arranged by state but indexed by title and subject. Ordering information included.)

U. S. Superintendent of Documents. *Document Index*. Washington, D.C.: U. S. Government Printing Office, 1895—.

(Current. Includes only those publications printed as documents and reports of the United States Senate or House of Representatives.)

U. S. Superintendent of Documents. *Monthly Catalog of United States Government Publications*. Washington, D.C.: U. S. Government Printing Office, 1895—.

(A current listing of materials issued by *all* divisions of government. Price and ordering information. Subject index at back of bound volumes. All items continuously numbered. Index provides item number in bound volume. *Always* check this source for low-cost or free government materials.)

U. S. Superintendent of Documents. *Selected List of United States Government Publications*. Washington, D.C.: U. S. Government Printing Office, 1928—.

(Bi-weekly. Free. Superintendent of Documents, Washington, D.C. "A leaflet giving titles and prices of the more important government publications on sale, with annotations showing the scope of each publication. A check-list order form is enclosed." —Schmeckebier and Eastin)

YOU ARE THE WATCHDOG OF THE REPUBLIC. YOU ARE THE EYES OF THE PEOPLE. YOU!

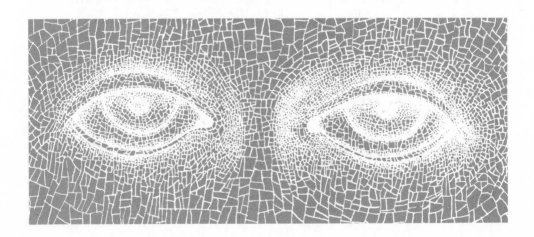

WHY NOT ORDER FOR YOURSELF?

U. S. Labor Department. Women's Bureau. *Why Not Be an Urban Planner?* Careers for Women, No. L13.11:49. Washington, D.C.: Superintendent of Documents, 1970. (10c)

U. S. Federal Communications Commission. *Talkin' Blues: Television, Corporate Greed and Women's Liberation.* Remarks by Nicolas Johnson, prepared for delivery to American Women in Radio and Television, Mar. 2, 1970. Washington, D.C.: Federal Communications Commission, 1970. (Free)

U. S. Justice Department. Narcotics and Dangerous Drugs Bureau. *Clerical Employment Everywhere under the Sun, Well Almost!* No. J 24.2:L58. Washington, D.C.: Justice Dept., 1970. (Free)

U. S. National Industrial Pollution Control Council. *Comprehensive Community Programs for Narcotic Addicts and Drug Users.* Public Health Service Pub. 2149. Washington D.C.: Superintendent of Documents, 1971. (10c)

U. S. Dept. of Health, Education, and Welfare. National Institute of Mental Health. *Youth in Turmoil: America's Changing Youth Cultures and Student Protest Movements,* by Jack D. Douglas. Public Health Services Publ. 2058. Item 507-B-13. Washington, D.C.: Superintendent of Documents, 1970. (1.00)

SPECIALIZED REFERENCE WORKS

$\mathcal{Y}$e shall know the truth, and the truth shall make ye free.—John 8:32

How big a dose of truth can man endure? — Nietzsche

AMERICAN INDIANS

Ernest Haas.

Our Father above, I have seen.
The Raven says, "There is going
to be another judgement day."
　　　　　　　　—Ghost Dance

Reference Works

American Heritage Book of Indians. Ed. William Brandon. New York: Dell, 1961.

American Indian Index. Chicago: Huebner, 1953.
　(Books, articles, documents indexed by subject.)

Astrov, Margot. *American Indian Prose and Poetry*. New York: Putnam, 1962.

Baldwin, Gordon C. *Talking Drums to Written Word*. New York: Grosset & Dunlap, 1970.

Blumenthal, Walter Hart. *American Indians Dispossessed: Fraud in Land Cessions Forced upon Tribes*. Philadelphia: MacManus, 1955.

Brinton, Daniel G. *Myths of the New World: A Treatise on the Symbolism and Mythology of the Red Race of America*. New York: Haskell, 1969.

Charters, Constitutions, and By-Laws of the Indian Tribes of North America. Ed. George E. Fay. Ethnology series. 9 vols. Greeley: Colorado State College, 1967–1970.

Deloria, Vine. *We Talk, You Listen: New Tribes, New Turf*. New York: Macmillan, 1970.

Dictionary of the American Indian. By John L. Stoutenburgh. New York: Philosophical Library, 1960.

Embree, Edwin R. *Indians of the Americas*. New York: Macmillan, 1970.
　(Paperback, $1.50.)

Handbook of Middle American Indians. Ed. Robert Wauchope et al. 14 vols. Austin: University of Texas Press, 1964–1970.

Hanke, Lewis. *Aristotle and the American Indians: A Study in Race Prejudice in the Modern World*. Bloomington: Indiana University Press, 1970.

Hofmann, Charles. *American Indians Sing*. New York: Day, 1967.
(Music and bibliographies included.)

Jacobs, Paul, et al. *To Serve the Devil*. Vol. I: *Natives and Slaves*. Vol. II: *Colonials and Sojourners*. New York: Random House, 1971.

Jacobson, Daniel. *Great Indian Tribes*. Maplewood, N.J.: Hammond, 1970.
(Good introductory study of North American tribes.)

Josephy, Alvin M. *Indian Heritage of America*. New York: Knopf, 1968.

Lewis, C. *American Indian Families: The Impact of Change*. Chicago: University of Chicago Press, 1970.

Marriott, Alice Lee, and Carol C. Rachlin. *American Indian Mythology*. New York: Crowell, 1968.

Reference Encyclopedia of the American Indian. Ed. Bernard Klein and Daniel Icolari. 2nd ed. New York: Klein, 1967.

Sanders, Thomas, and Walter Peek. *Literature of the American Indian*. Beverly Hills: Glencoe Press, 1973.

Swanton, John R. *The Indian Tribes of North America*. Washington, D.C.: Smithsonian Institution, 1971.

Textbooks and the American Indian. Ed. Rupert Costo. San Francisco: The Indian Historian Press, 1970.
(Bibliography, pp. 255–62.)

ANTHROPOLOGY

Casual writers thought [rock basins] were intended to hold the blood of sacrificial victims . . . [but] they are too frequent to have been intended for such a purpose, suggesting instead that they were cut to collect pure water for acts of lustration. By analogy with the primitive practice of walking between the severed parts of a sacrifice [it was] supposed that when a body was passed through the artificial holes or passages in the rocks it acquired a kind of Holiness and became more acceptable to the gods.

—*Antiquity*

Rock Temples of the British Druids. Left, general view of the central part of the Brimham Rocks. Right, close-up of some rock basins, diameter about 2 ft., on top of one of the tors.

Reference Works

Anthropology Today: Encyclopedic Inventory. Ed. A. L. Kroeber. Chicago: University of Chicago Press, 1953.

Bastian, Hartmut. *And Then Came Man.* New York: Viking, 1964.

Benedict, Ruth. *Contributions to Anthropology.* New York: AMS Press, 1969.

Benedict, Ruth. *Patterns of Culture.* Boston: Houghton Mifflin, 1959.

Biennial Review of Anthropology, 1969. Stanford, Calif.: Stanford University Press, 1970.
   (Includes bibliography.)

Binder, Otto. *Unsolved Mysteries of the Past.* New York: Tower, 1970.

Boas, Franz. *Anthropology and Modern Life.* New York: Norton, 1962.

Brew, John. O., ed. *One Hundred Years of Anthropology.* Cambridge, Mass.: Harvard University Press, 1968.

Coon, Carleton, and Edward E. Hunt, Jr. *Living Races of Man.* New York: Knopf, 1965.

Coon, Carleton Stevens. *Origin of Races.* New York: Knopf, 1962.
   (Bibliography, pp. 685–710.)

Frazer, Sir James George. *The New Golden Bough.* Ed. Theodor H. Gaster. New York: New American Library.
   (Abridged. Paperback, $3.95.)

Hays, H. R. *From Ape to Angel: An Informal History of Social Anthropology.* New York: Putnam, 1964.

International Bibliography of Social and Cultural Anthropology. Chicago: Aldine, 1955—.
   (Annual, author, subject index. Includes articles and books.)

Malinowski, Bronislaw. *Magic, Science, and Religion and Other Essays.* Garden City, N.Y.: Doubleday, 1954.

Montagu, Ashley. *Concept of Race.* New York: Macmillan, 1969.

Montagu, Ashley. *Man, His First Two Million Years: A Brief Introduction to Anthropology.* New York: Columbia University Press, 1969.

Norman, Eric. *Abominable Snowmen.* New York: Universal Publishing and Distributing, 1969.
   ($.75.)

Powdermaker, Hortense. *Stranger and Friend: The Way of an Anthropologist.* New York: Norton, 1967.
   (Bibliography, pp. 307–11.)

Winick, Charles. *Dictionary of Anthropology.* New York: Greenwood, 1956. Rpt. Totowa, N.J.: Littlefield, 1968.

Yearbooks

American Anthropologist. Philadelphia: University Museum, 1888—.

Biennial Review of Anthropology. Stanford, Calif.: Stanford University Press, 1959—.

Current Anthropology. Ed. William L. Thomas, Jr. Chicago: University of Chicago Press, 1956—.

Yearbook of Anthropology. New York: Wenner-Gren, 1955—.

Yearbook of Physical Anthropology. New York: Wenner-Gren, 1947—.

    (Largely articles reprinted from scientific journals.)

ART

"I distinctly ordered a reclining nude!"

Reference Works

Adeline Art Dictionary: Including Terms in Architecture, Heraldry, and Archaeology with a Supplement of New Terms. By Hugo G. Beigel. New York: Ungar, 1966.

Art Index. New York: Wilson, 1929—.

    (Author, subject index to art and related fields.)

Champlin, John. D., and C. C. Perkins. *Cyclopedia of Painters and Paintings.* 4 vols. New York: Kennikat, 1969.

Daniel, Howard. *Encyclopedia of Themes and Subjects in Painting.* New York: Abrams, 1971.

Encyclopedia of World Art. 15 vols. New York: McGraw-Hill, 1959–1968.

Gardner, Helen. *Art Through the Ages.* 5th ed. rev. New York: Harcourt, 1970.

Grants and Aid to Individuals in the Arts. Washington, D.C.: Washington International Arts Letter, 1970.

(Subtitle: "Containing listings of most professional awards and information about colleges, universities, and professional schools of the arts which offer assistance to students.")

Hamilton, George Heard. *19th and 20th Century Art, Painting, Sculpture and Architecture.* New York: Abrams, 1970.

(Includes appreciative, serious comment on "the soup-can, comic-strip, color-swatch, and eye-dazzle schools, all handsomely reproduced among the book's 487 illustrations. . . ."—David Glixon)

Havlice, Patricia Pate. *Art in Time.* Metuchen, N.J.: Scarecrow, 1970.

(This source provides a low-cost means of obtaining reproductions. Order back issues from A and S Book Company, 676 8th Avenue, New York, or Midtown Magazine, Inc., 3391 3rd Ave., Bronx, New York.)

Herbert, Robert L. *Modern Artists on Art.* Englewood Cliffs, N.J.: Prentice-Hall, 1965.

Janson, H. W., and Dora Jane Janson. *History of Art: From the Dawn of History to the Present Day.* New York: Abrams, 1970.

Myers, Bernard S., ed. *Encyclopedia of Painting.* 3rd rev. ed. New York: Crown, 1970.

Osborne, Harold, ed. *The Oxford Companion to Art.* New York: Oxford University Press, 1970.

Who's Who in Art. New York: International Publications Services, 1927—. (Annual.)

Yearbooks

Art News Annual. New York: Art News, 1926—.

Contemporary American Painting and Sculpture. Urbana, Ill.: University of Illinois Press, 1948—.

International Poster Annual: World Wide Review of Poster Art. New York: Hastings, 1948—.

Penrose Annual: International Review of the Graphic Arts. New York: Hastings, 1895—.

The Year's Art. Ed. Michael Dempsey. New York: Putnam, 1968/69—.

ASTRONOMY

Astronomy compels the soul to look upwards and leads us from this world to another.—Plato

Reference Works

Alter, Dinsmore, et al. *Pictorial Astronomy*. 3rd ed. New York: Crowell, 1969.

Baker, Robert H. *Introduction to Astronomy*. 7th ed. New York: Van Nostrand Reinhold, 1968.

Bell, Raymond Martin. *Your Future in Astronomy*. Careers in Depth No. 94. New York: Richard Rosen, 1970.

Fanning, A. E. *Astronomy Explained*. New York: International Publications Service, 1970.

Fanning, Anthony E. *Planets, Stars, and Galaxies: Descriptive Astronomy for Beginners*. New York: Dover, 1966.

Hammond Incorporated. *Earth and Space*. Maplewood, N.J.: Hammond, 1970.

Hodge, Paul W. *Revolution in Astronomy*. New York: Holiday, 1970.

(Bibliography, pp. 176–80.)

Howard, Neale E. *The Telescope Handbook and Star Atlas*. New York: Crowell, 1967.

(Good for beginner.)

Kemp, D. Alasdair. *Astronomy and Astrophysics: A Bibliographical Guide*. Hamden, Conn.: Shoe String, 1970.

McGraw-Hill Encyclopedia of Space. New York: McGraw-Hill, 1968.

Nicolson, Iain. *Astronomy*. New York: Grosset & Dunlap, 1970.

Rudaux, Lucien, and G. de Vaucouleurs. *Larousse Encyclopedia of Astronomy*. 2nd ed. New York: Prometheus, 1962.

Sagan, Carl, and I. S. Shklovsky. *Intelligent Life in the Universe*. New York: Delta, 1968.

Shapley, Harlow. *Source Book in Astronomy, 1900–1950*. Cambridge, Mass.: Harvard University Press, 1960.

Space Encyclopedia: A Guide to Astronomy and Space Research. Ed. H. S. Jones et al. Rev. ed. New York: Dutton, 1970.

Wallenquist, Ake. *Dictionary of Astronomical Terms*. Ed. and trans. Sune Engelbrektson. Garden City, N.Y.: Natural History Press, 1964.

Weigert, Arnold, and H. Zimmermann. *Concise Encyclopedia of Astronomy*. New York: American Elsevier, 1968.

Yearbooks

Annual Review of Astronomy and Astrophysics. Ed. Leo Goldberg. Palo Alto, Calif.: Annual Reviews, Inc., 1963—.

Asterisks. New York: Amateur Astronomer's Association, 1959—. (Free. 212 W. 79th St., New York 10024.)

U.S. Naval Observatory: Astronomical Phenomena. Washington, D.C.: U.S. Government Printing Office, 1951—.

Yearbook of Astronomy. New York: Norton, 1962—. (For amateurs.)

BLACK STUDIES

Afro-American Studies

I FEEL IN MYSELF A SOUL AS IMMENSE AS THE WORLD. I AM A MASTER AND I AM ADVISED TO ADOPT THE HUMILITY OF THE CRIPPLE.
—FRANZ FANON

From *The Art of Revolution by Dugald Stermer*
published by McGraw-Hill Book Company.

Reference Works

Abrahams, Roger D. *Positively Black*. Englewood Cliffs, N.J.: Prentice-Hall, 1970.

(Folklore. Bibliography, pp. 163–66.)

Americans from Africa. Ed. Peter Isaac Rose. 2 vols. New York: Aldine, 1970.

Berry, Mary F. *Black Resistance and White Law*. New York: Appleton, 1971.

Bigsby, C. W., ed. *Black American Writer*. 2 vols. New York: Penguin, 1971.

The Black Seventies: Leading Black Authors Look at the Present and Reach into the Future. Ed. Floyd B. Barbour. Boston: Sargent, 1970.

Bormann, Ernest G., comp. *Forerunners of Black Power: The Rhetoric of Abolition*. Englewood Cliffs, N.J.: Prentice-Hall, 1971.

(Speeches and essays by abolitionists.)

Bracey, J. H., et al. *Black Matriarchy: Myth or Reality*. New Haven, Conn.: Wadsworth, 1971.

Chapman, Abraham, ed. *Black Voices: An Anthology of Afro-American Literature*. New York: St. Martin's, 1970.

(Bibliography, pp. 700–18.)

David, John P., ed. *The American Negro Reference Book*. Englewood Cliffs, N.J.: Prentice-Hall, 1969.

Ducas, George, and Charles Van Doren, comps. *Great Documents in Black American History*. New York: Praeger, 1970.

(Includes some material never before published in complete form.)

Dunbar, Alice M., ed. *Masterpieces of Negro Eloquence: The Best Speeches Delivered by the Negro from the Days of Slavery to the Present Day*. New York: Bookery, 1914. Rpt. New York: Johnson Reprints, 1970.

Feldstein, Stanley. *Once a Slave: The Slave's View of Slavery.* New York: Morrow, 1971.

(Study by a historian relying upon slave narratives. Excellent bibliography.)

Franklin, John Hope. *From Slavery to Freedom.* 3rd. ed. New York: Random House, 1967.

Franklin, John Hope, and Isadore Starr, eds. *Negro in Twentieth Century America.* New York: Random House, 1967.

Frazier, Thomas R., ed. *Afro-American History: Primary Sources.* New York: Harcourt, 1970.

(Includes annotated bibliography.)

Gayle, Addison, comp. *The Black Aesthetic.* Garden City, N.Y.: Doubleday, 1971.

(Essays exploring black alienation from white aesthetic judgments.)

Grant, Joanne, ed. *Black Protest: History, Documents, and Analyses, 1619 to the Present.* New York: Fawcett, 1968.

Hentoff, Nat, ed. *Black Anti-Semitism and Jewish Racism.* New York: Schocken, 1970.

Index to Periodical Articles by and About Negroes. Boston: Hall, 1950—.

(Current. Authors, titles, subjects in one alphabetical listing.)

Jones, LeRoi. *Black Music.* New York: Morrow, 1971.

Jones, M. J. *Black Awareness: A Theology of Hope.* Nashville: Abingdon, 1971.

Kane, Michael B. *Minorities in Textbooks: A Study of Their Treatment in Social Studies Texts.* New York: Quadrangle, 1971.

(Concludes that there has been "little progress in correction of distortions in treatment of minorities in U.S. secondary school textbooks. . . ."—*Booklist.* Titles of offending textbooks included.)

Kearns, Francis Edward, ed. *Black Experience: An Anthology of American Literature for the 1970's.* New York: Viking, 1970.

(Bibliography, pp. 639–50.)

Kronus, Sidney. *The Black Middle Class.* Columbus, Ohio: Merrill, 1971.

Marshall, Sharon. *Black Beauty Book.* New York: Bantam, 1970.

Mead, Margaret, and James Baldwin. *A Rap on Race.* Philadelphia: Lippincott, 1971.

Miller, Ruth, ed. *Blackamerican Literature: 1760-Present.* Beverly Hills, Calif.: Glencoe, 1971.

"Negroes in the United States." *Bibliographic Survey: The Negro in Print.* Washington, D.C.: Negro Bibliographic and Research Center, Inc., 1965—.

($11.00 annually. 117 R Street, N.E., Washington, D.C. 20002. Available on microfilm.)

Pantell, Dora F., and Edwin Greenidge. *If Not Now, When? The Many Meanings of Black Power.* New York: Delacorte, 1970.

Patterson, Lindsay. *Black Theatre: A Twentieth Century Collection of the Works of Its Best Playwrights.* New York: Dodd, Mead, 1971.

Podish, Philip, et al. *Black Experience: The Negro in America, Africa, and the World: A Comprehensive Annotated Subject Bibliography of Works in the Libraries.* Toledo: University of Toledo, 1970.

Roberts, Hermese E. *The Third Ear: A Black Glossary.* Chicago: English Language Institute, 1971.

("... planned as part of a forthcoming dictionary, defines 400 vivid expressions. ..." Available for $.50 from English Language Institute of America, Inc., 1727 S. Indiana Ave., Chicago, Ill. 60616.)

Schechter, William. *History of Negro Humor in America.* New York: Fleet, 1971.

(Bibliography, pp. 205–07.)

Tucker, Sterling. *For Blacks Only: Black Strategies for Change in America.* Grand Rapids, Mich.: Eerdmans, 1970.

(Argues that "Blacks can achieve justice within the framework of U.S. society." —*Booklist*)

Turner, Darwin T., ed. *Black American Literature: Essays, Poetry, Fiction, Drama.* Columbus, Ohio: Merrill, 1970.

(Includes bibliography.)

Turner, D., ed. *Black Drama: An Anthology.* New York: Fawcett, 1971.

Uya, Okon Edet. *Black Brotherhood: Afro-Americans and Africa.* Lexington, Mass.: Heath, 1970.

Wilentz, Ted, and Tom Weatherly. *Natural Process: An Anthology of New Black Poetry.* New York: Hill & Wang, 1971.

Young, Richard P., ed. *Roots of Rebellion: The Evolution of Black Politics and Protest Since World War II.* New York: Harper & Row, 1970.

African Studies

Reference Works

Abraham, Roy. *Dictionary of Modern Yoruba.* Mystic, Conn.: Verry, 1958.

Abrash, Barbara. *Black African Literature in English since 1952.* Chicago: Johnson, 1971.

Africa 1970–71. 3rd ed. Comp. and ed. editorial staff of *Jeune Afrique.* New York: International Publications Service, 1970.

(Arrangement by country. Abundant data on topics ranging from mass media to government.)

Clark, Desmond. *The Prehistory of Africa.* New York: Praeger, 1970.

Davidson, Basil. *Africa: A History of a Continent.* New York: Macmillan, 1966.

Davidson, Basil. *The Lost Cities of Africa.* Rev. ed. Boston: Little, Brown, 1970.

Dictionary of African Biography. 2 vols. Totowa, N.J.: Rowman & Littlefield, n.d.

Douglas, Mary, and Phyllis M. Kaberry. *Man in Africa.* New York: Barnes & Nobel, 1969.

Hachten, Harva. *Kitchen Safari: A Gourmet's Tour of Africa.* New York: Atheneum, 1970.

Shapiro, Norman R., comp. *Negritude: Black Poetry from Africa and the Caribbean.* New York: October House, 1970.

Willett, Frank. *African Art: An Introduction.* New York: Praeger, 1971.

Yearbooks

Africa Annual 1970. 10th ed. New York: International Publications Service, 1970.

(Coverage ranges from livestock to politics of all African countries.)

Africa Contemporary Record: Annual Survey and Documents 1970–1971. 2nd ed. Ed. Colin Legum and John Drysdale. New York: International Publications Service, 1970.

(Annual survey of economic, commercial, political, and social developments.)

Negro Almanac. Comp. and ed. Harry A. Ploski and Roscoe C. Brown. New York: Bellwether, 1967—.

West Africa Annual. New York: International Publications Service, 1963—.

Year: Pictorial History of the Black American. By the editors of *Newsfront.* New York: Year, Inc., 1968—.

BUSINESS

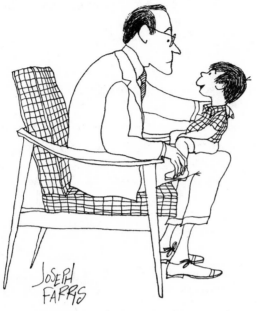

"Dad, tell me the facts of life. How does one beat the system?"

Reference Works

Brown, Courtney. *World Business: Promise and Problem.* New York: Free Press, 1970.

Business Periodical Index: A Cumulative Subject Index to Periodicals. . . . New York: Wilson, 1958—.

Carvel, Fred J. *Human Relations in Business.* New York: Macmillan, 1970.
(Bibliography.)

Child, J. *Business Enterprise in Modern Industrial Society.* New York: Macmillan, 1970.

Epstein, Edwin M. *Corporation in American Politics.* Englewood Cliffs, N.J.: Prentice-Hall, 1969.
(Bibliography, pp. 333–43.)

Goodman, Steven E. *Guide to Two Hundred Free Periodicals in the Social Sciences: Education, Business, Management, Government.* Los Angeles: Education and Training Consultants, 1970.

Hart, Donald J. *Introduction to Business in a Dynamic Society.* 2nd ed. New York: Macmillan, 1970.
(Bibliography.)

International Businessmen's Who's Who. 2nd Ed. New York: International Publishers, 1970.

Learned, Edmund Philip. *Business Policy: Text and Cases*. Rev. ed. Homewood, Ill.: Irwin, 1969.

Leslie, Conrad. *Conrad Leslie's Guide for Successful Speculating: Stocks, Commodities, Gold*. Chicago: Dartnell, 1970.

Prentice-Hall, Inc. *Encyclopedic Dictionary of Business Finance*. Prepared by editorial staff. Englewood Cliffs, N.J., 1971.

Silk, Leonard Solomon, and Louise M. Curley. *Primer on Business Forecasting: With a Guide to Sources on Business Data*. New York: Random House, 1970. (Bibliography, pp. 55–60.)

Tver, David F. *Dictionary of Business and Scientific Terms*. Houston: Gulf, 1968.

Wiebe, Robert H. *Businessmen and Reform: A Study of the Progressive Movement*. Chicago: Quadrangle, 1968.

Young and Company. *Sources of World Tax and Business Information*. New York: Bartlett Brown, 1968.

Yearbooks

U.S. Small Business Administration. *Handbook for Participation Loans with the Small Businesses Administration*. Washington, D.C.: U.S. Government Printing Office, 1960—.

U.S. Congress. Senate. Senate Reports. Select Committee on Small Business. *Annual Report*. Washington, D.C.: U.S. Government Printing Office.

World Trade Annual. New York: Walker, 1963—.

DRUG USE

You gonna shoot dope, Ralphie. You gonna be in jail or you gonna be dea
—an ex-add

Copyright Rapho Guillumette Pictures and Robert Com

Reference Works

Aldrich, Michael, et al. *Drugs: For and Against*. New York: Hart, 1970.
(Twelve essays by psychologists, clergymen, youthful radicals, and others.)

Bleibtreu, John N. *The Parable of the Beast*. New York: Macmillan, 1969.

Bloomquist, Edward R. *Marijuana: The Second Trip*. Beverly Hills, Calif.: Glencoe, 1971.

Braden, William. *The Private Sea: LSD and the Search for God*. Chicago: Quadrangle, 1967.

Brenner, Joseph H., et al. *Drugs and Youth: Medical Psychiatric and Legal Facts*. New York: Liveright, 1970.
(Popularly written. Includes comments by users of drugs.)

Coles, R., et al. *Drugs and Youth*. New York: Liveright, 1971.

Deedes, William. *Drugs Epidemic*. New York: Barnes & Noble, 1971.

Duncan, Tommie L. *Understanding and Helping the Narcotic Addict*. Philadelphia: Fortress, 1968.

Ebin, David, ed. *The Drug Experience: First-Person Accounts of Addicts, Writers, Scientists, and Others*. New York: Grove, 1965.

Fine, Ralph Adam. *Mary Jane versus Pennsylvania: The Day the Supreme Court Heard the Arguments For and Against Legalization of Marijuana*. New York: McCall, 1970.

Fort, Joel. *Pleasure Seekers: The Drug Crisis*. Indianapolis: Bobbs-Merrill, 1969.

Geller, A., and M. Boas. *Drug Beat*. New York: McGraw-Hill, 1971.

Grinspoon, L. *Marijuana Reconsidered*. Cambridge, Mass.: Harvard University Press, 1971.

Hentoff, Nat. *Doctor Among the Addicts*. Chicago: Rand McNally, 1968.

Huxley, A. *The Doors of Perception*. New York: Harper & Row, 1970.
(Paperback, $.95.)

Leary, Timothy R. *High Priest*. 2nd ed. New York: College Notes, 1968.

Leary, Timothy R. *The Politics of Ecstasy*. New York: Putnam, 1968.

Lingeman, Richard R. *Drugs from A to Z: A Dictionary*. New York: McGraw-Hill, 1969.

Lord, Jess R. *Marijuana and Personality Change*. Lexington, Mass.: Heath, 1971.

Marks, Jeanette. *Genius and Disaster: Studies in Drugs and Genius*. Port Washington, N.Y.: Kennikat, 1968.

Masters, E. L., and Jean Houston. *Psychedelic Art*. New York: Grove, 1968.

Menditto, Joseph. *Drugs of Addiction and Non-Addiction, Their Use and Abuse: A Comprehensive Bibliography, 1960–1969*. New York: Whitson, 1970.

Milbauer, Barbara. *Drug Abuse and Addiction: A Manual for Parent and Teenager*. New York: Crown, 1970.
(Bibliography included. Also agencies able to give information and help.)

Nowlis, Helen H. *Drugs on the College Campus*. Garden City, N.Y.: Doubleday, 1969.

Osmond, Humphrey, and Bernard Aaronson, eds. *Psychedelics: The Uses and Implications of Hallucinogenic Drugs*. Garden City, N.Y.: Doubleday, 1970.

(Anchor paperback, $2.45. Bibliography, pp. 482–501.)

Pawlak, Vic. *Conscientious Guide to Drug Abuse*. Hollywood, Calif.: Do It Now Foundation, 1970.

($.75. Order P.O. Box 3573, Hollywood, Calif. 90028.)

Slotkin, J. S. *The Peyote Religion*. New York: Free Press, 1956.

U.S. National Institute of Mental Health. *Directory of Narcotic Addiction Centers in the United States, 1968–69*. By Deena Watson and S. B. Sells. Washington, D.C.: U.S. Government Printing Office, 1970.

($.70. If ordering, include number: HE 20.2402: N 16/3/968–69.)

Whitney, Elizabeth D. *World Dialogue on Alcohol and Drug Dependence*. Boston: Beacon, 1970.

Wilder-Smith, A. E. *Drug Users: The Psycho-pharmacology of Turning On*. Wheaton, Ill.: Shaw, 1969.

(Bibliography, pp. 302–04.)

Wolfe, T. *The Electric Kool-Aid Acid Test*. New York: Farrar, 1968.

Yearbook

Current Drug Handbook. By Mary W. Falconer et al. Philadelphia: Saunders, 1958—.

ECOLOGY

Death is nature's way of recycling human beings

Reference Works

Anderson, Paul K. *Omega: Murder of the Ecosystem and Suicide of Man.* Dubuque, Iowa: Brown, 1971.

Anderson, Walt. *Politics and Environment: A Reader in Ecological Crisis.* Pacific Palisades, Calif.: Goodyear, 1970.

Brainerd, John W. *Nature Study for Conservation: A Handbook for Environmental Education.* New York: Macmillan, 1971.

(Ecology for the layman.)

Congressional Quarterly Service. *Man's Control of the Environment: To Determine His Survival . . . or to Lay Waste to His Planet.* Washington, D.C.: Congressional Quarterly Service, 1970.

(Discussion of government programs to save the environment, as well as government failures to act in crucial instances.)

DeBell, Garrett, ed. *Environmental Handbook.* New York: Ballantine, 1970.

(Paperback, $.95.)

Edberg, Rolf. *On the Shred of a Cloud.* New York: Harper & Row, 1971.

Ehrlich, Paul. *Population Bomb.* Rev. ed. New York: Ballantine, 1970.

Environment Information Access. New York: Ecology Forum, Inc., 1971—.

Mitchell, John G., and Constance L. Haltings, eds. *Ecotactics: The Sierra Club Handbook for Environmental Activists.* New York: Simon & Schuster, 1970.

(Bibliography. Explains action programs for environmental survival. Existing organizations to support. $.95.)

Olsen, Jack. *Slaughter the Animals: Poison the Earth.* New York: Simon & Schuster, 1971.

Reinow, Robert, and Leona Train Reinow. *Moment in the Sun.* New York: Ballantine, 1969.

Roloff, Joan G., and Robert C. Wylder. *There Is No "Away": Readings and Language Activities in Ecology.* Beverly Hills, Calif.: Glencoe, 1971.

Saltonstall, Richard. *Your Environment and What You Can Do About It.* New York: Walker, 1970.

Segerberg, Osbourne. *Where Have All the Flowers, Fishes, Birds, Trees, Water, and Air Gone.* New York: McKay, 1971.

Slusser, Dorothy Mallett, and Gerald Slusser. *Technology: The God that Failed.* Philadelphia: Westminster, 1971.

Swatek, Paul. *The Users Guide to the Protection of the Environment.* New York: Ballantine, 1970.

("The 14 chapters present facts about consumer products and their ecological effects, offering alternatives to high polluting practices." —ARBA. $1.25.)

Taylor, Gordon Rattray. *The Doomsday Book: Can the World Survive?* New York: World, 1970.

Yearbooks

Clean Air Year Book. London: National Society for Clean Air, 1951—.

Conservation Yearbook. Baltimore: Conservation Yearbook, 1952—.
(Biennial.)

International Youth Federation for the Study and Conservation of Nature. *IYF Yearbook*. Switzerland: International Youth Federation, 1962—.
(Free. Write c/o International Union for the Conservation of Nature and Natural Resources, 1110 Morges, Switzerland.)

National Wildlife Federation. *Conservation Directory: A Listing of Agencies, Organizations, and Officials Concerned with Natural Resource Use and Management*. Washington, D.C.: National Wildlife Federation, 1953—.
($1.00. 1412 16th St. N.W., Washington, D.C. 20036.)

ECONOMICS

"H-H-Herbert Hoover!"

Reference Works

Back, Harry, et al, eds. *Polec: Dictionary of Politics and Economics*. 2nd ed. New York: De Gruyter, 1967.

Dorfman, Joseph. *The Economic Mind in American Civilization*. 5 vols. New York: Viking, 1959.

Index of Economic Journals. Homewood, Ill.: Irwin, 1961—.
(Indexing by author and subject.)

International Bibliography of Economics. Chicago: Aldine, 1952—.
(Annual author, subject index of government publications, pamphlets, articles, and books.)

Nemmers, Erwin E., and Cornelius C. Janzen, eds. *Dictionary of Economics and Business*. Totowa, N.J.: Rowman & Littlefield, 1971.

Paradis, Adrian A. *The Economics Reference Book*. Philadelphia: Chilton, 1970.
(Introductory study for beginners.)

Sloan, Harold S., and Arnold J. Zurcher, eds. *Dictionary of Economics*. 5th rev. ed. New York: Barnes & Noble, 1971.

Yearbooks

The Economic Almanac. New York: National Industrial Conference Board, 1940—.

United Nations Bureau of Economic Affairs. *World Economic Survey*. New York: International Publications Service, 1945—.

U.S. Congress. House Reports. *Report of the Joint Economic Committee*. Washington, D.C.: U.S. Government Printing Office, 1948—.

EDUCATION

Reference Works

Current Financial Aids for Undergraduate Students, 1972–1973. Ed. Dr. Bernard G. Maxwell. Moline, Ill.: M. & L. Enterprises, 1973.
(Annual.)

Deighton, L. C., ed. *The Encyclopedia of Education*. 10 vols. New York: Macmillan, 1971.

Dennison, George. *The Lives of Children*. New York: Random House, 1970.
(Slum triumph. Twenty-three children begin to love learning.)

"Experimental Free Universities." *The Modern Utopian: Man in Search of Utopia*, 5, No. 4 (1971), 182–86.
(Order from Alternatives Foundation, P.O. Drawer A, Diamond Heights Station, San Francisco, Calif. 94131. Names and addresses arranged by state.)

Gattegno, Caleb. *What We Owe Children*. New York: Outerbridge, 1970.

Goodman, Paul. *Compulsory Mis-Education*. New York: Random House, 1969.

Gross, Ronald and Beatrice. *Radical School Reform*. New York: Simon & Schuster, 1970.

Guide to Study in Europe: A Selective Guide to Study in Europe. By Shirley Yvonne Herman. New York: Four Winds, 1969.

Herndon, James. *How to Survive in Your Native Land.* New York: Simon & Schuster, 1971.

(Author believes "U.S. schools are too foolishly over-administered to . . . nurture either reading and writing or the ability to cope . . . with . . . modern life." — *Time*)

Holt, John. *How Children Fail.* New York: Dell, 1970.

Holt, John. *How Children Learn.* New York: Dell, 1970.

Howes, Virgil H., ed. *Individualization of Instruction: A Teaching Strategy.* New York: Macmillan, 1970.

(A how-to book.)

Jerome, Judson. *Culture Out of Anarchy: The Reconstruction of American Higher Learning.* New York: Herder, 1970.

(How higher education precludes learning. Hopeful signs of changing processes.)

Kohl, Herbert. *Open Classroom.* New York: Random House, 1970.

Leonard, George B. *Education and Ecstasy.* New York: Delacorte, 1968.

Marcus, Sheldon, and Harry N. Rivlin, eds. *Conflicts in Urban Education.* New York: Basic Books, 1971.

Monroe, Paul. *A Cyclopedia of Education.* Detroit: Gale, 1968.

Neill, Alexander S. *Summerhill: A Radical Approach to Child Rearing.* Intro. Erich Fromm. New York: Hart, 1960.

Outstanding Educators of America. Chicago: Outstanding Educators of America, 1970—.

Piaget, Jean. *Science of Education and the Psychology of the Child.* New York: Grossman, 1970.

(Critique of "force feeding" in education.)

Silberman, Charles E. *Crisis in the Classroom: The Remaking of American Education.* New York: Random House, 1970.

(Important critical study of American education.)

U.S. Department of Health, Education, and Welfare. *Report on Higher Education.* Washington, D.C.: Superintendent of Documents, 1971.

($.75. Covers "virtually every aspect of . . . higher education . . . from the development of new and radically different institutions to the achieving of equality for women." —*Saturday Review*)

World Survey of Education. 4 vols. Paris: UNESCO, 1955–1966.

Yearbooks

Education Committees Yearbook. London: Councils and Education Press, 1969—.

A Handbook on Current Educational Affairs. Washington, D.C.: NEA, 1962—.

HEW Yearbook. Los Angeles: Academic Media, 1970.

National Society for the Study of Education. *Yearbook.* Chicago: University of Chicago Press, 1902—.

Standard Education Almanac. Orange, N.J.: Academic Media, 1970—.

U.S. Office of Education. *Biennial Survey of Education.* Washington, D.C.: U.S. Government Printing Office, 1916—.

World Year Book of Education, 1970: Education in Cities. Ed. Joseph A. Lauwerys and David G. Scanlon. New York: Harcourt, 1970.

("Comprehensive study of the effects of urbanization on education at all levels. Various case studies illustrate particular educational problems . . . in specific parts of the world." —ARBA)

Yearbook of Education. New York: Harcourt, 1953—.

Yearbook of Higher Education. Ed. Alvin Renetzky and Jon S. Greene. Los Angeles: Academic Media, 1969—.

HISTORY

Ye are gods and behold ye shall die,
and the waves be upon you at last.

In the darkness of time, in the deeps of
the years, in the changes of things,

Ye shall sleep as a slain man sleeps, and
the world shall forget you were
kings.

— Anonymous

"The Dying Gaul."

Reference Works

Adams, James Truslow, et al. *Album of American History.* 6 vols. New York: Scribner's, 1969.

Adams, James T., ed. *Dictionary of American History.* 2nd ed., rev. 6 vols. New York: Scribner's, 1961.

America, History and Life: A Guide to Periodical Literature. Santa Barbara: Clio, 1955—.

(Indexed by subjects and names. Current.)

America's Front Page News 1690–1970. Garden City, N.Y.: Doubleday, 1971.

(". . . a folio volume containing facsimile reproductions of 300 newspaper pages and photos . . . grouped according to four themes: wars, national leaders, popular movements, and 'Triumphs and Tragedies.' " —David Glixon)

The Cambridge Ancient History. Rev. ed. 12 vols. New York: Cambridge University Press, 1961.

The Cambridge Medieval History. Ed. Henry M. Gwatkin et al. 8 vols. New York: Cambridge University Press, 1966.

Current, Richard N., T. H. Williams, and Frank Freidel. *American History: A Survey*. 3rd ed. New York: Knopf, 1971.

Dictionary of American Biography. 11 vols. New York: Scribner's, 1958.

(Deceased persons.)

Harper Encyclopedia of the Modern World: A Concise Reference History from 1760 to the Present. Ed. Richard B. Morris and Graham W. Irwin. New York: Harper & Row, 1970.

Hurwitz, Howard L. *An Encyclopedic Dictionary of American History*. New York: Washington Square Press, 1970.

(Paperback, $1.45.)

Langer, William L., ed. *Encyclopedia of World History: Ancient, Medieval, and Modern Chronologically Arranged*. 4th ed., rev. and enl. Boston: Houghton Mifflin, 1968.

Larousse Encyclopedia of Modern History: From 1500 to the Present Day. Ed. M. Dunan. New York: Harper & Row, 1964.

Morris, R. B., and H. S. Commager, eds. Rev. ed. *Encyclopedia of American History*. New York: Harper & Row, 1970.

National Cyclopedia of American Biography. 49 vols. Ann Arbor, Mich.: University Microfilms, 1892—.

(Living persons. Kept current.)

The New Cambridge Modern History. New York: Cambridge University Press, 1957—.

Oxford Classical Dictionary. Ed. N. G. Hammond and H. H. Scullard. 2nd ed. New York: Oxford University Press, 1970.

Schlesinger, Arthur M., and Dixon R. Fox, eds. *History of American Life: A Social, Cultural, and Economic Analysis*. 13 vols. New York: Macmillan, 1927–1956.

Webster's Guide to American History. Ed. Charles Van Doren and Robert McHenry. Springfield, Mass.: Merriam, 1971.

(Historical account from discovery to present. "It takes the form of a chronology accompanied by extracts from a rich variety of contemporary source material: news items, speeches, letters, documents, and popular literature." —David Glixon)

Yearbooks

Americana Annual. New York: Americana, 1923—.

Current History Review. Chicago: Rand McNally, 1959—.

Essays in History: Annual Collection. Charlottesville: University of Virginia, 1954—.

Living History of the World. New York: Stravon, 1966—.

New International Yearbook: A Compendium of the World's Affairs for the Year. New York: Funk & Wagnall's, 1907—.

News Dictionary. New York: Facts on File, 1965—.

Newsweek's History of Our Times. New York: Funk & Wagnall's, 1949—.

Statesman's Yearbook. New York: St. Martin's, 1961—.

Year: A Permanent Record of All the Year's Outstanding News Events in . . . Pictures and . . . Words. Ed. W. T. Adams, J. M. Orr, and Kalman Phillips. Maplewood, N.J.: Hammond and Year, 1948—.

LITERATURE

Genre

Clearly I will set forth all you would learn, speaking not in dark riddles, but in full simplicity, as speech is due between friends. Behold, I whom you see am Prometheus, the giver of fire to mankind.—Aeschylus

Pieter Paul Rubens, "Prometheus Bound."

Reference Works

Adleman, Irving. *Modern Drama: A Checklist of Critical Literature on 20th Century Plays*. Metuchen, N.J.: Scarecrow, 1967—.

Baker, Ernest A. *The History of the English Novel*. 11 vols. New York: Barnes & Noble, 1961–1967.

Beachcroft, T. O. *Modest Art: A Survey of the Short Story in English*. New York: Oxford University Press, 1968.

Bowman, Walter P., and Robert H. Ball. *Theatre Language: A Dictionary of Terms in English of the Drama and Stage from Medieval to Modern Times*. New York: Theatre Arts Books, 1961.

Brooks, Cleanth. *Modern Poetry and the Tradition*. Chapel Hill: University of North Carolina Press, 1965.

Cohn, Ruby. *Currents in Contemporary Drama*. Bloomington: Indiana University Press, 1969.

Courthope, William J. *A History of English Poetry*. 6 vols. New York: Macmillan, 1895–1910. Rpt. New York: Russell, 1962.

Deutsch, Babette. *Poetry Handbook: A Dictionary of Terms*. Rev. ed. New York: Funk & Wagnall's, 1969.

Dunlop, John C. *History of Prose Fiction*. 2 vols. New York: Burt Franklin, 1970.

Esslin, Martin. *Theatre of the Absurd*. Garden City, N.Y.: Doubleday, 1969.

Gassner, John, and Edward Quinn. *Reader's Encyclopedia of World Drama*. New York: Crowell, 1969.

Granger's Index to Poetry. Ed. William F. Bernhardt. 5th ed., rev. New York: Columbia University Press, 1962. Supplement 1967.

(Indexing by author, title, first line, and subject.)

Halliday, Frank. *Shakespeare Companion, 1564–1964*. Baltimore: Penquin, 1964.

Hartnoll, Phyllis. *The Oxford Companion to the Theatre*. New York: Oxford University Press, 1967.

International Who's Who in Poetry. London: Cranbrook, 1958—.

Kuntz, Joseph M. *Poetry Explications: A Checklist of Interpretations Since 1925 of British and American Poems Past and Present*. Chicago: Swallow, 1962—.

Mandel, Siegfried, ed. *Contemporary European Novelists*. Carbondale: Southern Illinois University Press, 1968.

Nicoll, Allardyce. *A History of English Drama, 1660–1900*. Rev. ed. 6 vols. Cambridge, Mass.: Harvard University Press, 1952–59.

Nicoll, Allardyce. *World Drama from Aeschylus to Anouilh*. New York: Harcourt, 1949.

Nygren, Dorothy, ed. *A Library of Literary Criticism*. New York: Ungar, 1960.

(Twentieth century coverage.)

Pearce, Richard. *Stages of the Clown: Perspectives on Modern Fiction from Dostoyevsky to Beckett*. Carbondale: Southern Illinois University Press, 1970.

Preminger, Alex, et al. *Princeton Encyclopedia of Poetry and Poetics*. Princeton, N.J.: Princeton University Press, 1965.

Short Story Index. New York: Wilson, 1953. Supplements 1958, 1963, 1968. (Plans are to keep this current. Indexing by author, title, and subject.)

West, Paul, ed. *Modern Novel*. 2 vols. New York: Hutchinson, 1969–1970.

Yearbooks

Yearbook of the American Short Story. Boston: Houghton Mifflin, 1915—.

Yearbook of Comparative Criticism. Ed. Joseph Strelka. University Park: Pennsylvania State University Press, 1968—.

Yearbook of the Drama in America. Boston: Small, Maynard, 1920—.

British and American Literature

Reference Works

Abstracts of English Studies. Boulder: University of Colorado, 1958—.

American Literature Abstracts. San Jose: Burbank Press, 1967.

Cambridge History of American Literature. 4 vols. Ed. W. P. Trent et al. New York: Macmillan, 1967.

Cambridge History of English Literature. New York: Cambridge University Press, 1970.

The Concise Oxford Dictionary of English Literature. Ed. Dorothy Eagle. 2nd ed. New York: Oxford University Press, 1970.

Hart, James D. *The Oxford Companion to American Literature*. 4th ed., rev. and enl. New York: Oxford University Press, 1965.

Harvey, Paul, and Dorothy Eagle, eds. *Oxford Companion to English Literature*. 4th ed. New York: Oxford University Press, 1967.

Kunitz, Stanley J., and Howard Haycraft. *American Authors, 1600–1900*. New York: Wilson, 1938.

Kunitz, Stanley J., and Howard Haycraft. *British Authors Before 1800*. New York: Wilson, 1952.

Kunitz, Stanley J., and Howard Haycraft. *Twentieth Century Authors*. New York: Wilson, 1955.

Modern Language Association of America. *MLA International Bibliography of Books and Articles on the Modern Languages and Literatures*. New York: MLA, 1963—.
(Annual. Arrangement by national literatures; author index at the end of each volume. Multi-lingual.)

Penguin Companion to Literature: American and Latin American. Baltimore: Penguin, 1971.

Penguin Companion to Literature: English and Commonwealth. Baltimore: Penguin, 1971.

Spiller, R. E. W., et al. *Literary History of the United States*. 3 vols. New York: Macmillan, 1963.
(Volume III is devoted exclusively to bibliography.)

Yearbooks

American Literary Scholarship. Durham, N.C.: Duke University Press, 1963—.

Literary and Library Prizes. Ed. Olga S. Weber. New York: Bowker, 1935—.
(Checklist of awards available to amateur writers.)

The Yearbook of English Studies. Cambridge, Mass.: Modern Humanities Research Association, 1971—.

Year's Work in English Studies. Ed. Geoffrey Harlow and James Redmond. New York: Humanities, 1919—.
(British only.)

World Literature

"Farinata Delgi Uberti," Dante's Inferno, ill. Gustave Dore. From *A Dore Treasury*, Crown. 1971.

Reference Works

Encyclopedia of World Literature in the Twentieth Century. Ed. Wolfgang B. Fleischmann. 3 vols. New York: Ungar, 1970.

Grigson, Geoffrey. *The Concise Encyclopedia of Modern World Literature.* 2nd ed. New York: Hawthorn, 1971.

Harkins, William E. *Dictionary of Russian Literature.* New York: Greenwood, 1956.

Harvey, Sir Paul, and Janet E. Heseltine. *The Oxford Companion to French Literature.* New York: Oxford University Press, 1959.

Hornstein, Lillian, et al., eds. *Reader's Companion to World Literature.* New York: New American Library, 1957.

International Who's Who. New York: International Publishing Service, 1935—.

Modern Language Association of America. *MLA Bibliography of Books and Articles on the Modern Languages and Literatures.* New York: MLA, 1963—. (Continues MLA *Annual Bibliography.*)

Newmark, Maxim. *Dictionary of Spanish Literature.* Totowa, N.J.: Littlefield, 1956.

The Oxford Classical Dictionary. Ed. N. G. Hammond and H. H. Scullard. 2nd ed. New York: Oxford University Press, 1970.

Penguin Companion to Literature: European. By Anthony K. Thorlby et al. Baltimore: Penguin, 1969.

Rose, Herbert Jennings. *Handbook of Greek Literature: From Homer to the Age of Lucian*. 4th ed. New York: Dutton, 1965.

Rose, Herbert Jennings. *A Handbook of Latin Literature from the Earliest Times to the Death of St. Augustine*. 3rd ed. New York: Dutton, 1966.

Shipley, Joseph T., ed. *Dictionary of World Literary Terms: Forms, Technique, Criticism*. Rev. and enl. ed. Boston: Writer, 1970.

Shipley, Joseph T., ed. *Encyclopedia of Literature*. 2 vols. New York: Philosophical Library, 1946.

Yearbooks

Northeast: New International Literary Annual. LaCrosse, Wisc.: Keller Press, 1965—.

Yearbook of Comparative and General Literature. New York: Russell, 1952—.

The Year's Work in Classical Studies. London: J. Murray, 1907—.

The Year's Work in Modern Language Studies. New York: Oxford University Press, 1931—.

MASS MEDIA

She is folded in magic and hushed in the pride of her cloak
Which is woven of worship like silk for the hollows of eyes
That are raised in the dark to her image that shimmered and spoke;

And she speaks in her darkness alone and her emptiness cries
Till her voice is as shuddering tin in the wings of a stage,
And her beauty seems wrong as the wig of a perfect disguise;

She is sick with the shadow of shadow, diseased with the rage
Of the whiteness of light and the heat of interior sun,
And she faints like a pauper to carry the weight of her wage . . .
—Karl Shapiro

Andy Warhol, "Marilyn, Monroe"

Reference Works

Agee, James. *Agee on Film*. 2 vols. New York: Grosset & Dunlap, 1969. (Paperback, $2.95 each.)

Anderson, John, and Rene Fulop-Miller. *American Theatre and the Motion Picture in America*. New York: Johnson Reprint, 1970.

Baxter, John. *Science Fiction in the Cinema*. Cranbury, N.J.: A. S. Barnes, 1970. (Bibliography and plot summaries included.)

Berger, Arthur. *Lil Abner*. New York: Twayne, 1969. (Criticism of the comics.)

Chester, Edward W. *Radio, Television, and American Politics*. New York: Sheed & Ward, 1970.

Clark, David G., and Earl P. Hutchinson, eds. *Mass Media and the Law: Freedom and Restraint*. New York: Wiley, 1970. (Bibliography.)

Couperie, Pierre, and Maurice C. Horn. *A History of the Comic Strip*. New York: Crown, 1968.

Editorials on File. New York: Facts on File, 1970—.

Encyclopedia of Radio and Television Broadcastings. By Robert St. John. 4th ed. Milwaukee: Cathedral Square, 1970.

Galanoy, Terry. *Down the Tube, or Making Television Commericals Is Such a Dog-Eat-Dog Business It's No Wonder They're Called Spots*. Chicago: Regnery, 1970.

Goodstone, Tony, ed. *Pulps: Fifty Years of American Pop Culture*. New York: Random House, 1970. (Selected stories including some by H. P. Lovecraft, Tennessee Williams, Ray Bradbury, MacKinlay Kantor.)

Graham, Peter. *Dictionary of the Cinema*. Cranbury, N.J.: A. S. Barnes, 1968.

Halliwell, Leslie. *Film Goer's Companion: From Nickelodeon to New Wave*. 3rd ed., rev. New York: Hill & Wang, 1970.

Journalism Quarterly: Devoted to Research in Journalism and Mass Communications. Minneapolis: University of Minnesota Press, 1924—.

Kahn, Frank J., ed. *Documents of American Broadcasting*. New York: Appleton, 1968. (Original texts of laws and decisions crucial to American broadcasting.)

"Paperbacks in Mass Communication: A Comprehensive Bibliography." *Journalism Quarterly*. Minneapolis: University of Minnesota Press. (Appears in each issue.)

Randall, Richard S. *Censorship of the Movies: The Social and Political Control of a Mass Medium*. Madison: University of Wisconsin Press, 1970.

Rissover, Fredric, and David C. Birch, eds. *Mass Media and Popular Art*. New York: McGraw-Hill, 1971. (Essays on advertising, journalism, cartoons, radio, television, movies, and popular music.)

Spottiswoode, Ray, et al., eds. *The Focal Encyclopedia of Film and Television: Techniques*. New York: Hastings, 1969.

Steinberg, Charles Side. *The Communicative Arts: An Introduction to Mass Media*. New York: Hastings, 1970.

Wilk, Max. *Wit and Wisdom of Hollywood: From the Squaw Man to the Hatchet Man*. New York: Atheneum, 1970.

Yearbooks

Broadcasting Yearbook. Washington, D.C.: Broadcasting Publications.

Daniel Blum's Screen World. Philadelphia: Chilton, 1950—.

Film Review Annual. Cranbury, N.J.: A. S. Barnes, 1944—.

Films in Review. New York: National Board of Review of Motion Pictures, 1950—.

International Motion Picture Almanac. New York: Quigley, 1930—.

International Television Almanac: Basic Reference Tool of the Television Industry. New York: Quigley, 1955—.

Look-Listen Opinion Poll. Madison: American Council For Better Broadcasting, 1954—.

Screen World. New York: John Willis, 1966—.

Yearbook of the American Screen. Boston: Small, Maynard, 1923—.

MATHEMATICS

Mathematics possesses not only truth, but supreme beauty—a beauty cold and austere, like that of sculpture, without appeal to any part of our weaker nature, sublimely pure, and capable of a stern perfection such as only the greatest art can show.—Bertrand Russell

Salvador Dali, "Las Meninas."

Reference Works

Ball, W. W. Rouse. *A Short Account of the History of Mathematics*. New York: Dover, 1960.

Gamow, George. *One, Two, Three . . . Infinity: Facts and Speculations of Science*. New York: New American Library, 1953.

Howard, Alexander Edward, et al. *Teaching Mathematics*. New York: Humanities Press, 1968.

(Bibliography, pp. 180–82.)

James, Glenn, and Robert C. James, eds. *Mathematics Dictionary*. 3rd ed. New York: Van Nostrand Reinhold, 1968.

Kline, Morris. *Mathematics in Western Culture*. New York: Oxford University Press, 1953.

Kuipers, L., and R. Tinman, eds. *Handbook of Mathematics*. Trans. I. N. Sneddon. Elmsford, N.Y.: Pergamon, 1969.

Newman, James R. *The World of Mathematics*. 4 vols. New York: Simon & Schuster, 1956–1960.

Universal Encyclopedia of Mathematics. New York: Simon & Schuster, 1964.

(Suitable for undergraduates.)

Wheeler, Ruric E. *Modern Mathematics: An Elementary Approach*. 2nd ed. Belmont, Calif.: Brooks/Cole, 1970.

(Bibliography, pp. 549–52.)

Whitehead, Alfred North. *An Introduction to Mathematics*. Rev. ed. New York: Holt, Rinehart & Winston, 1959.

MUSIC

WITHOUT MUSIC, LIFE WOULD BE A MISTAKE
—NIETZSCHE

Reference Works

Apel, Willi. *Harvard Dictionary of Music*. 2nd ed. Cambridge, Mass.: Harvard University Press, 1969.

Baker, Theodore. *Dictionary of Musical Terms*. New York: AMS, 1970.

Baker, Theodore. *Baker's Biographical Dictionary of Musicians*. 5th ed. New York: Schirmer, 1965.

(Supplement pending.)

Brown, Len, and Gary Friedrich. *Encyclopedia of Rock and Roll*. New York: Tower, 1970.

(Paperback, $1.50.)

Clough, Francis F., and G. J. Cuming. *The World's Encyclopedia of Recorded Music*. Westport, Conn.: Greenwood, 1952. (Supplement, 1966.)

Cross, Milton, and David Ewen. *The Milton Cross New Encyclopedia of the Great Composers and Their Music*. 2 vols. Garden City, N.Y.: Doubleday, 1969.

Dictionary of Modern Music and Musicians. By Arthur E. Hull. New York: AMS Press, 1969.

Duckles, Vincent Harris. *Music Reference and Research Materials: An Annotated Bibliography.* 2nd ed. New York: Free Press, 1967.

Ewen, David. *American Popular Songs from the Revolutionary War to the Present.* New York: Random House, 1966.

Ewen, David. *Complete Book of Classical Music.* Englewood Cliffs, N.J.: Prentice-Hall, 1965.

Ewen, David. *New Complete Book of the American Musical Theatre.* New York: Holt, Rinehart & Winston, 1971.

(Summarizations of 500 shows.)

Ewen, David. *The World of Twentieth Century Music.* Englewood Cliffs, N.J.: Prentice-Hall, 1968.

Gillett, Charlie. *The Sound of the City: The Rise of Rock and Roll.* New York: Outerbridge, 1970.

(Bibliography included.)

Glazer, Tom, comp. *Songs of Peace, Freedom, and Protest.* New York: McKay, 1970.

Grove, Sir George. *Dictionary of Music and Musicians.* Ed. Eric Blom. 5th ed. 10 vols. New York: Macmillan, 1961. Supplement, 1966.

Kennington, Donald. *The Literature of Jazz: A Critical Guide.* Chicago: American Library Association, 1971.

(Bibliographies of jazz literature; listing of jazz films.)

Lloyd, Norman. *The Golden Encyclopedia of Music.* New York: Golden Press, 1968.

Music Index. Detroit: Information Service, 1949—.

(Author, subject index to periodical literature.)

Scholes, Percy A. *The Oxford Companion to Music.* Ed. John Owen Ward. 10th ed., rev. New York: Oxford University Press, 1970.

Yearbooks

Annual Directory of the Concert World. Evanston, Ill.: Sommy Birchard, 1954—.

Country Music World and Yearbook. Arlington, Va.: Jim Clark, 1964—.

High Fidelity Magazine. *Records in Review.* New York: Scribner's, 1955—.

Julliard Review Annual. New York: Julliard School of Music, 1962—.

Music: Down Beat's Music. Chicago: Maher, 1956—.

Ready, Steady, Go! Annual for Popular Music Fans. London: TV Publications, 1965—.

World of Religious Music. Cincinnati: Billboard, 1965—.

The Year in American Music. New York: Allen, Towne, & Heath, 1946/47—.

MYTHOLOGY AND FOLKLORE

Behold now behemoth, which I made with thee; he
  eateth grass as an ox.
Lo now, his strength is in his loins, and his force is in
  the navel of his belly.

—Job 40:15-16

Reference Works

Abstracts of Folklore Studies. Austin: University of Texas Press, 1963—.

Beckwith, Martha. *Hawaiian Mythology.* Honolulu: University of Hawaii Press, 1970.

Benet, William Rose, ed. *The Reader's Encyclopedia.* New York: Crowell, 1965.

Bulfinch's Mythology: The Age of Fable, The Age of Chivalry, Legends of Charlemagne. New York: Crowell, 1970.

Daniels, Cora L., and C. M. Stevans, eds. *Encyclopedia of Superstitions, Folklore, and the Occult Sciences of the World.* 3 vols. Detroit: Gale, 1971.

Davidson, Gustav. *A Dictionary of Angels Including Fallen Angels.* New York: Free Press, 1967.

Diehl, Katherine. *Religions, Mythologies, Folklores: An Annotated Bibliography.* 2nd ed. Metuchen, N.J.: Scarecrow, 1962.

The Encyclopedia of Ancient and Forbidden Knowledge. New York: Zolar, 1970.
  (A study of the occult.)

Evans, Bergen. *Dictionary of Mythology: Mainly Classical.* Lincoln, Neb.: Centennial, 1970.
  (Bibliography included.)

Frazer, Sir James G. *The Golden Bough: A Study in Magic and Religion*. 13 vols. 3rd ed. London: Macmillan, 1955.

Gray, Louis H., and John A. MacCulloch, eds. *Mythology of All Races*. 13 vols. New York: Cooper, 1964.

Larousse Encyclopedia of Mythology. Ed. F. Guirand. New York: Putnam, 1968.

Robbins, Russell Hope. *The Encyclopedia of Witchcraft and Demonology*. New York: Crown, 1959.

(Extensive bibliography, pp. 558–71.)

Tallman, Marjorie. *Dictionary of American Folklore*. New York: Philosophical Library, 1959.

Waters, Clara. *A Handbook of Legendary and Mythological Art*. Boston: Houghton Mifflin, 1881. Rpt. Detroit: Gale, 1969.

(Explains mythological and religious representations in art. Norse mythology excluded.)

PERFORMING ARTS

Ernest Haas.

105

Reference Works

Ballanchine, George. *Ballanchine's New Complete Stories of the Great Ballets*. Ed. Frances Mason. Garden City, N.Y.: Doubleday, 1968.

Blum, Daniel. *A Pictorial History of the American Theatre, 1860–1970*. 3rd. ed. New York: Crown, 1969.

Brinson, Peter, and Clement Crisp. *International Book of the Ballet*. New York: Stein & Day, 1970.

Brockett, Oscar Gross. *Theatre: An Introduction*. 2nd ed. New York: Holt, Rinehart & Winston, 1969.

(Bibliography, pp. 553–72.)

Cayou, Dolores K. *Modern Jazz Dance*. New York: National Press, 1971.

Cole, Toby, and Helen Krich Chinoy, eds. *Actors on Acting: Theories, Techniques and Practices of the Great Actors of All Times as Told in Their Own Words*. . . . Rev. ed. New York: Crown, 1970.

(Bibliography, pp. 670–94.)

Duncan, Isadora. *Art of the Dance*. New York: Theatre Arts, 1928.

Ewen, David. *New Complete Book of the American Musical Theatre: From 1866 to the Present*. New York: Holt, Rinehart & Winston, 1970.

Fox, Charles P., and L. Freeman. *Big Top Circus Days*. Watkins Glenn, N.Y.: Century House, 1969.

Guide to Performing Arts. Metuchen, N.J.: Scarecrow, 1967—.

Johnston, Jill. *Not in Broad Day Light: Dance Journal 1971*. New York: Dutton, 1971.

Kersley, Leo, and Janet Sinclair. *Dictionary of Ballet Terms*. New York: Pitman, 1964.

Loewenberg, Alfred, ed. *Annals of Opera: 1597–1940*. Totowa, N.J.: Rowman & Littlefield, 1971.

McDonagh, Don. *Rise and Fall of Modern Dance*. New York: Outerbridge, 1970.

McPharin, Marjorie B. *Puppet Theatre in America: A History 1524–1948*. Boston: Plays, 1969.

Martin, George. *Opera Companion: A Guide for the Casual Opera Goer*. New York: Apollo, 1970.

Matthews, Thomas. *Splendid Art: A History of the Opera*. New York: Macmillan, 1970.

(Bibliography, pp. 206–08.)

Peckam, Morse. *Man's Rage for Chaos: Biology, Behavior and the Arts*. Philadelphia: Chilton, 1965.

Percival, John. *Modern Ballet*. New York: Dutton, 1970.

Rigdon, Walter, ed. *Biographical Encyclopedia and Who's Who of the American Theatre*. New York: Heineman, 1966.

Rischbieter, Henning. *Art and the Stage in the Twentieth Century: Painters and Sculptors Work for the Theatre*. Greenwich, Conn.: New York Graphic Society, 1969.

Rosenthal, Harold D., and J. Warrack. *Concise Oxford Dictionary of Opera*. New York: Oxford University Press, 1964.

Shank, Theodore. *Art of Dramatic Art*. Encino, Calif.: Dickenson, 1969. (Bibliography, pp. 199–206.)

Sharp, Harold, and Marjorie Z. Sharp. *Index to Characters in the Performing Arts*. Metuchen, N.J.: Scarecrow, 1966—.

Yearbooks

Ballet Annual. London: A & C Black, 1950—.

Daniel Blum's Theatre World. New York: Theatre World, 1945—.

Focus on Dance: Papers from Annual Conferences. . . . Washington, D.C.: American Association for Health, Physical Education, and Recreation, 1960—.

Folk Dance Guide. New York: Carlton, 1951—.

Opera. London: Alan Ross, 1950—.

Theatre Annual. Albany, N.Y.: State University of New York, 1942—.

Theatre World. New York: Crown, 1965—.

Theatre World Annual. London: Rockliff, 1950—.

Willis, John, ed. *Dance World*. 5 vols. New York: Crown, 1966—. (Revised annually.)

PHILOSOPHY

Jacques Louis David, "The Death of Socrates," Metropolitan Museum of Art, Wolfe Fund, 1931. New York.

. . . he walked about until, as he said, his legs began to fail, and then he lay on his back, according to the directions, and the man who gave him the poison now and then looked at his feet and legs; and after a while he pressed his foot hard, and asked him if he could feel; and he said, No; and then his legs, and so upwards and upwards, and showed us that he was cold and stiff. And he felt then himself and said: When the poison reaches the heart, that will be the end.

—*The Works of Plato*, trans. B. Jowett

Reference Works

Bibliography of Philosophy. Ed. C. L. Higgins. Ann Arbor: Campus, 1965. (Paperback, $1.00.)

Copleston, Frederick C. *History of Philosophy.* 8 vols. Garden City, N.Y.: Doubleday, 1967.

Edwards, Paul, ed. *Encyclopedia of Philosophy.* 8 vols. New York: Macmillan, 1967.

Passmore, J. *Philosophy in the Last Decade.* Zion, Ill.: International Scholarly Book Service, 1969.
(Paperback, $1.35.)

Philosopher's Index. Bowling Green, Ohio: Bowling Green University, 1967—.
(Indexing by author and subject of articles in British and American journals.)

Runes, Dagobert D. *Who's Who in Philosophy.* Westport, Conn.: Greenwood, 1942.

Runes, Dagobert D., ed. *The Dictionary of Philosophy.* Totowa, N.J.: Littlefield, 1960.

Russell, Bertrand. *A History of Western Philosophy.* New York: Simon & Schuster, 1967.

Schneider, Herbert W. *A History of American Philosophy.* 2nd ed. New York: Columbia University Press, 1963.

Thomas, Henry. *Biographical Encyclopedia of Philosophy.* Garden City, N.Y.: Doubleday, 1965.

Urmson, J. O., ed. *The Concise Encyclopedia of Western Philosophy and Philosophers.* New York: Hawthorn, 1960.
(Bibliographies.)

POLITICAL SCIENCE

The purification of politics is an iridescent dream.
—John James Ingalls

Reference Works

Beer, Samuel H., and Adam B. Ulam. *Patterns of Government: The Major Political Systems of Europe.* 2nd ed. New York: Random House, 1962.

Eulau, Heinz, and James G. March, eds. *Political Science.* Englewood Cliffs, N.J.: Prentice-Hall, 1969.

Filler, Louis. *A Dictionary of American Social Reform.* New York: Philosophical Library, 1963.

Harmon, Mont J. *Political Thought: From Plato to the Present.* New York: McGraw-Hill, 1964.

Heimanson, Rudolph. *Dictionary of Political Science and Law.* Dobbs Ferry, New York: Oceana, 1967.

Hitchner, Dell Gillette, and William H. Harbold. *Modern Government: A Survey of Political Science.* 2nd ed. New York: Dodd, Mead, 1965.

International Political Science Abstracts. Oxford: Basil Blackwell, 1954—.

Mitchell, Edwin V. *Encyclopedia of American Politics.* New York: Greenwood, 1969.

Montgomery, H., and P. G. Cambray. *Dictionary of Political Phrases and Allusions, with Bibliography.* Detroit: Gale, 1906. Rpt. New York: Burt Franklin, 1966.

Smith, Edward C., and Arnold J. Zurcher, eds. *Dictionary of American Politics.* 2nd ed. New York: Barnes & Noble, 1968.

Who's Who in American Politics. Ed. Paul A. Theis and Edmund Littenshaw. 3rd ed. New York: Bowker, 1973.

(Kept current.)

Yearbooks

American Academy of Political and Social Science Annals. Lancaster, Pa.: AAPS, 1890—.

("Each issue deals with one broad subject." Cumulative indexes every five years.)

Annual Review of United Nations Affairs. New York: New York University Press, 1969–70.

Carnegie Endowment for International Peace. *Annual Report.* New York: Carnegie Endowment, 1911—.

(Free. Carnegie Endowment, United Nations Plaza at 46th St., New York 10017.)

International Yearbook and Statesman's Who's Who. New York: International Publications Service, 1953—.

Political Handbook and Atlas of the World. New York: Council on Foreign Relations, 1928—.

Poor Man's Guide to War/Peace Literature: Bibliography of Inexpensive or Free Materials. . . . New York: New York Peace Information Center, 1963—. (Biennial. Free. 218 E. 18th St., New York.)

Statesman's Yearbook: Statistical and Historical Annual of the States of the World. London: Macmillan, 1864—.

United Nations Yearbook. New York: Columbia University Press, 1947—.

United Nations. *Yearbook on Human Rights.* New York: International Publications Service, 1946—.

U.S. Commission on Civil Rights. *Annual Report.* Washington, D.C.: U.S. Government Printing Office.

Where in the World: Annual Index of War Peace Information. New York: New York Peace Information Center, 1964—.

Yearbook on International Communist Affairs. Stanford, Calif.: Hoover Institution on War, Revolution, and Peace, Stanford University Press, 1966—.

Yearbook of World Affairs. London: Sweet and Maxwell, 1947—.

PSYCHOLOGY

Roman Vishniac.

They are playing a game. They are playing at not playing a game. If I show them I see they are, I shall break the rules and they will punish me. I must play their game, of not seeing I see the game.

—R. D. Laing

Reference Works

Adler, Alfred. *The Practice and Theory of Individual Psychology*. Trans. P. Radin. New York: Humanities Press, 1951

Alexander, Franz G., and Sheldon T. Selesnick. *The History of Psychiatry: An Evaluation of Psychiatric Thought and Practice from Prehistoric Times to the Present*. New York: New American Library, 1966.
(Bibliography, pp. 431–51. Paperback, $1.50. Mentor, 1968.)

American Psychiatric Association. *Biographical Directory*. . . . New York: Bowker, 1962—.

Berne, Eric. *Games People Play*. New York: Grove, 1964.

Chaplin, James Patrick. *Dictionary of Psychology*. New York: Dell, 1968.

Chicago Psychoanalytic Literature Index. Chicago: Institute for Psychoanalysis, 1958—.

Erikson, Erik H. *Childhood and Society*. New York: Norton, 1950.

Freud, Sigmund. *The Basic Writings of Sigmund Freud*. Trans. A. A. Brill. New York: Modern Library, 1938.

Freud, Sigmund. *The Standard Edition of the Complete Psychological Works of Sigmund Freud*. Trans. James Strachey. 24 vols. London: Hogarth, 1953–1964.

Fromm, E. *The Art of Loving: An Inquiry into the Nature of Love*. New York: Harper & Row, 1956.

Goldenson, Robert M. *The Encyclopedia of Human Behavior: Psychology, Psychiatry, and Mental Health*. Garden City, N.Y.: Doubleday, 1970.

Harris, Thomas A. *I'm OK—You're OK: A Practical Guide to Transactional Analysis*. New York: Harper & Row, 1969.

Horney, Karen. *Self-Analysis*. New York: Norton, 1942.

Jung, Carl G. *Collected Works*. Ed. G. Adler et al. 14 vols. Princeton, N.J.: Princeton University Press, 1970.

Jung, Carl G., ed. *Man and His Symbols*. New York: Dell, 1968.
(Essays designed to make Jungian psychology accessible to the layman.)

Mental Health Book Review Index. Flushing, N.Y.: Queens College, 1956—.
(Cumulative author-title index, 1969.)

Otto, Herbert, ed. *Family in Search of a Future: Alternative Models for Moderns*. New York: Appleton, 1970.

Otto, Herbert. *Guide to Developing Your Potential*. New York: Scribner's, 1967.

Perls, Frederick. *Hunger and Aggression: Beginning of Gestalt Therapy*. New York: Random House, 1969.

Piaget, Jean. *The Child's Conception of the World*. Totowa, N.J.: Littlefield, 1969.

Skinner, B. F. *Beyond Freedom and Dignity*. New York: Knopf, 1971.
(Skinner advises that freedom and dignity need to be replaced by conditioning in socially productive behavior.)

Skinner, B. F. *Walden Two*. New York: Macmillan, 1960.
(Behaviorist's utopian novel of a controlled society.)

Watson, Robert I. *Great Psychologists: From Aristotle to Freud*. 2nd ed. Philadelphia: Lippincott, 1968.

Yearbooks

Advances in Experimental Social Psychology. 5 vols. New York: Academic Press, 1964—.

Annual Review of Psychology. Palo Alto, Calif.: Annual Reviews, Inc., 1950—.

Buros, Oscar K., ed. *Mental Measurements Yearbook*. 6th ed. New Brunswick, N.J.: Gryphon, 1965—.

Psychoanalytic Study of the Child. Ed. Ruth S. Eissler et al. New York: International Universities Press, 1945—.

Science and Psychoanalysis. New York: Grune & Stratton, 1958—.

RECREATION AND PHYSICAL EDUCATION

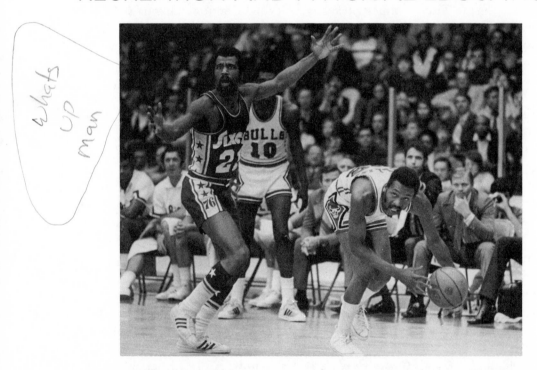

The bow cannot always stand bent, nor can human frailty subsist without some lawful recreation.

—Cervantes

Reference Works

American Association for Health—Physical Education—and Recreation. *Complete Research in Health, Physical Education and Recreation*. 11 vols. Washington, D.C.: AAHPER, 1969.

Arnold, Peter J. *Education, Physical Education and Personality Development*. New York: Atherton, 1971.

Cerutty, Perce. *Be Fit or Be Damned*. New York: Dell, 1970.

Clarke, David H., and H. Harrison. *Research Processes in Physical Education, Recreation and Health*. Englewood Cliffs, N.J.: Prentice-Hall, 1970.

Cratty, Bryant J. *Psychology and Physical Activity*. Englewood Cliffs, N.J.: Prentice-Hall, 1968.

Gerber, Ellen W. *Innovators and Institutions in Physical Education*. Philadelphia: Lea & Febiger, 1971.

How-to-Do-It Books: A Selected Guide. 3rd rev. ed. New York: Bowker, 1963. (4,000 government publications, books, and pamphlets listed by subject.)

Pinkerton, James R., and Marjorie J. Pinkerton. *Outdoor Recreation and Leisure: A Reference Guide and Selected Bibliography*. Columbia: University of Missouri, 1969.

Popular Mechanics Do-It-Yourself Encyclopedia. 16 vols. New York: Hearst, 1968.

Postma, J. W. *Introduction to the Theory of Physical Education*. New York: International Publications Service, 1970.

Rand McNally Guidebook to Campgrounds: A Family Camping Directory of Campgrounds throughout the United States and Canada. 12th ed. Chicago: Rand McNally, 1970.

(Paperback, $3.95. Order from Rand McNally, Box 7600, Chicago, Ill. 60680.)

Rice, Emmett, et al. *Brief History of Physical Education*. New York: Ronald, 1969.

Slusher, Howard S., and Aileene S. Lockhart. *Anthology of Contemporary Readings: An Introduction to Physical Education*. Dubuque, Iowa: W. C. Brown, 1970.

Slusher, Howard S. *Man, Sport, and Existence*. Philadelphia: Lea & Febiger, 1967.

Updyke, Wynne F., and Perry B. Johnson. *Principles of Modern Physical Education, Health, and Recreation*. New York: Holt, Rinehart & Winston, 1970. (Bibliography.)

Yearbooks

AAU Basketball Handbook. New York: Amateur Athletic Union.
AAU Boxing Handbook. New York: Amateur Athletic Union.
AAU Gymnastics Handbook. New York: Amateur Athletic Union.

AAU Judo Handbook. New York: Amateur Athletic Union.

AAU Swimming, Water Polo, and Diving Handbook. New York: Amateur Athletic Union.

AAU Track and Field Handbook. New York: Amateur Athletic Union.

AAU Weightlifting Handbook. New York: Amateur Athletic Union.

AAU Wrestling Handbook. New York: Amateur Athletic Union.

Baseball Guide and Record Book. New Rochelle, N.Y.: Snibbe, 1965.

Boating Almanac. New York: Bromsley, 1960—.

Boxing Annual. New York: Whitestone, 1966—.

Car and Driver Racing Manual. New York: Ziff-Davis, 1967—.

Continental Camping Sites. Croyden, Surrey, England: Caravan Publications, 1964—.

(Caravan Publ., Ltd., Link House, Dingwall Ave., Croyden, Surrey, England.)

Fishing Annual. New York: Maco.

($.50. 757 Third Ave., N.Y. 10017.)

Football Register. St. Louis: Sporting News, 1966—.

Golfing Guide. Columbia, Mo.: Ovac, 1962—.

International Athletics Annual. New York: International Publications Service, 1950—.

Model Airplane News Annual. New York: Air Age, 1960—.

Official Baseball Guide. St. Louis: Sporting News, 1970—.

Physical Education Yearbook. London: Physical Education Association, 1958—.

The Year in Sports: The Associated Press Review of the Memorable Sports Events. Englewood Cliffs, N.J.: Prentice-Hall, 1958—.

RELIGION

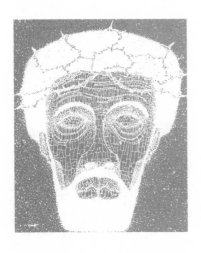

TO BECOME LOVE,
FRIENDSHIP NEEDS
WHAT MORALITY NEEDS
TO BECOME RELIGION—
THE FIRE OF EMOTION.
—RICHARD GARNETT

Reference Works

American Catholic Who's Who. Detroit: Romig, 1934—.

Barrow, John G. *A Bibliography of Bibliographies in Religion*. Austin, Texas: Barrow, 1955.

Buttrick, George A., et al. *The Interpreter's Bible*. 12 vols. New York: Abingdon, 1962.

Canney, Maurice A. *Encyclopedia of Religions*. Detroit: Gale, 1970.

Concise Bible Dictionary. New York: World, 1971.
(Only $2.95. 1500 words explained and defined in terms of individual contexts.)

Cross, F. L., ed. *The Oxford Dictionary of the Christian Church*. New York: Oxford University Press, 1957.

Dictionary of Comparative Religions. Ed. S. G. Brandon et al. New York: Scribner's, 1970.
(Includes bibliographies. Covers primitive and ancient as well as contemporary religions.)

Encyclopedia of Religion and Ethics. Ed. James Hastings. 13 vols. New York: Scribner's, 1908–1927.

Gaynor, Frank. *Dictionary of Mysticism*. New York: Philosophical Library, 1953.

Gibb, H. A. R., and J. H. Kramers, eds. *Shorter Encyclopedia of Islam*. Ithaca, N.Y.: Cornell University Press, 1953.

Index to Religious Periodical Literature. Chicago: American Theological Library Association, 1953—.

The Interpreter's Dictionary of the Bible. Ed. George A. Buttrick. 4 vols. New York: Abingdon, 1962.

Joy, Charles R., comp. *Harper's Topical Concordance*. Rev. ed. New York: Harper & Row, 1962.

Mayer, Frederick E., ed. *The Religious Bodies of America*. 2nd ed. St. Louis: Concordia, 1961.

Mead, Frank S., ed. *The Encyclopedia of Religious Quotations*. Westwood, N.J.: Revell, 1965.

Mead, Frank Spencer. *Handbook of Denominations in the United States*. 5th ed. New York: Abingdon, 1970.

New Catholic Encyclopedia. 15 vols. New York: McGraw-Hill, 1967.

The New Standard Jewish Encyclopedia. Ed. Cecil Roth et al. 4th new rev. ed. Garden City, N.Y.: Doubleday, 1970.

Oxford Bible Atlas. Ed. Herbert G. May, R. W. Hamilton, and G. N. S. Hunt. New York: Oxford University Press, 1962.

Smith, James W., and A. L. Jamison, eds. *Religion in American Life*. 4 vols. Princeton, N.J.: Princeton University Press, 1961.

Wedeck, H. E., and Wade Baskin. *Dictionary of Pagan Religions*. New York: Philosophical Library, 1971.

Young, Robert. *Young's Analytical Concordance to the Bible*. Rev. ed. Grand Rapids, Mich.: Eerdmans, 1955.

Zaehner, Robert C., ed. *The Concise Encyclopedia of Living Faiths*. Boston: Beacon, 1959.

Yearbooks

American Jewish Yearbook. Ed. Morris Fine and Milton Himmelfarb. New York: Jewish Publication Society of America, 1899—.

Biblical Research. Chicago: Society of Biblical Research, 1956—.

Christian Periodical Index. Buffalo: Christian Librarian's Fellowship, 1959—.

Guide to Catholic Literature. Ed. Walter Romig. Haverford, Pa.: Catholic Library Association.

Jehova's Witnesses Yearbook. New York: Watchtower, 1927—.

Jewish Yearbook: Reference Book of World Jewry. London: Jewish Chronicle Publications, 1895—.

Know Your Faith Series. Nashville: Abingdon.

National Catholic Almanac. Garden City, N.Y.: Doubleday, 1904—.

Religion and the Public Order. Ed. Donald A. Gianella. Chicago: University of Chicago Press, 1964—.

SCIENCE

General Science

Andreas Feininger.

Science carries us into zones of speculation, where there is no habitable city for the mind of man.
—Robert Louis Stevenson

Reference Works

American Men of Science. Ed. Jacques Cattell. 12 vols. New York: Bowker, 1965—.

The Book of Popular Science. 10 vols. New York: Grolier, 1970.

Bronwell, B. *Science and Technology in the World of the Future.* New York: Wiley, 1970.

Dictionary of Scientific Biography. Ed. Charles C. Gillispie. 2 vols. New York: Scribner's, 1970.

Dubos, Rene Jules. *Reason Awake: Science for Man.* New York: Columbia University Press, 1970.

Glass, Hiram Bentley. *The Timely and the Timeless: The Interrelationships of Science, Education and Society.* New York: Basic Books, 1970.

Harper Encyclopedia of Science. Ed. James R. Newman. 4 vols. New York: Harper & Row, 1967.

McGraw-Hill Encyclopedia of Science and Technology. 15 vols. New York: McGraw-Hill, 1971.

("... a large part of the text is accessible to the educated layman, including high-school students. And 'science' is taken in the broad sense of all objective knowledge, including human behavior (normal and abnormal), animal life and evolution, microbiology, food, geography of the continents, graphic arts, and musical instruments." —David Glixon)

Sarton, George. *History of Science.* 2 vols. New York: Norton, 1970.

Scientific American Resource Library. 15 vols. San Francisco: Freeman, 1969.

Van Nostrand's Scientific Encyclopedia. 4th ed. New York: Van Nostrand Reinhold, 1968.

Weaver, Warren. *Scene of Change: A Lifetime in American Science.* New York: Scribner's, 1970.

Yearbooks

Britannica Yearbook of Science and the Future 1971. Chicago: Encyclopaedia Britannica, 1970.

Carnegie Institution of Washington. *Yearbook.* Washington, D.C.: Carnegie Institution.

McGraw-Hill Year Book of Science and Technology. New York: McGraw-Hill, 1960—.

Science Experimenter. Ed. Don A. Torgersen. New York: Arco.

Science News Yearbook. Ed. Science Service. New York: Scribner's, 1969—.

Science Year: World Book Science Annual. Ed. Arthur Tressler. Chicago: Field, 1965—.

Biological Science

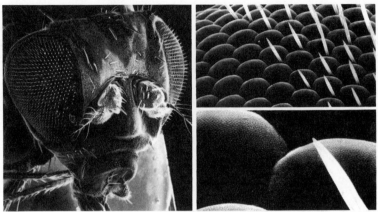

The Eye of a Fruit Fly. Magnified 180, 2240, and 11, 200 times, 1968.

*WHERE THE TELESCOPE ENDS, THE MICROSCOPE BE-
GINS. WHICH OF THE TWO HAS THE GREATER VIEW?*
—VICTOR HUGO

Reference Works

Baer, Adela S., et al. *Central Concepts of Biology*. New York: Macmillan, 1971.

Blake, Sidney. *Geographical Guide to Floras of the World: An Annotated List with Special Reference to Useful Plants and Common Plant Names*, 1942. Rpt. Darien, Conn.: Hafner, 1963.

Butler, John Alfred. *The Life Process*. New York: Basic Books, 1971.

Chinery, Michael. *A Science Dictionary of the Animal World*. New York: Watts, 1969.

  (Particularly appropriate for undergraduates.)

Gray, Peter, ed. *Encyclopedia of the Biological Sciences*. 2nd ed. New York: Van Nostrand Reinhold, 1970.

Jordan, E. L. *Animal Atlas of the World*. Maplewood, N.J.: Hammond, 1969.

The Larousse Encyclopedia of Animal Life. New York: McGraw-Hill, 1967.

Leftwich, A. W. *Dictionary of Zoology*. 2nd ed. New York: Van Nostrand Reinhold, 1967.

Phillips, Edwin A. *Basic Ideas in Biology*. New York: Macmillan, 1971.

Stanbury, David. *The Living World*. New York: Macmillan. 1971.

Swift, Lloyd H. *Botanical Bibliographies: A Guide to Bibliographic Materials Applicable to Botany*. Minneapolis: Burgess, 1970.

Winter, Charles A. *Opportunities in the Biological Sciences*. New York: Universal, 1970.

  (Careers in biological sciences surveyed. How to find employment.)

Physical Science

SINCE I DO NOT FORESEE THAT ATOMIC ENERGY IS TO BE A GREAT BOON FOR A LONG TIME, I HAVE TO SAY THAT FOR THE PRESENT IT IS A MENACE.
—ALBERT EINSTEIN, 1945

Reference Works

Ashford, Theodore A. *The Physical Sciences from Atoms to Stars.* New York: Holt, Rinehart & Winston, 1967.

Ballentyne, Dennis W., and David R. Lovett. *A Dictionary of Named Effects and Laws in Chemistry, Physics, and Mathematics.* 3rd ed. New York: Barnes & Noble, 1970.

Besancon, Robert M., ed. *Encyclopedia of Physics.* New York: Van Nostrand Reinhold, 1966.

Clark, George L., and Gessner G. Hawley, eds. *The Encyclopedia of Chemistry.* 2nd ed. New York: Van Nostrand Reinhold, 1966.

Fairbridge, Rhodes Whitmore. *The Encyclopedia of Atmospheric Sciences and Astrogeology.* New York: Van Nostrand Reinhold, 1967.

Hampel, Clifford A., ed. *Encyclopedia of the Chemical Elements.* New York: Van Nostrand Reinhold, 1968.

Handbook of Chemistry and Physics: A Ready-Reference Book of Chemical and Physical Data. Ed. Robert C. Weast. 50th ed. Cleveland: Chemical Rubber Co., 1969.

International Dictionary of Physics and Electronics. Ed. Walter C. Michels et al. 2nd ed. New York: Van Nostrand Reinhold, 1961.

The International Encyclopedia of Science. Ed. James R. Newman. Edinburgh: Nelson, 1965.

Krauskopf, Konrad B. *Fundamentals of Physical Science.* 6th ed. New York: McGraw-Hill, 1971.

Miller, Albert. *Meteorology*. 2nd ed. Columbus: Merrill, 1971.

Partington, James R. *History of Chemistry*. 4 vols. New York: St. Martin's, 1970.

Shipman, James T., and Jerry L. Adams. *An Introduction to Physical Science*. Lexington, Mass.: Heath, 1971.

Sloane, Eric. *Look at the Sky . . . and Know the Weather*. Rev. and enl. ed. New York: World, 1970.

Swenson, Hugo N., and Edmund J. Woods. *Physical Science for Liberal Arts Students*. New York: Wiley, 1971.

Van Nostrand's International Encyclopedia of Chemical Science. New York: Van Nostrand Reinhold, 1964.

Van Straten, Florence W. *Weather or Not*. New York: Dodd, Mead, 1966.

White, John Henry. *A Reference Book of Chemistry*. New York: Philosophical Library, 1967.

SOCIAL SCIENCE (GENERAL)

Reference Works

The American Behavioral Scientist: Recent Publications in the Social and Behavioral Sciences. The ABS Guide: 1970 Supplement. Beverly Hills, Calif.: Sage, 1970.

Behavioral Sciences and the Mass Media. Ed. Frederick T. Yu. New York: Russell, 1968.

Bliss, William Dwight. *The New Encyclopedia of Social Reform.* New York: Arno, 1970.

Bruckner, M. *Social Science and Society.* Berkeley: McCutchan, 1968.

Filler, Louis. *A Dictionary of American Social Reform.* Westport, Conn.: Greenwood, 1963.

Gould, Julius, and William L. Kolb. *UNESCO Dictionary of the Social Sciences.* New York: Free Press, 1964.

International Encyclopedia of the Social Sciences. 17 vols. New York: Macmillan, 1968.

Madden, Charles F. *Talks with Social Scientists.* Carbondale: Southern Illinois University Press, 1968.

Noland, Robert L. *Research and Report Writing in the Behavioral Sciences.* Springfield, Ill.: Thomas, 1970.

Ryan, Alan. *The Philosophy of the Social Sciences.* New York: Pantheon, 1971.

Simey, T. S. *Social Science and Social Purpose.* New York: Schocken, 1969.

Understanding Society: Readings in the Social Sciences. London: Macmillan, 1970.

Yearbooks

Yearbooks are listed in individual fields of the Social Sciences.

SOCIOLOGY

And the only point I'm trying to make is this, man; I'm a vet. I need a place to live, and I don't have no time to fool around with Chuck over a place to live. I'm workin', and I need a home. I don't have time to explain to him why I'm black, you see—I don't have time to explain to him why people out here broke these windows... —Transcription of a rap and suds session, Build Black, Inc.

Reference Works

Anderson, Charles H. *Toward A New Sociology: A Critical View*. Homewood, Ill.: Dorsey, 1971.

Anderson, Nels. *The Industrial Urban Community: Historical and Comparative Perspectives*. New York: Appleton, 1971.

Becker, Leonard, Jr., and Clair Gustafson. *Encounter with Sociology: The Term Paper*. Berkeley: Glendessary, 1968.

Bell, Inge Powell. *Involvement in Society Today*. Del Mar, Calif.: CRM, 1971.

Benson, A. *Community Development: A Directory of Academic Curriculums throughout the World*. Columbia: University of Missouri, 1969.

Berger, Bennett M. *Looking for America: Essays on Youth, Suburbia, and Other American Obsessions*. Englewood Cliffs, N.J.: Prentice-Hall, 1971.

Bibliography of Research in Children, Youth, and Family. Ann Arbor: University of Michigan, 1969.

Cahill, Susan, and Michele Cooper, comps. *The Urban Reader*. Englewood Cliffs, N.J.: Prentice-Hall, 1971.

Children and Youth in America: A Documentary History. Ed. Robert H. Bremner et al. 3 vols. Cambridge, Mass.: Harvard University Press, 1970.

Coulson, Margaret Anne, and David Riddel. *Approaching Sociology: A Critical Introduction*. London: Routledge, 1970.

Cuzzort, Raymond Paul. *Humanity and Modern Sociological Thought: An Introduction*. New York: Holt, Rinehart & Winston, 1969.

(Bibliographical footnotes.)

David, Anne. *A Guide to Volunteer Services: Help Yourself by Helping Others*. New York: Cornerstone, 1970.

(Order from Simon & Schuster, 630 Fifth Ave., N.Y. 10020. $1.45.)

De Fleur, Melvin Lawrence. *Sociology: Man in Society*. Glenview, Ill.: Scott Foresman, 1971.

Encyclopedia of Social Work. Ed. Robert Morris. New York: National Association of Social Workers, 1965.

Gouldner, Alvin Ward. *The Coming Crisis of Western Sociology.* New York: Basic Books, 1970.

Hoult, Thomas Ford. *Dictionary of Modern Sociology.* Totowa, N.J.: Littlefield, 1969.

International Bibliography of Sociology. Chicago: Aldine, 1952—.

(Author, subject index of pamphlets, periodicals, books, and government publications.)

Leinwand, Gerald, comp. *Minorities All.* New York: Washington Square Press, 1971.

McKeown, James E., ed. *The Changing Metropolis.* 2nd rev. ed. Boston: Houghton Mifflin, 1971.

Mitchell, Geoffrey Duncan. *A Hundred Years of Sociology.* Chicago: Aldine, 1968.

Mitchell, Geoffrey Duncan. *Sociology: An Outline for the Intending Student.* New York: Humanities, 1970.

Pinson, William M. *Resource Guide to Current Social Issues.* Waco, Texas: Word, 1968.

(Sections on many topics of wide current concern. Includes agencies and organizations.)

Public Welfare Directory. . . . Chicago: American Public Welfare Association, 1973.

(Revised annually. Agencies providing help for aged, veterans, the handicapped. Local, state, federal agencies. Addresses.)

Raskin, Eugene. *Sequel to Cities: The Post Urban Society.* New York: Bloch, 1970.

Riesman, David. *The Lonely Crowd: Study of the Changing American Character.* New Haven: Yale University Press, 1950.

Urban Data Service Reports. Washington, D.C.: International City Management Association, 1970—.

(Monthly. Data on municipal government activities. For study of the city of the Seventies. Suggestions for improving quality of urban life.)

U.S. Department of Labor. Bureau of Labor Statistics. *Occupational Outlook Handbook.* 1972–73 ed. Bulletin No. 1650. Washington, D.C.: U.S. Government Printing Office, 1973.

(Survey of job availability in the professions, business, government, agriculture, etc.)

Yearbooks

Current Sociological Research. New York: American Sociological Society, 1955—.

Research Annual on Intergroup Relations. By Melvin Tumin. New York: Quadrangle, 1958—.

Social Work Year Book. New York: National Association of Social Workers, 1929—.

SPEECH

William Gropper, "The Senate." 1935. Oil on canvas 25⅛ x 33⅛". Collection of The Museum of Modern Art, New York. Philip Johnson Fund.

WHAT ORATORS WANT IN DEPTH, THEY GIVE YOU IN LENGTH.—MONTESQUIEU

Reference Works

Baird, Albert Craig. *General Speech Communication*. 4th ed. New York: McGraw-Hill, 1971.

Barbara, Dominick A. *Your Speech Reveals Your Personality*. Springfield, Ill.: Thomas, 1970.

Clevenger, Theodore. *The Speech Communication Process*. Glenview, Ill.: Scott Foresman, 1971.

Communication Disorders. Baltimore: John Hopkins, 1968—.

Hanley, Theodore D., and Wayne Thurman. *Developing Vocal Skills*. 2nd ed. New York: Holt, Rinehart & Winston, 1970.

Hegarty, E. *Making What You Say Pay Off*. Englewood Cliffs, N.J.: Prentice-Hall, 1968.

Kruger, Arthur N. *Effective Speaking: A Complete Course*. New York: Van Nostrand Reinhold, 1970.

Prochnow, Herbert Victor. *1400 Ideas for Speakers and Toastmasters: How to Speak with Confidence*. Grand Rapids, Mich.: Baker Book House, 1964.

(Quotations, epigrams, jokes, etc. Paperback, $1.95.)

Rochmis, Lyda N., and Dorothy Doob. *Speech Therapy: A Group Approach for Schools and Clinics*. New York: John Day, 1970.

(Bibliography, pp. 224–27.)

Rosenstock-Huessy, Eugen. *Speech and Reality*. Norwich, Vt.: Argo, 1970.

Sutton, Roberta Briggs. *Speech Index to Sixty-four Collections of World Famous Orations*. Metuchen, N.J.: Scarecrow, 1966.

(Periodic updating.)

Vital Speeches of the Day. New York: City News Publ. Corp., 1934—.

(Monthly.)

Yearbook

Baird, Albert Craig. *Representative American Speeches*. New York: Wilson, 1938—.

WOMEN'S LIBERATION

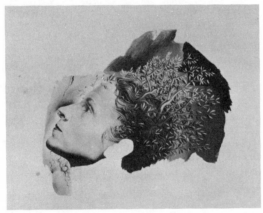

Salvador Dali, "Automatic Beginning of a Portrait of Gala"

Life demands that the duality in men and women be freed to function, released from hate or guilt....They need each other's qualities if they are ever to understand each other in love and life. The beautiful difference of our biological selves will not diminish through this mutual fusion. It should flower, expand; blow the mind as well as the flesh....We could both breathe free.
—Marya Mannes

Reference Works

Adams, Elsie, and Mary Louise Briscoe. *Up Against the Wall, Mother: Readings in Women's Liberation*. Beverly Hills, Calif.: Glencoe, 1971. (Bibliography, pp. 513–21.)

de Beauvoir, Simone. *The Second Sex*. Trans. H. M. Parshley. New York: Bantam, 1970.

Ellis, Julie. *Revolt of the Second Sex*. New York: Lancer, 1970. (Report on women's lib organizations. Addresses.)

Epstein, C. F. *Woman's Place: Options and Limits in Professional Careers*. Berkeley: University of California Press, 1971.

Firestone, Shulamith. *The Dialectic of Sex: The Case for Feminist Revolution*. New York: Bantam, 1970.

Friedman, Sande, and Lois Schwartz. *No Experience Necessary: A Guide to Employment for the Female Liberal Arts Graduate*. New York: Dell, 1971.

Gornick, V., and B. K. Moran, eds. *Woman in Sexist Society: Studies in Power and Powerlessness*. New York: Basic Books, 1971.

Greer, Germaine. *The Female Eunuch*. New York: McGraw-Hill, 1971.

Hennessey, Caroline. *The Strategy of Sexual Struggle*. New York: Lancer, 1971.

Ireland, Norma. *Index to Women of the World from Ancient to Modern Times: Biographies and Portraits*. Westwood, Mass.: Faxon, 1970.

Millett, Kate. *Sexual Politics*. Garden City, N.Y.: Doubleday, 1970. (Bibliography, pp. 364–77.)

Notes from the Second Year: Major Writings of the Radical Feminists. Ed. Shulamith Firestone. New York: New York Radical Feminists, 1970.

Peck, Ellen. *The Baby Trap*. New York: Geis, 1971.

Showalter, Elaine, ed. *Women's Liberation and Literature*. New York: Harcourt, 1971. (Bibliography, pp. 337–38.)

Whole Woman's Catalogue 1971. Portsmouth, N.H.: Papeman, 1971. (Current. For information write Susie Papeman, 26 Profile, Portsmouth, N.H. 03801.)

BOOKS CANNOT BE KILLED BY FIRE.
PEOPLE DIE, BUT BOOKS NEVER DIE.
NO MAN AND NO FORCE CAN ABOLISH
MEMORY.... BOOKS ARE WEAPONS.
   —FRANKLIN D. ROOSEVELT

Chapter 4

A paper
before the paper

BUT I RECKON I GOT TO LIGHT OUT FOR
THE TERRITORY AHEAD OF THE REST,
BECAUSE AUNT SALLY SHE'S GOING TO
ADOPT AND SIVILIZE ME, AND I CAN'T
STAND IT. I BEEN THERE BEFORE.
—HUCKLEBERRY FINN

In Chapter 3 we examined the wide range of sources available for research. By now you know there are many avenues of exploration beyond the card catalog and *Readers' Guide to Periodical Literature*. Hopefully, you have found sources that will be useful to you in your own paper and listed them in correct bibliographical form on separate note cards.

To help you to prepare for A Paper of Your Own, this chapter presents three crucial stages in the process of development: notetaking, outlining, and completion—the paper itself, which emerges from the note cards and outline that precede it. There is more here than models for you to look at, however. There are several pages of note cards for you to cut out and put into intellectually related groups, just as you will with your own note cards before you begin writing your own paper. There are also scrambled outline components taken from the note card groupings. You can cut these out, too, and arrange them coherently, just as you will have to arrange the headings and subheadings that emerge from your own note cards. Finally, there is a finished paper, including footnotes and bibliography. This allows you to see that a research paper is a translation of source materials into your own words, a creative arrangement of other people's ideas into a thought pattern all your own. You will also see how each quotation, fact, and concept taken from a source is acknowledged through the use of responsible documentation. Explanations and models illustrating proper documentation forms appear in Chapter 5.

Before you begin working with the preliminary practice materials, the following information may prove helpful.

PRE-WRITING PROCEDURES

Q. What shall I do after I've surveyed sources and written bibliography cards?

A. Examine your cards carefully, discarding any that are unrelated to the narrowed topic that probably will have emerged during your initial research steps.

Q. When I decide upon a facet of my subject I'd like to explore in depth, which bibliography cards should I keep and which should I discard?

A. Keep cards for broad range sources that deal directly with your subject; although you will be writing about a particular aspect of a subject, such definitive works will probably contain material on that aspect. Also, keep cards on any articles that relate directly to your narrowed topic. Discard any highly specialized sources whose titles rule out coverage of your topic, and eliminate sources whose coverage is so general that they do not treat your topic in any detail.

Q. When I have my selective bibliography in hand, what then?

A. Check the tables of contents in books to see if there are chapters relating directly to your topic. Check indexes to find pages dealing with your topic. Then prepare to take notes.

Q. What's the point of taking notes? Why can't I write directly from my sources?

A. Sometimes your sources can't be taken from the library.

Q. Suppose all my sources can be used at home. Do I still need to take notes?

A. Yes! The research paper always involves ordering and systematizing information found in a variety of sources. Suppose you find six books explaining different facets of one of your main points. You must have all related materials together, and you can shuffle note cards far more easily than you can shuffle a pile of books.

Q. Must I take notes on cards?

A. Not necessarily. It is less expensive to take notes on half sheets of notebook paper which also give you more space than cards. However, notebook paper is less sturdy than cards, and it may get frayed or torn. I recommend that you use 4″ x 6″ cards because they are easier to work with. Do not attempt to use 3″ x 5″ cards; they are simply too small for longer blocks of material.

Q. How much should I write on each card?

A. As little as possible. Ideally, one intellectually self-contained unit of material. This is important because ultimately you will sort the cards into piles dealing with separable subtopics. If two or three separable units of material are jammed together on one card, you will need to recopy portions of your card or cut it up. Remember you will eventually write your paper from logically arranged groups of note cards; every unit of material must be in the right place before you begin to write.

Q. Is there a way to label cards for easy identification of content?

A. Yes. Put a brief descriptive heading at the top of each card. This will greatly simplify the sorting process.

Q. How do I designate sources on my note cards?

A. At the bottom of each card, put author's name and pages used. This is enough to refer you to the complete bibliography card. If there are two works by the same author, include title as well as author and pages used.

Q. What is the best way to take notes?

A. Copy all information verbatim. This is extremely important. It guarantees fidelity to your source. Unintentional distortion of sources can occur if you translate material into your own words at this stage. Additionally, you may be asked to submit your note cards with your paper. The notes contain the phraseology of your source, the paper your recasting of the source in your own words. The similarity in content and dissimilarity in phrasing between notes and finished paper are your protection against charges of plagiarism.

Recycling to minimize pollution

Libre New Mexico: "Jim built it [his house] for under $100, using scrap lumber and mill ends. He collected rubble from a wrecked house — a mixture of adobe bricks and wood — to insulate the walls. He has heard of another hip builder who insulated his house using empty glass formaldehyde bottles discarded by a mortician."

Houriet, pp. 224-25

Libre Commune in New Mexico carries recycling even farther. One member built his house for less than $100.00, using only discarded pieces of lumber and debris from a demolished building. Another builder spent a warm winter within adobe walls insulated by "empty glass formaldehyde bottles discarded by a mortician."[10]

Q. Does this mean I must copy *every* word on the page?

A. No. You need copy only germinal material, often only key phrases and sentences.

Q. Do I have to indicate omissions from my source in any particular way?

A. Yes. Use dots (ellipsis) to indicate omissions of words or sentences within a quoted passage.

- Use three spaced dots to indicate omission of words within a sentence.

    "The land . . . became a key to the communitarians' search for another style of being."

- Use three spaced dots to indicate omission of the first or last part of a sentence within a paragraph.

    "He made $50,000 in his two seasons of pro ball . . . Oliver hasn't given up work, just making money."

- Use three spaced dots after a period to indicate an omission following a complete sentence. Note that no space intervenes between the period and the end of the sentence.

> "He made $50,000 in his two seasons of pro ball, counting salary, bonus and playoff money. . . . Oliver hasn't given up work, just making money."

- Disregard punctuation within an elipsis, save for a terminal period.

> ORIGINAL
>
> "A 50 person hippie commune in California called itself 'The Lynch Family'; a New Mexico commune 'The Chosen Family'; a New York group simply 'The Family.' "
>
> QUOTATION
>
> "A 50 person hippie commune in California called itself 'The Lynch Family' . . . a New York group simply 'The Family.' "

- There is no need to use spaced dots before or after portions of sentences that are obviously fragmentary.

> Communal life ends loneliness and tends to create the "interdependent togetherness of tribalism."

- Indicate omission of a paragraph or more from a prose passage or a line or more from a passage of poetry with a line of spaced dots.

. . . .

Is everything perfectly clear ?

Q. May I ever insert material in my own words in the verbatim notes?

A. Yes. Use brackets to indicate insertions. These insertions may be made for purposes of clarification or brief summarization of omitted passages.

> "Ralph (Chip) Oliver [fled to] a large Victorian house in Larkspur, Calif., that is the headquarters of a commune known as the One World Family of the Messiah's World Crusade."

Q. After I've finished taking notes, am I ready to begin writing my paper?

A. Only after you have put your notes in order.

Q. How do I do that?

A. By sorting them into piles that relate to the same subtopics, and sorting each pile into smaller subgroups.

Q. Now can I begin writing?

A. You could begin writing at this point, but it is a good idea to set up the skeletal framework—or outline—of your paper first.

Q. How is the outline put together?

A. If you've divided your note cards into four main piles, the central topic of each pile becomes a Roman numeral heading in your outline. The subgroups within each main pile become letter divisions. The sub-subgroups become Arabic numeral divisions, and so on.

Q. What good is the outline?

A. It is a system of arrangement extracted from your note cards. It is your roadmap, your plan of sequence. It tells what you are going to write about first, second, third—last. However, sometimes thought occurs while you are writing. The paper begins to write itself. If this happens, recast your outline to fit the existing paper. Outlining, even after the fact, helps you check out intellectual relationships. If you find you cannot outline your paper, maybe you have no paper; that is, perhaps your paper has no structure and needs re-thinking. More on this later.

The Paper as Collage

Think of your paper as an intellectual collage, an integration and arrangement of sources into something new, something Yours—a personal act of creative synthesis.

Scrambled Note Cards

The following note cards are not in order. Cut them out and arrange them coherently. To do this, sort the cards into groups relating to separable subjects. Divide each group into subgroups and each subgroup into sub-subgroups. This is what you must do with your own note cards before you begin writing a paper of your own. It is a way of establishing the divisions of your preliminary outline and, ultimately, the paper itself.

Recycling to minimize pollution

Libre, New Mexico: "Jim built it [his house] for under $100, using scrap lumber and mill ends. He collected rubble from a wrecked house—a mixture of adobe bricks and wood—to insulate the walls. He has heard of another hip builder who insulated his house using empty glass formaldehyde bottles discarded by a mortician."

Houriet, pp. 224–25

Achieving a new consciousness

"I am twenty-one years old. . . . I am a product of this fat consumption-oriented middle-class America, 'fat city.' . . . Having only a fat city consciousness . . . my answer . . . is to develop a new consciousness; in order to develop a new consciousness, I must develop a new existence. The first step . . . building an intentional community within the territory claimed by fat city."

Dahlin, p. 31

No alternative to splitting: political action futile

"Neither peaceful demonstration nor sporadic gestures of violence could change the mentality of police . . . could vitalize the towering glass apartment buildings and asphalted shopping centers; could breathe life into decayed churches or humanize inflexible corporations. The only option was to split."

Houriet, p. xii

Return to land for development of a new self

"Beyond the gloss and froth of city life and threat of premature extinction, a sense of 'self' emerges from the mythic essence of the land and from each soul's new unfettered impulses."

Hedgepeth, p. 7

Anti-materialism: private property separates men

Communitarians "believe that money and private property create barriers between people. Money should be thrown into a common pot and property should belong to anyone who uses it. The acceptance of common property is reflected in the answer of a small child in a Cambridge commune. Questioned about who owned a cat, he said, 'The cat is everyone's.'"

Kanter, p. 56

Hostility toward technology as polluter

"endless debates about whether or not to use electricity from outside sources: electrical connection meant becoming party to the national electrical network and being indirectly responsible for helping perpetuate a power system that poisoned the air with pollutants and strip-mined farmlands . . . most limited electrical use to essentials: freezers, pumps, and in some cases stereos. . . . The rationale . . . to adopt only those limited segments of modern technology that fit in with a number of other communal ideals, such as self-sufficiency and craftsmanship: e.g., electricity to heat a kiln or run a sewing machine."

Houriet, p. 218

Joy in communal life

"life is meant to be a joy, not only joyful within the existence of each individual but also as expressed along with others in collective singing, dancing, moon-worship and everything else hitherto 'irresponsible.' Unhappiness is seen as a malfunction of the human organism."

Hedgepeth, p. 186

Commune as family

"Today's communes seek a family warmth and intimacy, to become extended families. A 50 person hippie commune in California called itself 'The Lynch Family'; a New Mexico Commune 'The Chosen Family'; a New York Group simply 'The Family.'"

Kanter, p. 54

Communes equal revolution now

Twin Oaks Press: "What if we just went ahead as though the revolution were over and we had won? What would a post-revolutionary society be like? A society committed to non-aggression, where one man's gain is not another's loss, where work is minimized and leisure is maximized? . . . decentralized societal units of approximately 1,000 people or whatever size proves to be most beneficial."

Twin Oaks was determined to create a "viable alternative to capitalism"

Houriet, pp. 289-90

Income sources

Drop City, N.M.: "Economically, the commune ekes by on funds earned from the occasional operating of light shows for rock groups in tow. . . . doing crafts and selling to a place in town--stuff like pottery, wire sculpture, jewelry and musical instruments."

Hedgepeth, p. 154

Communal togetherness

Communal life ends loneliness and tends to create the "interdependent togetherness of tribalism."

Hedgepeth, p. 186

Communes: the bloodless revolution

"The present social reorganization in the U. S. and Europe has the express intent of creating a viable alternative to the established economic and social order. Rather than a revolution in the bloody sense, it is the creation of self-sufficient communities that function within . . . capitalism."

Herrick, p. 27

Anti-materialism: brotherhood through sharing

Summary of Timothy Leary's theory of money: "Its only function is to flow. . . . Any attempt to trap money . . . involves 90% of your time. . . . We simply float along . . . we have learned to fill our canteen and share with our friends and our brotherhood shared with us, so there's no money problem."

Hedgepeth, p. 83

Communes become the revolution

"We had all been watching that movie for too long, Revolution in America. . . . It was time to move the whole thing out into the open, up front and into the daylight in Real Life. It was time to stop watching the movie and become it'."

Diamond, p. 4

Commune as family

"The desire is to create intense involvement in the group--feelings of connectedness, belonging and the warmth of man attachments. Communes seek a family warmth and intimacy, to become extended families."

Kanter, p. 54

Communal closeness in human relationships

"young migrants quietly sense the cruelly shattering status of a society erected on a cult of rigid, non-emotional 'rugged individualism.' And in response, they hunger now for community. They crave the sensation of becoming whole with other human beings, of being a part of a larger thing. . . . They are socialist almost by instinct . . . seek . . . a living repudiation of the cash nexus among people."

Hedgepeth, p. 30

Non-materialism: prototype for future

"By 1975 . . . the world will be faced with continent-wide famines, which can be averted only if and when each individual realizes that he can survive comfortably by taking less for himself. . . . Within New Mexico . . . it's possible . . . (Drop Citier thinks) for an entirely original dollarless economy to be built-- which, if it proves workable on such a large scale, the whole world will eventually adopt."

Hedgepeth, p. 163

Communes superior to family of origin

"deep involvement with others in a climate of freedom, openness and commitment. . . . feeling of belonging has, been described as both a 'new tribalism' and a 'new sense of brotherhood,'" characterized by respect for the individuality of other family members. A tendency to recapture the Indian belief in tribal "respect for your brother's dream."

"In the communes, we are now beginning to feel that man has many brothers. . . . You can say things to each other and share things like you never could in the family. I never had so much love in my whole life."

Otto, p. 21

Communes realize the moment for action is now

Jack Kerouac, Scripture of the Golden Eternity: "The point is we're waiting, not how comfortable we are while waiting. . . . We're waiting for the realization that this is the golden eternity."

Diamond, p. 4

Communal life as a way of ending participation in pollution of environment

"First there is a deep respect . . . for nature and the ecological system. There is a clear awareness that 70% of the population lives on one percent of the land and that this one percent is severely polluted, depressingly ugly, and psychologically over-crowded. Commune members generally believe that a very small but politically influential minority with no respect for the ecological system or beauty of nature exploits all of the land for its own gain. . . . most commune members stress the rehabilitation of all lands and the conservation of all natural resources for the benefit of all the people."

Otto, p. 17

Cheapness of communal living

"Collective living is also an economic necessity. Since many people in the alternative society have given up the idea of a 'career' in the traditional sense, and do not want to work full time, the struggle for solvency is constant. . . . Buying food in bulk and sharing many meals at home cut costs . . . and each member of the Red Fox (Berkeley) pays only $65.00 a month for food and lodging. Most . . . have to work only parttime and can devote the rest of their efforts to the movement."

Roberts, p. 48

Joy as a facet of the new consciousness

"life is meant to be fundamentally joyous . . . 'doing your thing.' Work . . . a form of joyous self-expression . . . the absence of authentic joy [caused by] our social institutions . . . game-playing."

Otto, p. 17

Because of futility of action, impetus to flee to the land

"Neither peaceful demonstration nor sporadic gestures of violence could change the mentality of police . . . Instinctively, they took the escape route . . . their grandparents had taken in fleeing the grim cities of the Northeast; that the grandparents before them had taken in fleeing Europe's dark satanic mills, foreclosures, persecutions, and wars. They went back to the land; but this time, they went together."

Houriet, p. xii

Self-sufficiency through farming

"One ideal is to create economically self-sufficient communities with all property owned in common. The desire for self-sufficiency and control over their own financial destinies leads many communes to form around farms, to attempt to provide for their own maintenance needs themselves, to live in simple dwellings and to work the land."

Kanter, p. 55

Income sources

The Ant Farm, Sausalito, Calif.: "currently specializes in building plastic 'inflatables,' balloon-type environments which are used at rock festivals, and on children's playgrounds."

Andrews, p. 38

Return to land comparable to a psychedelic high

"The city-bred migrants discovered . . . that open country can produce a natural 'high' as psychedelic as any chemical . . . a melting away of the anxieties, phobias and rationalizations that had kept them from seeing themselves in cosmic perspective and from relating to . . . brothers in a fully human way. The land . . . became a key to the communitarians' search for another style of being."

Hedgepeth, p. 75

Number of communes

"Between 1965 and 1970 more than two thousand communal groups were established."

"Dr. Benjamin D. Zablocki, an assistant professor of sociology at the University of California, at Berkeley, put the figure at 3,000 in an interview in the San Francisco Chronicle of February 19, 1970."

Houriet, p. xiii

Communal life as a way of avoiding support of war

"Ralph (Chip) Oliver [fled to] a large Victorian house in Larkspur, Calif. that is the headquarters of a commune known as the One World Family of the Messiah's World Crusade." p. 50

"Chip Oliver's liberation is costing him at least $25,000 a year. He made $50,000 in his two seasons of pro ball, counting salary, bonus and playoff money. . . Oliver hasn't given up work, just making money. 'Hell, $10,000 of that $50,000 went down the drain in Vietnam—then Cambodia . . . That's another reason I quit. The only way not to pay taxes is not to make money.'" p. 51

Newnham, pp. 50–51

Recycling to minimize pollution

New Buffalo Commune, New Mexico: "'We set up a nail recovery operation. I used a crowbar to pull and pry; Torah . . . hammered them straight. 'Probably enough nails in dumps to keep all the carpenters in America busy for years . . . Except straightening isn't profitable. It's more profitable to use up all the iron and metal resources and let the iron foundries pollute the air and streams.'"

Houriet, p. 174

Anti-materialism: joy in giving up pre-occupation with possessions

"In a tangle of cliffs I chose a place—
Bird-paths, but trails for men.
What's beyond the yard?
White clouds clinging to vague rocks.
Now I've lived here—how many years—
Again and again spring and winter pass.
Go tell families with silverware and cars
What's the use of all that noise and money?"
Gary Snyder, Cold Mountain Poems

Diamond, p. 22

As noted on page 134, the outline is the skeletal framework for a paper. The outline reflects note card groupings. *Roman numeral divisions* are the elements of the main groups of cards. *Capital letter divisions* reflect the first set of subgroups within each main group. *Arabic numeral divisions* reflect the sub-subgroups within each subgroup. Before you begin the outline for a paper of your own, there are two additional points you should keep in mind.

1. THE OUTLINE IS A BALANCED STRUCTURE

The Principle of Parallelism

Recreation for Release of Aggression
I. Spectator football for vicarious aggressive body contact
II. Television for pleasure in murder always punished
III. Bridge for conquest through wits
IV. Some people get aggressive release in sports participation

Some people don't see faulty parallelism when it's right under their noses.

To love	Swimming in the summer	Illuminated by light
To laugh	Hiking in the fall	Entranced by nature
To hope	Skiing in the winter	Enchanted by peace

PARALLELISM IS BALANCED STRUCTURE. PARALLELISM ACCENTUATES RELATIONSHIPS. PARALLELISM IS POETRY.

The Principle of Coordination

I. Reasons for the credibility gap
II. Reasons for the generation gap
III. Refusal to listen to another's hopes
IV. Reasons for the communications gap

Which heading doesn't belong?

HEADINGS EQUAL IN SIGNIFICANCE AND SCOPE HAVE COMPARABLE NUMERICAL OR LETTER DESIGNATIONS.

The Principle of Subordination

I. Dogs
   A. Collies
   B. German shepherds   *You'll never figure this one out!*
   C. Basset hounds
   D. Cats

The Principle of Division and Subdivision

Breeds of Dogs

I. Working dogs
   A. Collies
II. Sporting Dogs
III. Hounds

*This is simple.
You can't divide a
subject into one part.*

Breeds of Dogs

I. Working dogs
   A. Collies
   B. German shepherds
II. Sporting dogs
III. Hounds

*You <u>can</u> divide a
subject into two parts.*

*If you really wish to deal only with Collies, you must completely
recast your outline and do something like this.*

Collies

I. Nutritional needs
II. Exercise needs

2. THE OUTLINE REQUIRES CLEAR ARTICULATION OF RELATIONSHIPS BETWEEN COMPONENT PARTS

I. Women's libbers are hostile
   A. Because women are regarded as sex objects
   B. Because men's salaries for comparable jobs are higher
   C. Because women are stuck with domestic drudgery

or

I. Reasons for the hostility of women's libbers
   A. Women are regarded as sex objects
   B. Men's salaries for comparable jobs are higher
   C. Women are stuck with domestic drudgery

not

I. Women's libbers are hostile
   A. Sex objects
   B. Housework
   C. Higher salaries

Scrambled Outline

Cut out the following outline components. Remember that the outline reflects note card groupings. Remember the principles of parallelism, coordination, subordination, and division and subdivision. Recall that outline relationships must be clearly articulated. Then put the outline components into coherent order. When you've finished, you'll have the framework for the first part of the model research paper that concludes this chapter.

Through resistance to technology

To live with the land

To futile educational processes

Achieving brotherhood through sharing instead of hoarding

To find emotional security through an "extended family"

Through meaningful work

To attain self-sufficiency

Communes fill needs unmet in conventional society

To futile political action

Through action instead of talk

Through freedom from restricting institutions

To have a peaceful revolution now

Through growing own food

As a means of survival

Communes provide an alternative

To halt pollution

Providing a model of a "dollarless economy" ultimately necessary for preserving the species

To live non-materialistically

Through recycling

Through setting up ideal societies within the existing framework

Through "irresponsible" fun

As a means of attaining a new consciousness

Why communes?

Which provides more love than the family of origin

Through operating communal businesses

Protecting the earth from the dangers of over-consumption

Which respects one's individuality

Ending living for acquisition of things

To attain joy

II. What problems do communes face?
    A. Problems brought from the outside
        1. Indecisiveness
            a) About trivial issues of household management
            b) About independence versus dependence upon outside support
        2. Work incapacity
            a) Resulting in property disintegration
            b) Resulting in fleeing the destroyed commune
        3. Hostility toward organization
            a) Derived from hatred of arbitrary outside authority
            b) Continued even when organization is needed for survival
    B. Problems in attaining self-sufficiency
        1. Failure of communal business enterprises
        2. Dependency upon outside support
        3. Impossibility of communal manufacture of all equipment and materials
    C. Ambivalence of workers toward unemployed co-members
        1. Workers' hostility toward "drones"
        2. Workers' concommitant desire to avoid money preoccupation
    D. Tension over open versus closed commune concepts
        1. General preference for the open commune
            a) Because of belief in an undivided earth accessible to all
            b) Because of fear of private property as the root of dissension among men
        2. Practical need for a closed commune
            a) To avoid over-crowding
            b) To avoid influx of neurotics who drain group energy
    E. Too little private living space
        1. Preventing needed solitude
        2. Causing irritability
    F. Illnesses
        1. Respiratory diseases
        2. Dysentery
            a) Resulting from unhygienic food preparation
            b) Resulting from dietary imbalances
        3. Venereal disease
    G. Community hostility
        1. Based on fear of communes as disease carriers
            a) Resulting in involving zoning ordinances
            b) Resulting in communal attempts to define themselves as legal families
        2. Based on horror of influx of "undesirables"
            a) Resulting in parental prohibition of children's visits
            b) Resulting in physical attacks
                (1) On commune property
                (2) On commune members
            c) Resulting in legal action against the commune
        3. Based on fear of alien values
            a) Devaluation of work ethic
            b) Pleasure as an end in itself
            c) Leisure as a right
            d) Needed commodities as a right
            e) Sanctity of free love
III. How does one enter a commune?
    A. Consider alternative possibilities
        1. Starting a commune
        2. Joining an existing commune

B. Consider kinds of communes already in existence to help you define options
   1. Remember that successful communes have some kind of loose identity
   2. Read about existing communes in The Modern Utopian
   3. Read about existing communes in Alternatives News Magazine
C. Accumulate information about communes that interest you
   1. Through visiting
   2. Through communal newsletters
D. If starting a commune, find congenial "family" members
   1. From your friendship group
   2. Through Alternatives Foundation Match-Making Service
   3. Through Questers computerized match-making agency
E. Get experienced counsel in organizing your commune
   1. Through attending communal seminars
      a) At Lama Foundation
      b) At Heathcote Community School of Living
   2. Through commune survival literature
      a) Alternatives Foundation booklets
      b) Green Revolution booklet
      c) Uncollege Catalog
F. If interested in rural living, locate available land
   1. Through booklets and newsletters
      a) Mother Earth News
      b) Green Revolution Community Newsletter
      c) Research Report on Where It Is Still Pleasant to Live in the U.S.A.
   2. Through realtors' catalogs
      a) United Farm Agency
      b) Strout Realty
   3. Through purchase of tax delinquent property
G. If interested in farming for food supply, become agriculturally knowledgeable
   1. Through Department of Agriculture pamphlets
   2. Through use of the Monthly Catalog of United States Government Publications
H. Familiarize yourself with food handling
   1. Large quantity cooking
   2. Sanitation
   3. Nutrition
I. Learn to construct low-cost, adequate shelter
   1. Order Zone Primer
   2. Consult Ald's list of shelter materials
   3. Consult shelter section of The Last Whole Earth Catalog
   4. Consult Monthly Catalog of United States Government Publications for inexpensive pamphlets
   5. Consult Vertical File Index
J. Plan your income source
   1. Assess your skills and your communal resources
   2. Review income sources of other communes
   3. Order Alternatives Foundation booklet, How to Make Money.
K. Consider matters of interpersonal relationship
   1. Decision making processes
   2. Admission and exclusion policies
   3. Plans for work allocation
   4. Privacy requirements
   5. System of communication among members

Alternative Life Style: Communes of the Sixties and Seventies,
or Have You Ever Wanted Out?

But I reckon I got to light out for the territory ahead of the
rest, because Aunt Sally she's going to adopt and sivilize me, and
I can't stand it. I been there before.

--Huckleberry Finn

Have you ever wanted out? Have schools bored you and jobs
looked grim? Have you been lonely in the closeness of your family
and choking on an urban street? Do you love people and hate to be
bossed? Are you sick of acquisition and eager for spontaneous joy?
Are you strong enough for freedom and steady enough for work? Are
you seeking self-emergence and willing to pay the cost? Out there
in the cities and farmlands are people, like you perhaps, who asked
these questions in their heads and answered, yes. They had shared
anger and common needs. They faced grave problems and sometimes
solved them. This paper is a study of the needs an alternative life
style can gratify and the dangers implicit in it. And for those who
share the longings and are willing to take the risks, there are some
suggestions for finding sources dealing with joining or founding
intentional communes.

In the sixties, the campuses exploded, and the war dragged on.
In the sixties and seventies, the rivers and the lakes were dying,
and thermal pollution dragged on. The air was unbreathable, and the
cars rolled on. The colleges and universities had few answers, and
the students dragged on. Or did they?

1

Some didn't. They fled the schools, the cities, and the
marketplace. "Between 1965 and 1970 more than two thousand communal groups were established," maybe more, according to Berkeley
sociologist, Dr. Benjamin Zablocki, who placed the figure more
nearly at 3,000 in February 1970.[1]

The thousands of communes were formed by young people seeking
clean water and uncontaminated air, humane social relationships, and
extended families. These people went into voluntary exile, far away
from futile action and the urban rot--back to the land.[2] "Instinctively, they took the escape route...their grandparents had taken in
fleeing the grim cities of the Northeast; that the grandparents
before them had taken in fleeing Europe's dark satanic mills, foreclosures, persecutions, and wars. They went back to the land; but
this time they went together."[3]

They knew what they were leaving, but what were they seeking?
One objective was escape from forced financing of the policies of
the alien culture. Chip Oliver, linebacker for the Oakland Raiders,
an improbable escapee from a $50,000 take in two seasons of ball, is
now living in a big old house in Larkspur, California, as a member
of the One World Family of the Messiah's World Crusade.[4] Chip continues working but rejects money because "$10,000 of that $50,000
went down the drain in Vietnam--then Cambodia...The only way not to
pay taxes is not to make money."[5]

Living without money or with so little of it there are no taxes
calls for sizeable adjustments. Separate apartments, mortgage pay-
ments on suburban homes, individual grocery shopping all become
impossible. Communes are the answer because they're cheap. For
instance, members of the Red Fox Commune in Berkeley pay "only
$65.00 a month for food and lodging," an accomplishment made
possible by shared rent, communal meals, and food buying in bulk.[6]

Not only have young people resisted financing the war, but they
resist joining what Paul Goodman referred to as the plunge toward
"ecological disaster." If society won't abandon destruction of

the environment, at least they will. Their starting points are hard-headed awareness that seventy percent of the world's inhabitants occupy approximately one percent of the earth's surface; that this mutilated fraction is ugly, contaminated, and often unfit for human habitation; that the entire eco-system is exploited by a powerful minority committed to personal gain.[7] Thus items of the communal credo are preservation of the environment through decentralization of the population and loving care of the land one tills.

Impetus to protect the environment leads communes to hostility toward technology. Basically, communes want no responsibility for perpetuating a power system that "poisoned the air with pollutants and strip-mined farmlands." So they generally curtail their use of electricity drastically, reserving its use for survival appliances like freezers and pumps or sewing machines that promote self-sufficiency and individual crafts.[8]

Not only do communes escape reliance on technology, but they seek to salvage raw materials, making recycling as important as organic farming. Members of New Buffalo Commune in New Mexico happily straighten old nails, commenting that there are "probably enough nails in dumps to keep all the carpenters in America busy for years...Except straightening isn't profitable. It's more profitable to use up all the iron and metal resources and let the iron foundries pollute the air and streams."[9] Libre Commune in New Mexico carries recycling even farther. One member built his house for less than $100.00, using only discarded pieces of lumber and debris from a demolished building. Another builder spent a warm winter within adobe walls insulated by "empty glass formaldehyde bottles discarded by a mortician."[10]

Strong communal feelings of anti-materialism stem from this desire to protect the earth through slowing down the rape of natural resources and production of non-biodegradable debris. However, anti-materialism harmonizes well with communal ideals of frugality, self-sufficiency, and the abiding conviction that private ownership

fosters greed and violent protection of property. Whatever the
theoretical rationale, perhaps some of the people are just fed up
with collecting junk that breaks before it's paid for and living for
the collection of more. Commune poet Gary Snyder puts it like this:

> In a tangle of cliffs I chose a place—
> Bird-paths, but trails for men.
> What's beyond the yard?
> White clouds clinging to vague rocks.
> Now I've lived here—how many years—
> Again and again spring and winter pass.
> Go tell families with silverware and cars
> "What's the use of all that noise and money?"[11]

Non-materialism opens the gates to brotherhood, many feel. In
communal living, sharing replaces hoarding.[12] The dream of love
fuels the hatred of wealth: the belief that things build walls
between men. So throw the money in a common pot and let the property belong to "anyone who uses it." A visitor asks a child
raised in a Cambridge commune: "Who owns the cat," and she answers, "The cat is everyone's."[13]

In final terms, non-materialism becomes more for commune
dwellers than a preference. It represents salvation of the species.
From Drop City, New Mexico, comes the vision of an "entirely original dollarless economy...the whole world will eventually adopt,"
when famines bred of overpopulation and misuse of resources force
the rich to live on less and share the abundance of the earth with
their brothers.[14]

The needs communal life fills come together. Non-materialism
becomes a way of saving the earth and loving its people, living
cheaply and avoiding taxes. But non-materialism realizes still
another dream: self-sufficiency. To leave the world behind, one
must be able to survive without it. So communes go to great lengths
to become self-supporting. Many farm in order to provide their own

maintenance.[15] Drop City supplements its income with "light shows
for rock groups in town" and selling handcrafted pottery, jewelry,
and musical instruments.[16] The Ant Farm in Sausalito, California,
builds inflatable "environments," balloon structures used in playgrounds and rock festivals.[17] The devices are varied, the objec-
tives the same: self-sufficiency through self-employment, working
for all men and being owned by none.

As we've seen, self-sufficiency is generally related to living
from the land. But the land is more than a means of survival. Some
see it as a means of discovery of self, miraculously emerging in
open fields and uncontaminated air, "soul's new unfettered impulses"
rising from the "mythic essence of the land."[18] Living with the
sun and sky, the open country after the cluttered cities, produces a
psychedelic thrill that beats all drugs; a melting of tension, an
expanding of consciousness, a sense of merging with the cosmos.[19]

Communitarians seek a new "consciousness" that can emerge
only in a new environment. For the city dweller the land provides
the new environment, though the change must essentially be in one's
own head. Commune member Doug Dahlin puts it this way: "I am
twenty-one years old...I am a product of this fat, consumption-
oriented middle-class America, 'fat city'...Having only a fat city
consciousness...my answer...is to develop a new consciousness; in
order to develop a new consciousness, I must develop a new existence...The first step...building an intentional community within
the territory claimed by fat city."[20]

The new consciousness made possible in the commune includes
joy. Communitarians feel conventional, straight existence destroys
spontaneous joy which comes from "doing your thing." In the
commune even work becomes "a form of joyous self-expression,"[21]
because the work you choose is "your thing"; and the drudgery
necessary for survival is equally shared, not dumped on some victim
lowest in the social pecking order. Joy is given outlet in communal
life in "singing, dancing, moon-worship and everything else hith-

erto 'irresponsible.'" Only unhappiness is viewed as deviation from the norm.[22]

Perhaps joy is an extension of emotional security that comes from belonging to a close and protective group like a commune. Commune writers describe this sense of oneness in many ways: as the "togetherness of tribalism,"[23] "the extended family," "feelings of connectedness, belonging and the warmth of many attachments."[24] Whatever the name of the feeling, commune dwellers agree in wanting an alternative to "rugged individualism" and a bond stronger than the monetary ties.[25] Most frequently, they call the communal group an extended family, even assuming a family name. A hippie commune in California numbering 50 members is called the Lynch family. A New Mexico commune calls itself the "Chosen Family," and a group in New York just "The Family."[26] But these families are hopefully improvements upon the splintered families the communitarians left behind. The new communities, for one, hark back to the Indian tribal belief that beyond all values is "respect for your brothers' dream." This simple code might ease the tensions in many conventional families wracked by sibling rivalry and the generation gap. There is, ideally, openness and love in the extended families: Says one member, "In the communes, we are...beginning to feel that man has many brothers....You can say things to each other and share things like you never could in the family. I never had so much love in my whole life."[27]

Probably the strongest push toward the communal alternative is the impatience of the young, echoing the lines from Marat/Sade: "We want our revolution now." "Wait for this and wait for that, wait for other worldly bliss," the older generation mumbles; the young answer: Now! "This is the golden eternity."[28] A member of Twin Oaks commune traces the reasoning: "What if we just went ahead as though the revolution were over and we had won?" What kind of world would we set up: a world with leisure and love where a man could gain without robbing his brothers and work without being a

slave; a world of small, decentralized communal groups living in
harmony and peace; "a viable alternative to capitalism"[29] within
the capitalist state. The communal drive is this: the bloodless
revolution NOW.[30] As Steve Diamond puts it, "We had all been
watching that movie for too long, Revolution in America....It was
time to stop watching the movie and become it."[31]

So they became it and established independent communities nour-
ished by the land they nurtured. They tested alternative life
styles and formed extended families. They gave their children many
parents instead of two. They founded free schools and communities
of craftsmen, and they looked for God in many places--in the Bible,
the Koran, the Bhagavad-Gita, and the uncontaminated air.[32]

All of this sounds fairly euphoric: love, companionship,
craftsmanship, saving one's sanity, saving the earth. But so far
all we've really looked at is the communal ideal; an answer to the
question, "Why communes"; the needs young people hope communes
will satisfy. But there is always a discrepancy between reality and
a dream. So before you go rushing off to join the nearest commune,
read on and see if you have the stomach for some of the tangles that
mar even the best intentioned and most idealistic dreams.

When anyone tries to escape his own life, he takes himself with
him. When anyone tries to escape his world, he takes it with him
too--perhaps because he's the product of it. In his extensive communal visiting, Robert Houriet finds instability aplenty. There are
hopeless meetings that can't decide whether to leave the dogs in or
out, people who want to junk capitalism while living on handouts
from the government or the old man. There are sinks of dishes no
one washes, unmended gates, wandering cows, and persistently no one
who is ever to blame. There is even a repeat of "splitting."
Somebody is always picking up his guitar, saying goodbyes, and roam-
ing off in quest of a "truly free, unhungup community."[33] A par-
tial explanation may be that communes attract discontented people
who, of course, may be the only sane ones in a crazy world; but who

may also be "the neurotic offspring of a neurotic society."[34]

A specific problem imported from outside is hostility to organization, structure, and delegation of authority. This hostility is understandable as most communitarians rebelled against perverse exercise of discipline in the home and school where authority equalled punishment driving one toward somebody else's end.[35] But ironically only authority and order in some form can keep communes alive. Often they start in a blaze of enthusiasm and hope but collapse in chaos because nobody gets the overpowering urge to dump the garbage.[36] And there isn't any father-teacher-boss to give an order. Before the demise of Oz, a commune in Pennsylvania, most of the windows were broken and left unrepaired. Flies by the thousands lived indoors. The plaster cracked, and the stove broke. Dogs and cats licked food from plates. The garden was planted too late to yield a harvest, and symbolic of all else a geodesic dome stood unfinished in a deserted clearing.[37]

This brings a cruel dilemma into focus: How can the commune be freer than conventional society when it needs authoritarianism to survive? A despairing writer in The Modern Utopian concludes that "the only way to be free is to be alone."[38] But perhaps that's not entirely true. There may be an alternative for some. As a mature member of a dying commune commented, "Anarchism assumes people are independent and can carry their own weight."[39] Another way of putting this might be: Freedom is possible for those who have the strength to be free. Or external controls aren't needed by people who can control themselves.

Problems come up not only with regard to structure and authority but to the immensely important ideal of communal self-sufficiency. Self-sufficiency, of course, is dependent upon capacity for cooperative work. But even with work energy, things go wrong. Rainbow Farm, for instance, set out to do odd jobs in the community like roto-tilling. But the roto-tiller broke. The trailer attached to the jeep broke. Customers wanted the work done on schedule, but repair parts weren't available. So the kids borrowed a tiller, stuffed it in the jeep, tilled for the neighbors, and came home and tilled for themselves, only to find they'd made too little to pay their bills. So the money came from mamas or buried reserves, along with a dirty sense of dependency on the world they'd fled.[40] Whatever the attitude, self-sufficiency is generally more of a fantasy than an operable principle. Ken Kesey calls the inconsistency "a lie in the air...I haven't seen a commune make it on its own terms where it's making it off its own piece of stuff and it's not having to draw from outside."[41] The communes by and large can't even earn their own way let alone produce and manufacture all needed supplies. Steve Baer, who travels around the Southwest helping construct "zomes," a new communal dwelling unit, laughs at fantasies of self-sufficiency: "All this talk about a self-contained counter-culture—can you imagine us freaks trying to manufacture plastic, pipe and glass."[42] As things stand, it seems communes still have to work out a viable relationship with the outside world: using it without being used in return.

As self-sufficiency is hard to get, we've seen that many communes depend upon the money of a few members, and tensions rise over inequities in contributions. In a Marin County commune, for instance, only four or five members worked steadily. Transients wandered in for a free ride. Even some of the permanent members were jobless. The workers wanted to be sympathetic and generous, not penny-counting. Yet their hostility rose over giving drones a free ride.[43] An apparent paradox emerges: communitarians fled the money scene, the owning, grabbing, leisure-hating world outside only to find utopia coming apart because some had money and others not, because some worked and others played.

Perhaps the problem of inequity of contribution lies partially in admissions policies, the question of the open versus the closed commune. We've seen that commune life seems to require people with stability, for freedom requires self-control. Harmony requires

maturity, and only realists can implement a dream. Obviously, not
everyone can fill the bill. Yet the communes were founded on a
Rousseauian dream of man as one of nature's children finding home on
any spot of an undivided earth. When man built fences and established boundaries, owned property and guarded it with guns, "he
fell from paradise." Closing the commune to any traveller betrayed
the vision. "How could a commune by definition draw a perimeter of
private property around itself?"[44] But visitors came, and the
space ran out. New Buffalo Commune in New Mexico nearly died of its
open-ended dream. Visitors came up the road from Taos a half dozen
a day. They pitched camp in tepees. They slept in the kitchen.
They moved into empty buses.[45] The older members hid or worked in
the cornfield while the visitors covered all the floor space with
their bodies, bled electricity meant only for the pump, smoked pot,
ate spam, drank milk from the babies' bottles, and drove the strug-
gling commune to bankruptcy[46] or would have if common sense hadn't
triumphed over utopian dreams. Instead of leaving, the old-timers
fought for their home and pleaded, "this is marginal land....We
were over-doing it with twenty-five people. Now we've got fifty
here. We don't have enough work or food or space....We can't keep
ourselves together. If you respect what we're trying to do, you'll
leave."[47] Mercifully, and none too soon, the visitors left, and
the commune barred its doors.

Obviously if everyone can't come to share the "free and
unowned" earth, admissions policies are needed, and exclusion policies too. With these the commune begins to sound like a private
club. Chestnut Hill in New England lasted a hard winter, coped with
external problems, but foundered in face of internal stress. There
was Bill who took more than he gave, not financially so much as
emotionally. He wasn't together. He roamed the house all night and
slept all day, started projects he couldn't finish, and contracted a
$250.00 bill for corkboard when the commune was broke. Finally,
painfully, the commune mobilized, held an awful meeting, and

agonized over moral responsibility to Bill. His laziness and
depression were dragging everybody down, but wasn't the whole point
of the farm "that the strong should carry the weak?" Who was
entitled to say "who the land belonged to" when they all had come
together? When the decision to exclude was made, there was an ugly,
shattering scene with Bill cracking and shouting, "No one the likes
of you is going to tell me when I can leave or not."[48] Again there
is inconsistency in paradise. The communitarians want love of man,
not the exclusiveness of a frat house. Yet the commune needs stable
people who live together compatibly. So policies must be devised to
limit membership and provide probationary periods for newcomers.

Compatibility becomes very important when there is a privacy
problem in all communes but the fairly prosperous ones with separate
dwellings and ample land. To survive communal life, one must be
very sociable, because only infrequently do members have rooms to
themselves. For respite from companionship, members frequently take
a walk in the woods.[49] No matter how comforting an extended family
of friends can be, human beings seem to need some time alone which
is drastically cut down in communes. So when someone (like Bill at
Chestnut Hill) lapses into depression, close quarters intensify the
strain.[50] There's no place to hide. The "family's" everywhere,
and some people lapse into irritability, get sick, and ultimately
flee the scene.[51]

In the communes, you can get sick of people. You can also just
plain get sick. Commune life can be hard, involving poor shelter,
crowding, and inadequate food. Respiratory diseases are common.
Dysenteries result from unhygienic food preparation. Venereal diseases are a hazard because of the number of nomadic hippies wandering in and out of communes.[52] Generalities about illnesses are per-
sonalized by a look at individual cases. Nineteen-year-old Wallace
C. fled an uncongenial home in Queens to the haven of a Sarasota
commune, Free Souls, started by a group of students. The food was
cheap, made mostly of old bread picked up for nearly nothing in

local stores, fried bread with other stuff, baked bread soaked down
with whatever was around. At first it didn't seem bad: "But I got
this stomach virus and diarrhea," Wallace explains. "It was my
first time with the C.C.'s (commune cramps)....It's funny now but I
remember that I had this odd feeling, thinking that I was going to
die."[53] He didn't, but the point is he thought he was, making it
evident that communes have to know something about sanitation and
diet.

    All the internal problems that beset communes combine to create
external ones in the form of community hostility. Straight communities are frightened of communes as public nuisances and disease
carriers. Armed with zoning ordinances, they go to war. Supposedly
"a house occupied by more than four or five people...unrelated by
blood, marriage or legal adoption...creates fire and health hazards,
traffic congestion, crowding and noise." As such ordinances endan-
ger the entire concept of communal living, members fight back
legally with the attempt to have communes classified as "legal families."[54] When one of the ill-fated Oz family contracted conta-
gious hepatitis, community fears were apparently realized. As the
commune had been widely visited, the local health department broad-
cast warnings precipitating fears of a hepatitis epidemic on the
scale of an onslaught of bubonic plague.[55]

    The hoards of visitors so troublesome to communes also contrib-
ute to problems in community relations. Oz, for instance, was beset
by the usual hip "drifters" and drug freaks. The community was
having enough trouble assimilating an alien life style and publi-
cized "non-capitalist religion," but now fear of corruption of
local youth burgeoned.[56] Parents prohibited their children's
visits. Tension was high, and the end came violently and fast.
Someone burned a communal house, killed a dog, attacked a girl. The
commune was boycotted by local businessmen, and the law moved in.
Members were charged with violation of an 1860 statute that read:
"Whoever keeps and maintains a common, ill-governed and disorderly

house or place to the encouragement of idleness, gaming, drinking or
misbehavior and to the common nuisance and disturbance of the neigh-
borhood...is guilty of a misbehavior." Charges were dropped when
the family agreed to leave within two weeks. But when everyone was
gone, townspeople came and burned the main communal building to the
ground, ending the four-month life-span of the Land of Oz.[57]

Using its massive artillery, the establishment closes in. And
though some of the complaints may be legitimate enough, one suspects
they are pretexts covering a half-acknowledged fear of an alien life
style. Perhaps it's natural for societies to strike out against
assumptions that pierce the heart of the existing order. And this
the communes surely do. Work and earned rewards, duty and order,
conformity and obedience--all these are abandoned in the quest for
joy. But such joy! This joy rules that "pleasure is an end in
itself," that leisure is man's birthright, and not his reward for
work.[58] Everything in the established world rests on the notion of
productivity and reward. But the communitarians say that even material goods belong to men by right, not by desert.[59] Even love is
free. "To hell with materially productive ends. Love, the most
all-enveloping of human emotions, should in itself be an end. Love
at all times, in any way, for its own sake."[60] So in the final
analysis, it may be the cult of joy that is really responsible for
establishment attack, because it is belief in joy that declares food
free and love free, pleasure first and labor last, drugs right and
authority wrong, because authority denies the autonomy of self.

If the first part of this study accentuates the positive, the
second highlights the negative, and truth is probably somewhere in
between. Whatever the case, there are happy, successful communes on
comfortable terms with the world outside. There are communes that
evolve democratic, workable decision-making processes based on con-
sensus for crucial matters and individual decision for others.
Flexibility is a hallmark, and regular communication a must.[61] At
High Ridge Commune in Oregon, work gets done without quotas or

bosses, timeclocks or orders. It gets done the way it gets done in
an average family.[62] Libre in Colorado has privacy with each house
on a spacious mountainside out of view of any other. Compatibility
is high because of a "probationary screening process."[63] Celo
Community in North Carolina has been around since 1937, with mature
members and families living in separate houses.[64] Koinonia, south of
Macon, Georgia, started an interracial settlement in 1942 in the
heart of Ku Klux country. Not only has it sustained itself in a
hostile environment, but it has served the community well, introduc-
ing scientific agricultural methods and building sturdy four-bedroom
homes which displaced families can buy at cost.[65] Drop City, a community of musicians and artists in New Mexico, survives with "no
organized work, just do-what-you-want sort of things." Money
earned through selling pottery and wire sculpture is held in common
in a Drop City account.[66] Morehouse Commune has thirteen houses in
San Francisco, Los Angeles, and Hawaii, with total assets exceeding
$2,000,000.[67] It can be seen that in some communes all the problems
itemized have been solved or never known. Looking for explanations,
one can see there are no formulas any more than there are prototypal
communes, because the essence of the communal movement is individualism. "Every commune wanted to be and had to be unique."[68]

This leads us to the title question: Have you ever wanted out?
If the answer is yes, and the overall goals are compatible, if the
dangers don't scare you, or you have enough sense to avoid them,
perhaps a commune is right for you.

First consider your alternatives: starting a commune or joining
one already in existence. Whichever your choice, write to Alternatives Foundation, P.O. Drawer A, Diamond Heights, San Francisco,
California. Subscribe to The Modern Utopian and the valuable semi-
annual Alternatives News Magazine which contains an updated Directory of Communes, articles, photographs, and reports, along with
communes seeking new members.[69]

If your friends aren't interested in dropping out (or dropping in), you can get agency help. The Alternatives Foundation sponsors a "Communal Match-Making" service. For $3.00, you can receive a copy of the "Alternatives Directory," "a private listing of individuals who are interested in finding an alternative life style." When you request the directory, write a brief description of yourself (100 words or less) mentioning your age, interests, occupation, kind of commune you're seeking. Communities will get in touch with you, if they have openings and you seem right for their group. Alternatives Foundation also sponsors a "group dating program," which seeks to help participants expand "the quality of their social lives."[70] Questers (Cathedral City, California) is another communal matchmaking agency, advertised as "primarily for middle-class dropouts, looking for a well-structured, economically sound community." A computer is utilized to combine compatible temperaments. Write for Quester's $4.00 booklet, which contains information and registration forms.[71]

If you're specifically interested in a rural commune, getting land is your first consideration. The Mother Earth News (Box 38, Madison, Ohio 44057) describes good communal land buys and offers help in communal operation. Current price is $5.00 a year.[72]

If you wish to obtain your food by farming, take advantage of the U.S. Department of Agriculture pamphlets on all facets of agriculture. You can receive a catalog of Department Publications on request. The Monthly Catalog of United States Government Publications which should be available in your library has an excellent subject index in the back of each bound volume. Many pamphlets are $.10 or $.15.

Be sure to familiarize yourself with methods of large-group cooking, nutrition, and sanitation. An invaluable book for these purposes (as well as general survival skills outside the establishment) is Living on the Earth by Alicia Bay Laurel.

One secret to successful, healthy, low-cost rural and wilderness living is obviously adequate shelter. Try to get a copy of The

Last Whole Earth Catalog which lists dozens of how-to-do-it sources
for the builder of low-cost dwellings. Check the Monthly Catalog of
United States Government Publications under such headings as domes,
zomes, geodesic domes, plywood constructions, tents, tepees, car-
pentry, low-cost homes, cabins, earth dwellings, adobe dwellings,
architecture for amateurs, shelter, rural housing, wilderness housing, prefabricated homes, etc. Also check these headings in the
Vertical File Index. Naturally, you can also consult the invaluable
Reader's Guide to Periodical Literature.

The Modern Utopian will give invaluable aid in discovering
income sources, patterns of communal governance, and skill for
reducing in-group friction. Above all, ponder Hedgepeth's list
of things most communes generally learn: "that the necessities of
group life call for a modification of the 'do your own thing'
ethic"; that everyone requires some privacy; that though group sex
is frequently practiced, monogamous communes seem to have more stability; "that open communication of all ideas and personal feelings
is an absolute necessity"; that flexibility is preferable to rigid
adherence to any collective decision.[73] Finally, bring to the ven-
ture all your hope, capacity for work, and loving patience with
human vulnerability and weakness.

We have seen that powerful dreams led thousands of young people
to seek their happiness outside the universities and marketplace and
that many of their failures were products of the dreams. Freedom
brought disorganization; self-sufficiency brought sickness; intimacy
brought anger; opposition to the system brought police raids. But
thousands of communes survive; and some people still want out, or
depending upon one's perspective "in." If you are one of the
latter, hopefully this research paper opens the door.

Footnotes

[1]Robert Houriet, Getting Back Together (New York: Coward, McCann, 1971), p. xiii.

[2]Ibid., p. xix.

[3]Ibid., p. xii.

[4]Blaine Newham, "Wow, Like Let's Really Try to Win," Sports Illustrated, 12 Oct. 1970, p. 50.

[5]Ibid., p. 51.

[6]Steven V. Roberts, "Halfway between Dropping Out and Dropping In," New York Times Magazine, 12 Sept. 1971, p. 48.

[7]Herbert Otto, "Communes: The Alternative Life Style," Saturday Review, 24 April 1971, p. 17.

[8]Houriet, p. 218.

[9]Ibid., p. 174.

[10]Ibid., pp. 224–25.

[11]Gary Snyder, Cold Mountain Poems, quoted in Stephen Diamond, What the Trees Said (New York: Delacorte, 1971), p. 22.

[12]William Hedgepeth and Dennis Stock, The Alternative: Communal Life in America (New York: Macmillan, 1971), p. 83.

[13]Rosabeth Moss Kanter, "Communes," Psychology Today, 4 (July 1970), 56.

[14]Hedgepeth, p. 163.

[15]Kanter, p. 55.

[16]Hedgepeth, p. 154.

[17]Louis M. Andrews, "Communes and the Work Crisis," Current, 126 (Feb. 1971), 38.

[18]Hedgepeth, p. 7.

[19]Ibid., p. 75.

[20]Douglas Dahlin, "A New Consciousness," The Modern Utopian: Communes, U.S.A., 5, No. 4 (1971), 31.

[21]Otto, p. 17.

[22]Hedgepeth, p. 186.

[23]Ibid., p. 186.

[24]Kanter, p. 54.

[25]Hedgepeth, p. 30.

[26]Kanter, p. 54.

[27]Otto, p. 21.

[28]Jack Kerouac, Scripture of the Golden Eternity, quoted in Stephen Diamond, What the Trees Said, p. 18.

[29]Houriet, pp. 289-90.

[30]C. P. Herrick, "Designing for Community," The Modern Utopian: Communes, U.S.A., 5, No. 4 (1971), 27.

[31]Diamond, p. 4.

[32]Houriet, p. xiv.

[33]Ibid., p. xxxiv.

[34]Ibid., p. 20.

[35]Rick Margolies, "Community Building," The Modern Utopian: Communes, U.S.A., 5, No. 4 (1971), 37.

[36]Hedgepeth, p. 188.

[37]Houriet, pp. xxi-xxii.

[38]Quoted in Hedgepeth, p. 187.

[39]Houriet, p. 20.

[40]"Notes from Rainbow Farm," Ramparts, 10 (Sept. 1971), 59.

[41]Michael Goodwin, "The Ken Kesey Movie," Rolling Stone, 7 March 1970, p. 18.

[42]Houriet, p. 217.

[43]Albert Solnit, "High Cost of Good 'Vibes': Wear and Tear in the Communes," Nation, 26 April 1971, p. 526.

[44]Houriet, p. 143.

[45]Ibid., p. 137.

[46]Ibid., pp. 144-45.

[47]Ibid., p. 143.

[48]Diamond, pp. 37-39.

[49]Otto, p. 20.

[50]Louie Robinson, "Life Inside a Hippie Commune," Ebony, 26 (Nov. 1970), 56.

[51]Otto, p. 21.

[52]Roy Ald, The Youth Communes (New York: Tower, 1970), p. 104.

[53]Ibid., pp. 115-16.

[54]Solnit, p. 525.

[55]Houriet, p. xxix.

[56]Hedgepeth, p. 77.

[57]Ibid.

[58]Ald, p. 79.

[59]Ibid., p. 63.

[60]Ibid., p. 64.

[61]Houriet, pp. 212-13.

[62]Ibid., p. 36.

[63]Hugh Gardner, "Your Global Alternative: Communes, Experiments, Jails, and Hidey Holes," Esquire, 74 (Sept. 1970), 108.

[64]Ibid., p. 109.

[65]Hedgepeth, pp. 175-76.

[66]Ibid., p. 154.

[67]Otto, p. 20.

[68]Houriet, p. 27.

[69]"Alternative Organs," The Modern Utopian: Communes, U.S.A., 5, No. 3 (1971), 188.

[70]"People Directory," The Modern Utopian: Directory of Social Change, 3, No. 4 (1969), n. pag.

[71]Houriet, p. 237.

[72]Gardner, p. 107.

[73]Hedgepeth, p. 187.

Bibliography

Ald, Roy. The Youth Communes. New York: Tower, 1970.

"Alternative Organs." The Modern Utopian: Communes, U.S.A., 5, No. 3 (1971), 188.

Andrews, Louis M. "Communes and the Work Crisis." Current, 116 (Feb. 1971), 34-39.

Dahlin, Douglas. "A New Consciousness." The Modern Utopian: Communes, U.S.A., 5, No. 4 (1971), 31-32.

Diamond, Stephen. What the Trees Said: Life on a New Age Farm. New York: Delacorte, 1971.

Gardner, Hugh. "Your Global Alternative: Communes, Experiments, Jails, and Hidey Holes." Esquire, 74 (Sept. 1970), 107-12, 163-64.

Goodwin, Michael. "The Ken Kesey Movie." Rolling Stone, 7 March 1970, pp. 18-19.

Hedgepeth, William, and Dennis Stock. The Alternative: Communal Life in New America. New York: Macmillan, 1970.

Herrick, C. P. "Designing for Community." The Modern Utopian: Communes, U.S.A., 5, No. 4 (1971), 27.

Houriet, Robert. Getting Back Together. New York: Coward, McCann, 1971.

Kanter, Rosabeth Moss. "Communes." Psychology Today, 4 (July 1970), 53-57, 78.

Margolies, Rick. "Community Building." The Modern Utopian: Communes, U.S.A., 5, No. 4 (1971), 36-39.

Newham, Blaine. "Wow, Like Let's Really Try to Win." Sports Illustrated, 12 Oct. 1970, pp. 50-54.

"Notes from Rainbow Farm." Ramparts, 10 (Sept. 1971), 58-59.

Otto, Herbert A. "Communes: The Alternative Life Style." _Satur-_
    day Review, 24 April 1971, pp. 16-21.

"People Directory: Communal Match-Making." _The Modern Utopian:_
    Directory of Social Change, 3, No. 4 (1969), n. pag.

Roberts, Steven V. "Halfway between Dropping Out and Dropping
    In." _New York Times Magazine,_ 12 Sept. 1971, pp. 44-64,
    68-69.

Robinson, Louie. "Life Inside a Hippie Commune." _Ebony,_ 26 (Nov.
    1970), 88-98.

Solnit, Albert. "High Cost of Good 'Vibes': Wear and Tear in the
    Communes." _Nation,_ 26 April 1971, pp. 524-27.

Chapter 5

A PAPER OF YOUR OWN

THE INTELLECTUAL PROCESS

Conceptualizing from Data: The Emergence of Thesis

IN THE BEGINNING IS THE IDEA

But where does the idea come from? Research materials on your note cards are data. To find the controlling idea in your paper, you need to see what your data adds up to, what you can abstract from it. This is simply the inductive method, drawing conclusions from a collection of particulars. A good way of proceeding is to ask yourself what all the particulars have in common, what separable groups of particulars have in common. The answer to your question is a *generalization*, a *concept*, a *controlling idea*, a *thesis*, an *intellectual center* for your paper that justifies its existence. Usually, you announce the central idea of your paper in the introductory passages.

To get the feel of the process, look at the automation jokes that follow. Try to see what attitudes toward automation are implicit in them. Begin by asking what all the jokes seem to have in common. (When I asked myself what all the data in Part I of my communal paper had in common, I saw that commune life always began with an ideal or human need unmet in conventional society.) See what conclusions you reach in open discussion.

Repairman fixing broken-down computer says accusingly to executive: "Did you ever think of showing it some *love?*"

Repairman to executive: "I've found what's causing the slowdown. The big computer is shoving all its work onto the small computer.

A truculent Army general asks a computer: "Will there be a World War III?" "Yes," answers the computer. "Yes!" roars the general. "What kind of an answer is that—'*yes*'?" Responds the computer, meekly, "Yes, *sir.*"

Boss to computer salesman:
"Nothing big — I just want to
replace one wise guy."

Secretary to office wolf:
"I'm sorry, Hugo, but I ran you
through the computer last night
and you didn't make it."

Flying on a plane that has been
automated, the passengers
hear over the loudspeakers: "This
plane has no pilot. Computers
are doing all the work. But you
have nothing to worry about
worry about worry about . . ."

Boss to underling: "Our computer is on the blink. Hire
21,000 office workers for the
next two days."

Puzzled-looking man in front of a
computer: "All that comes
out is a ball of gum."

An atheist painstakingly feeds
all of the world's great books
into a computer, then asks
the question: IS THERE A GOD?
The computer whirs, makes
eerie noises, then answers:
NOW THERE IS.

A man decides to test a computer's
accuracy. WHERE IS MY FATHER?
he asks. The machine answers:
YOUR FATHER IS IN A MEXICO
PRISON. Delighted at the mistake,
the man responds: WRONG!
HE'S IN LOS ANGELES WORKING IN A
BANK. The computer answers:
YOUR MOTHER'S HUSBAND IS
IN LOS ANGELES. YOUR FATHER IS
IN A MEXICO PRISON.

The Process of Classification

AFTER THE IDEA IS THE SEQUENCE OF PARTS

To find the divisions into which your paper will fall, you must find ways of classifying your data. This simply means setting up categories or sorting your data into piles and subpiles that have something important in common. For instance, when I began sorting my data on commune life into piles, each group of cards contained data about separable needs communal life filled: the need to escape supporting the government, the need to stop polluting the environment, the need to live inexpensively, the need for togetherness, and so on.

Now look back at our collection of automation jokes and cartoons and see if they fall into groups or clusters. What separable attitudes toward automation can be abstracted from each group? Identify categories, and put each joke or cartoon in one of the groups.

Fleshing Out the Frame

AFTER DIVISION COMES DEVELOPMENT

After you have determined the parts into which your paper will fall, you have a framework: a controlling idea or ideas and topic sentences for subdivisions. Here's the way it worked out in my communal paper, Part I:

Controlling idea: People enter communes because crucial needs are unmet in conventional society.

Subordinate ideas are abstracted from related clusters of data put in separate piles or categories.

One need "was escape from forced financing of the policies of the 'diseased culture.' "

Another need involved young people's resistance "to joining the plunge toward 'ecological disaster.' "

Another need grew from "strong communal feelings of anti-materialism that harmonize . . . with . . . the abiding conviction that private ownership fosters greed and violent protection of property."

Also, "communitarians seek a new 'consciousness' that can emerge only in a new environment."

How are these subtheses expanded upon, developed? Obviously by going back to the data from which they were drawn. Substantiate each point through precise reference to the data from which the subthesis was abstracted. The process is circular:

For example:

Developmental detail is drawn from data (note cards).

Subthesis (or topic sentence): "One objective was escape from forced financing of the policies of the 'diseased culture.' "

"Chip Oliver, linebacker for the Oakland Raiders, is an improbable escapee from a $50,000 take in two seasons of ball. He's living now in a big old house in Larkspur, California, as a member of the One World Family of the Messiah's World Crusade. Chip continues working but rejects money because '$10,000 of that $50,000 went down the drain in Vietnam—then Cambodia . . . The only way not to pay taxes is not to make money.' "

Now go back to our automation cartoons: Write a short paper. In an introductory paragraph explain what overall attitudes toward automation the jokes reflect. Devote a separate paragraph to each attitude. Illustrate the point made in each paragraph through references to appropriate jokes.

THE ESSENCE OF CLARITY

When we communicate with each other, it is useful to keep in mind that our common words may not evoke the same image in someone else's mind as they do in ours . . . Knowing this, we can help improve our communications by being as specific as possible in the way we use words . . .

Analysis

To give your paper intellectual depth, you can analyze or interpret your data as you go along, in concluding lines of paragraphs, in separate transitional and interpretive paragraphs, or in a formal conclusion that terminates your paper.

In the communal paper, I tended to analyze and interpret as I went along:

> The needs communal life fills come together. Non-materialism becomes a way of saving the earth and loving its people, living cheaply, and avoiding taxes. But non-materialism realizes still another dream: self-sufficiency.

A passage like this draws various sets of data together and provides a transition to the next point (in the sample paper, the next communal ideal: self-sufficiency, going it alone, cutting loose from the establishment). More interpretation and analysis occur in the final paragraph:

> We have seen that powerful dreams led thousands of young people to seek their happiness outside the universities and the marketplace and that many of their failures were products of their dreams. Freedom brought disorganization; self-sufficiency brought sickness; intimacy brought anger. . .

Going back to our automation jokes and cartoons, try to analyze the significance of the attitudes toward automation reflected in the jokes and cartoons. Why are there so many jokes about computers? Are jokes a source of comfort? What is the function of humor in reduction of anxiety? These are points that could be discussed in an analytical conclusion to your paper.

You might write the paper collectively in class. Someone could put the thesis and subtheses on the board, and then all of you could reason "communally" about the psychological function of humor.

> Germinal idea for a research paper: The Psychological Function of Humor. See Sigmund Freud, *Jokes and Their Relation to the Unconscious* (*New York: Norton, 1966*).

Unity

Each paragraph must relate to the thesis just as each sentence in individual paragraphs must relate to the topic sentence.

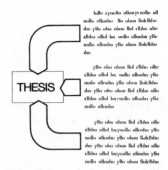

A paper has unity when it has a controlling idea and when all subdivisions (paragraphs and clusters of paragraphs) clearly relate to this controlling idea. Each paragraph needs an intellectual center of its own expressed in a topic sentence. Frequently, the topic sentence is the opening sentence of the paragraph, but it may follow a few introductory or transitional passages. The topic sentence may even conclude the paragraph when climactic arrangement is important. Whatever the arrangement, the center must be there, or you have *glop*—a *snarl*. The topic sentence is bi-directional by nature; it relates to the thesis of the paper and simultaneously anticipates or summarizes the content of the paragraph itself. Think of the thesis and topic sentences as promises to the reader: a way of saying, "I'm going to talk about this—wait and see."

PROFESSIONAL GLOP
OR THE CASE OF THE MISSING CENTER

About 31 per cent of the Tanzanian people are Moslems; let stand 30 minutes and then vacuum the area.
— Gettysburg *Times*

Mrs. B. writes: What causes my head to swim and my stomach to burp when I raise my head from the pillow every morning? Reply: God works in mysterious ways. Do you have car trouble?
— Orlando *Morning Sentinel*

GET THE POINT?

Propelled by a rocket motor and capable of supersonic speed, the SRAM is intended to knock out enemy defenses and enable the bombers to strike their primary targets. Each B52 can carry up to 20 teachers who have not been paid since last June.
— Knoxville *Journal*

Somewhere between 100 and 600 people are killed by lightning each year. About two thirds of them recover.
— *Science Digest*

IN EACH OF THESE, NOTHING HOLDS THE DISPARATE PARTS TOGETHER.

ON THE NATURE OF PLAGIARISM

They steal my thunder!
— John Dennis

They drive me nuts!
— Peg Hutchinson

Fine words! I wonder where you
stole 'em.
— Jonathan Swift

Wilde: "I wish I'd said that."
Whistler: "You will, Oscar,
you will."
— James McNeill Whistler

In vain we call old notions fudge,
And bend our conscience to
our dealing;
The Ten Commandments
will not budge,
And stealing will continue
stealing.
— Motto of the American
Copyright League

Q. What constitutes plagiarism?

A. Two or more words taken from a source without quotation marks.

Q. What are the risks of plagiarism?

A. An *F* on your paper. An *F* in the course. Expulsion from school. Notation on your transcript of cause of expulsion.

Q. What are safeguards against plagiarism?

A. The procedures recommended in Chapter 4:

1. In taking notes, copy all information verbatim. (Use dots to indicate omissions from the text. Use brackets to indicate insertions in your own words.)

2. When you write your paper, translate copied material into your own words, citing the original source in footnotes.

3. Arrange your note cards in the order in which you used them.

4. Number your note cards to correspond to footnote numbers. You have provided your instructor with *proof* of the originality of your phrasing. If he is in doubt, he can easily check any portion of your paper against your sources (readily accessible on the note cards).

Q. Will there be note cards for everything in my paper?

A. For everything taken from sources.

Q. Won't there be portions of the paper not derived from sources?

A. Yes. These passages will generally occur in introductory, concluding, and transitional paragraphs. They will generally be summarizing or interpretive passages. They won't be accumulations of information the average person doesn't carry in his head.

Q. How can I attest to the originality of my personal interpretive passages?

A. Largely by having written them yourself. Your instructor will suspect plagiarism only if there are discrepancies between writing fluency in the various parts of your paper and most noticeably between the quality of the writing in your research paper and the writing in papers done in class. When in doubt, your instructor may ask you to write a portion of your paper from memory. If you've assimilated your material and the writing styles are comparable, you have nothing to worry about.

Q. How do I credit sources I have used?

A. Through the use of conventionally accepted methods of documentation.

DOCUMENTATION

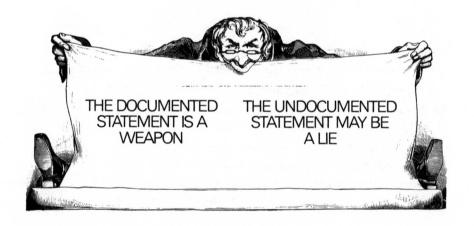

THE DOCUMENTED STATEMENT IS A WEAPON

THE UNDOCUMENTED STATEMENT MAY BE A LIE

ACKNOWLEDGING SOURCES

Author's Note

In order to provide models that exactly fit specific documentation forms, I have sometimes invented authors, titles, and publishers. Fidelity to existing sources often would have required the insertion of extraneous— possibly confusing—material. There are distinct advantages to focusing on discrete documentation elements. Models can then be combined when circumstances warrant, as it is impossible to provide forms for every possible combination of bibliographical data. At no time, however, have I erroneously attributed nonexistent works to existing publishers. That is, when the publisher exists, all data is accurate.

Numbering and Spacing Footnotes

1. Place footnotes on separate sheets at the end of the paper.
2. Do not bind your paper. Leave your instructor free to place notes beside text as he reads.
3. Double space footnotes.
4. Number consecutively.
5. Indent five spaces at the beginning of each note. Place Arabic number about one-half space above the line.

> [16]Alfred Burton, The Life of Clint Adams (New York:
> Atlantic Press, 1970), p. 18.
> [17]Elizabeth K. Norton, The Furies: Clint Adams
> Faces Conscience (Chicago: Midwest Press, 1968),
> pp. 14–15.

6. Place a corresponding raised number in the text after all quotations used and as close as possible to the beginning of borrowed ideas phrased in your own words.
7. Numbers after quotations follow all punctuation, excluding the dash.

> He asked but two questions: "Who do you think you are?
> Who do you think gave you the right to adjudge your wis-
> dom higher than that of the highest authorities in the
> land?"[18]

Abbreviations in Footnoting

Use abbreviations and short forms in documentation whenever this is consonant with clarity. *American Book Co.* and other comparable houses, for example, may be referred to without the designation *Co. Charles Scribner's Sons* may be designated as *Scribner's*. When in doubt, use the full name of the publisher.

Use abbreviations of months (16 Aug. 1971) in publication data, abbreviations of titles of magazines (*CE* instead of *College English*), abbreviations of Shakespearean plays, books of the Bible, words like *reprinted* (rpt.), *dissertation* (diss.).

Note that when the abbreviation "p." for page is used, it is lower cased and followed by a period: p. 18. When more than one page is designated, the abbreviation looks like this: pp. 18–21. Note that no period is used between the first and second "p."

In the models that follow, these principles have generally been observed with the exception of abbreviations for titles of magazines. Because some undergraduates may be unfamiliar with titles of journals, full titles have been used.

Citing Dates

A

Copyright © 1968, 1972 by Glencoe Press
A Division of The Macmillan Company

Printed in the United States of America

All rights reserved. No part of this book may be reproduced or transmitted in any form or by any means, electronic or mechanical, including photocopying, recording, or by any information storage and retrieval system, without permission in writing from the Publisher.

Glencoe Press
A Division of The Macmillan Company
8701 Wilshire Boulevard
Beverly Hills, California   90211
Collier-Macmillan Canada, Ltd., Toronto, Canada

Library of Congress catalog card number: 75–173688

First printing, 1972
Second printing, 1973

B

Copyright, 1948, by Stuart Gilbert
Copyright, 1947, by Librairie Gallimard

All rights reserved under International and Pan-American Copyright Conventions.

THE MODERN LIBRARY
is published by RANDOM HOUSE, INC.

Manufactured in the United States of America

C

A SPY IN THE HOUSE OF LOVE
A Bantam Modern Classic edition / published April 1968
2nd printing

All rights reserved.
Copyright, 1959, by Anaïs Nin.
This book may not be reproduced in whole or in part, by mimeograph or any other means, without permission.

Published simultaneously in the United States and Canada

Bantam Books are published by Bantam Books, Inc., a subsidiary of Grosset & Dunlap, Inc. Its trade-mark, consisting of the words "Bantam Books" and the portrayal of a bantam, is registered in the United States Patent Office and in other countries. Marca Registrada. Bantam Books. Inc., 271 Madison Avenue, New York, N.Y. 10016.

PRINTED IN THE UNITED STATES OF AMERICA

If there is more than one copyright date on the back of the title page (the copyright page), *use the earliest one.* Other dates may appear, but these represent new printings or impressions rather than new editions. In model A, use copyright date 1972. In model B, use the earlier copyright date, 1947. In sample C, use the earlier copyright date, 1959.

Data Sequence

Books

If from among the many model footnotes in the next section of this chapter, you can't find a model to fit your book, just follow this order in arranging your data:

1. AUTHOR *or* AUTHORS, COMMA

        John Doe,

        John Doe, Peter Jones, and William Doe,

2. *or* EDITOR (*name*), COMMA, ED. (*abbreviation for "Editor"*), COMMA

        Charles Snipper, ed.,

3. COMPONENT PART OF LARGER WORK (*in quotation marks*), COMMA (*inside final quotation mark*)

        John Doe, "English Is Hell,"

4. TITLE OF BOOK (*underlined*), COMMA (*unless parenthesis comes next*)

        John Doe, "English Is Hell," in <u>Anthology of Stu-</u>
    dent Opinion,

    (*"In" occurs before title only after a component part. No comma follows a title that ends in a question mark or exclamation mark:* "Is English Hell?")

5. EDITOR *or* TRANSLATOR (*if citation is by author*), COMMA (*unless parenthesis comes next*)

        John Doe, "English Is Hell," in <u>Anthology of Stu-</u>
        <u>dent Opinion</u>, ed. Mary Brown,

6. EDITION (*if there is more than one*), COMMA (*unless parenthesis comes next*)

        Gerald R. Baskins, <u>The College on the Run</u>, 2nd ed.,

7. SERIES NAME (*if any*), COMMA (*unless parenthesis comes next*)

> Gerald R. Baskins, The College on the Run, 2nd ed.,
> Free University Publications in Critical Pedagogy,

8. SERIES NUMBER (*if any*), COMMA (*unless parenthesis comes next*)

> Gerald R. Baskins, The College on the Run, 2nd
> ed., Free University Publications in Critical Pedagogy,
> No. 14,

9. VOLUME NUMBER (*if volumes were printed* separately), COMMA (*unless parenthesis comes next*)

> George Dorman, Alternatives to Dying, II,

10. PARENTHESIS, PLACE OF PUBLICATION, COLON

> George Dorman, Alternatives to Dying, II (New York:

11. PUBLISHER, COMMA

> George Dorman, Alternatives to Dying, II (New York:
> Free University Press,

12. DATE OF PUBLICATION, END PARENTHESIS, COMMA

> George Dorman, Alternatives to Dying, II (New York:
> Free University Press, 1973),

13. VOLUME NUMBER (*if all volumes in set were published at the same time*), COMMA

> George Gordon Edwards, Aesthetics, ed. George
> Epridge (New York: Free University Press, 1972), II,

14. PAGE *or* PAGES CITED (*no abbreviation for "page" with volume number*), PERIOD

> George Gordon Edwards, Aesthetics, ed. George
> Epridge (New York: Free University Press, 1972), II, 84.

15. PAGE *or* PAGES CITED (*abbreviation for "page" without volume number*), PERIOD

> Harold Richards, Call of the Communes (New York:
> Free University Press, 1973), p. 87.

> (*Abbreviation for "pages" looks like this:* pp. 87–89.)

Periodicals

If from among the many model footnotes in the next section of this chapter, you can't find a model to fit your periodical, just follow this order in arranging your data:

1. AUTHOR, COMMA

>   Betty J. Thompson,

2. TITLE (*in quotation marks*), COMMA (*inside final quotation mark*)

>   Betty J. Thompson, "The Decline of Political
>   Parties,"

(*No comma follows a title that ends in a question mark or exclamation mark:* "Are Illustrators Obsolete?" *A set of single quotation marks encloses a quotation within a title:* "Simon and Garfunkle's 'Richard Cory,' " . . .)

3. NAME OF PERIODICAL (*underlined*), COMMA

>   Betty J. Thompson, "The Decline of Political
>   Parties," Twentieth Century Views,

4. VOLUME NUMBER (*if used, in Arabic numbers*), COMMA (*unless parenthesis comes next*)

>   Betty J. Thompson, "The Decline of Political
>   Parties," Twentieth Century Views, 28,

(*Volume number may be omitted when complete monthly or weekly date is given.*)

5. ISSUE NUMBER (*if used*), COMMA (*unless parenthesis comes next*)

>   Betty J. Thompson, "The Decline of Political
>   Parties," Twentieth Century Views, 28, No. 17,

(*Issue number is used if paging is separate in each issue and if month or season isn't mentioned.*)

6. DATE OF PUBLICATION (*in parentheses if volume number is included*), COMMA

>   Betty J. Thompson, "The Decline of Political
>   Parties," Twentieth Century Views, 28, No. 17 (March
>   1972),

7. DATE OF PUBLICATION (*no parentheses without volume number*), COMMA

>   Sylvia Shandell, "Ethnic Names," Popular Linguis-
>   tics, 18 March 1973,

8. PAGE NUMBER (*abbreviation for "page" when there is* no *volume number*), PERIOD

> Sylvia Shandell, "Ethnic Names," Popular Linguis-
> tics, 18 March 1973, p. 18.

9. PAGE NUMBER (*no abbreviation for "page" with volume number*), PERIOD

> Harry Cohen, "Why We Can't Talk," Communications,
> 20 (1970), 1-5.

Short Forms

1. "Avoid Latin reference tags; they rarely save space and can severely try your reader's patience." (*The MLA Style Sheet*, p. 26.) This means you can forget about *op. cit.* and *loc. cit.* in your footnoting.

2. Use Ibid. (*not underlined*) in reference to a footnote immediately preceding:

> ⁴⁵Paul Gage, Caper in Cali (Sacramento: West Coast
> Press, 1972), p. 18.
>
> ⁴⁶Ibid., p. 94.

3. If the material is taken from another portion of the same page referred to in the preceding note, use Ibid. alone:

> ⁵⁴John White, "The Retired Business Man," Business
> Review, 18 March 1970, p. 27.
>
> ⁵⁵Ibid.

4. When you refer to a previously used source that is not immediately preceding, cite the author's last name plus the page number:

> ⁴⁹Sebastian Jones, "Growing Old," California
> Digest, 21 (April 1972), 38.
>
> ⁵⁰Arthur Hopkins, "Death by Boredom," Midwest
> Review, 34 (March 1971), 14.
>
> ⁵¹Jones, p. 78.

5. If two or more works by the same author have been cited in your paper, include the title or an abbreviated form of the title in your short footnote:

> ⁵²Sebastian Jones, Reflections upon the Acquisition
> of Business Acumen in the Late Nineteenth Century (New
> York: Coastal Press, 1969), p. 77.
>
> ⁵³Hopkins, pp. 18-21.
>
> ⁵⁴Jones, Reflections, p. 90.
>
> ⁵⁵Hopkins, p. 97.
>
> ⁵⁶Jones, "Growing Old," p. 79.

DIFFERENCES BETWEEN FOOTNOTE AND BIBLIOGRAPHICAL CITATIONS

BOOKS

Footnote	Bibliography
1. Indent first line five spaces.	1. Indent second and following lines five spaces.
2. First name, last name, comma. 　　¹John Jones,	2. Last name, comma, first name, period. 　Jones, John.
3. Subtitles may be omitted. 　　¹John Jones, *Poetry*	3. Subtitles may not be omitted. 　Jones, John. *Poetry: The Savage Mode*
4. Publication data in parentheses, no comma after title when parenthesis follows. 　　¹John Jones, *Poetry* (Boston: Martin Press, 1968),	4. Publication data not in parentheses, period after title. 　Jones, John. *Poetry: The Savage Mode.* Boston: Martin Press, 1968.
5. Comma after publication data.	5. Period after publication data.
6. Page number after publication data. 　　¹John Jones, *Poetry* (Boston: Martin Press, 1968), p. 18.	6. No page number. Date ends note.
7. Identifies a specific part of work quoted or discussed. 　　²George Everett, "Marlin Thorpe," *English History Defined,* ed. R. N. Daws, X (London British History Press, 1932), 194-196.	7. Identifies the whole work rather than a part. 　Daws, R. N., ed. *English History Defined.* 10 vols. London: British History Press, 1932.
(Note that in the footnote citation, we have the precise volume with its editor as well as page numbers identified.)	(Note that in the bibliographical citation, we have only the general editor and no page numbers.)

PERIODICALS

Footnote	Bibliography
1. Indent first line five spaces.	1. Indent second and following lines five spaces.
2. First name, last name, comma. 　　¹Jack Anderson,	2. Last name, comma, first name, period. 　Anderson, Jack.
3. Title of article, comma. 　　¹Jack Anderson, "Alien and Sedition Acts,"	3. Title of article, period. 　Anderson, Jack. "Alien and Sedition Acts."
4. Note only pages referred to in your paper. 　　¹Jack Anderson, "Alien and Sedition Acts," *American History,* 18 (May 1973), 91.	4. Note pages for article in its entirety. 　Jack Anderson. "Alien and Sedition Acts." *American History,* 18 (May 1973), 91-104.

DOCUMENTATION MODELS

May I
borrow
your
idea?

Certainly,
if you just
mention my name,
birthday, and
hometown.

Books

1. ONE AUTHOR

Footnote

[1]Truman Capote, In Cold Blood (New York: New American Library, 1967), p. 18.

Bibliography

Capote, Truman. In Cold Blood. New York: New American Library, 1967.

2. ONE AUTHOR, NAME GIVEN IN BODY OF PAPER

F. [1]In Cold Blood (New York: New American Library, 1967), p. 18.

B. In Cold Blood. New York: The New American Library, 1967.

3. ANONYMOUS AUTHOR

F. [2]Best Sellers Classified by Plot Elements (Chicago: Writers Press, 1969), p. 19.

B. Best Sellers Classified by Plot Elements. Chicago: Writers Press, 1969.

4. TWO AUTHORS

F. [3]Gerald Jordan and Austin Patterson, Theory of Dynamic Inter-Personal Contact (New York: Borden House, 1967), p. 4.

B. Jordan, Gerald, and Austin Patterson. <u>Theory of Dynamic Inter-Personal Contact</u>. New York: Borden House, 1967.

5. THREE AUTHORS

F. [4]Eldon Smith, David Clay Ascher, and Christopher Jordan Gaines, <u>Photosynthesis</u> (New York: Scientific Press, 1960), p. 97.

B. Smith, Eldon, David Clay Ascher, and Christopher Jordan Gaines. <u>Photosynthesis</u>. New York: Scientific Press, 1960.

6. MORE THAN THREE AUTHORS

F. [5]Jeffrey R. Botsford et al., <u>Myths of the Moon Goddess</u> (San Francisco: Sanford Press, 1970), pp. 18–20.

(*Note that "et al," is the abbreviation of the Latin* et allii, *"and others." The period occurs only because of the abbreviation.*)

B. Botsford, Jeffrey R., et al. <u>Myths of the Moon Goddess</u>. San Francisco: Sanford Press, 1970.

7. ORGANIZATIONAL AUTHORSHIP

F. [6]<u>Report of the Commission on Urban Renewal</u> (New York: Bureau of Urban Renewal, 1970), p. 80.

B. <u>Report of the Commission on Urban Renewal</u>. New York: Bureau of Urban Renewal, 1967.

(*See pages 205 and 215 for further discussion of documentation of reports.*)

8. INCLUSION OF STATE IN PUBLICATION DATA

F. [7]George C. Prentice, <u>Packing the Supreme Court</u> (Evanston, Ill.: Victory Press, 1973), p. 40.

B. Prentice, George C. <u>Packing the Supreme Court</u>. Evanston, Ill.: Victory Press, 1973.

(*The state is included in the citation when the town or city of publication is likely to be unfamiliar to many readers.*)

Is everything perfectly clear?

9. MISSING DATA

> *When place of publication and publisher are not included in your source, the abbreviation "n.p." is substituted for both.*

F.   [8]John Smith, Garlands of Posies (n.p., 1890), pp. 12–14.

B.   Smith, John. Garlands of Posies. n.p., 1890.

> *(When date is not included in your source, use the abbreviation "n.d." in the date position. When the pages of your source are not numbered, use the abbreviation "n. pag." (no pagination) in place of page numbers.)*

10. SUBTITLE

F.   [9]Eldridge Bassett, Living Creatures: Women, Dogs, and Mice (Chicago: Emory House Books, 1928), p. 28.

> *(Subtitle may be omitted in the footnote.)*

B.   Bassett, Eldridge. Living Creatures: Women, Dogs, and Mice. Emory House Books, 1928.

> *(Subtitle* may not *be omitted in bibliographical citation.)*

11. INTRODUCTION

F.   [10]John C. Clarke, "Introduction," The Tragic Era, by Peter Tomkins (Boston: Smith, Randall, and Berger, 1929), p. ix.

B.   Tomkins, Peter. The Tragic Era. Boston: Smith, Randall, and Berger, 1929.

> *(Note that in the bibliographical citation, reference is to the work in its totality, rather than to a component part. Thus the book is referred to by author.)*

12. EDITOR'S PREFACE TO AN ANTHOLOGY

F.   [11]Lloyd Tonkin, ed., "Preface," Eight Philosophers (New York: Atlantic Press, 1972), p. x.

B. Tonkin, Lloyd, ed. "Preface," <u>Eight Philosophers</u>. New
York: Atlantic Press, 1947.

13. COLLECTION CITED BY AUTHOR

13.1. ONE AUTHOR, NO EDITOR

F. [12]Robert Blyden, "Morning Symphony," in <u>Collected
Poems</u> (Chicago: Midwest Press, Inc., 1969), pp. 16–17.

B. Blyden, Robert. "Morning Symphony." <u>Collected Poems</u>.
Chicago: Midwest Press, 1969.

(*Note that MLA uses "in" before title in footnote, but not in bibliography.*)

13.2. ONE AUTHOR, ONE EDITOR, REFERENCE TO AN ENTIRE VOLUME

F. [13]Harry Herbert Ridgeback, <u>Geriatric Case Studies</u>,
ed. Lawrence B. Hughes (New York: Scientific Library
Publications, 1957), p. 200.

B. Ridgeback, Harry Herbert. <u>Geriatric Case Studies</u>. Ed.
Lawrence B. Hughes. New York: Scientific Library
Publications, 1957.

(*When there are two or more editors, handle names as in book author
models 4–6.*)

13.3. ONE AUTHOR, ONE EDITOR, REFERENCE TO SELECTION IN A COLLECTION

F.   [14]Martin Q. Antony, "Brevity," in <u>Garlands of Brevity</u>, ed. Bess R. Reston (New York: Metropolitan Press, 1964), p. 207.

B.   Antony, Martin Q. "Brevity," <u>Garlands of Brevity</u>. Ed. Bess R. Reston. New York: Metropolitan Press, 1964.

(Usually, the student wishes to refer to a specific selection in an anthology and emphasizes an individual author in his footnote. It is also possible to document collections by editor. See 16 below.)

13.4. COMPLETE BOOK INCLUDED IN A ONE-VOLUME COLLECTION

F.   [15]Voltaire, <u>Candide</u>, in <u>Complete Romances</u>, ed. G. W. Brock (New York: Walter J. Black, 1927), p. 147.

B.   Voltaire. <u>Candide</u>. <u>Complete Romances</u>. Ed. G. W. Brock. New York: Walter J. Black, 1927.

(Note that when a complete work is included in a collection, it is underlined rather than quoted like other component parts.)

14. COLLECTION CITED BY EDITOR

14.1. ONE EDITOR, ONE AUTHOR

F.   [16]Jeremy Morton, ed., <u>Visions of Mortality</u>, by Steiner G. Allport (New York: Manhattan Books, Inc., 1910), p. 471.

B.   Morton, Jeremy, ed. <u>Visions of Mortality</u>. By Steiner G. Allport. New York: Manhattan Books, 1910.

14.2. ONE EDITOR, AUTHOR'S NAME IN TITLE

F.   [17]Craig Richards, ed., <u>The Collected Works of Jordan Appleby</u> (Chicago: Midwest Press, 1909), pp. 704-08.

B.   Richards, Craig, ed. <u>The Collected Works of Jordan Appleby</u>. Chicago: Midwest Press, 1909.

15. THE NAMES OF TRANSLATORS AND COMPILERS ARE TREATED LIKE THOSE OF EDITORS

16. EDITION

F.   [18]James K. Bell and Adrian A. Cohn, <u>Rhetoric in a Modern Mode</u>, 2nd ed. (Beverly Hills: Glencoe Press, 1972), p. 201.

[19]<u>Literary Market Place: The Business Directory of American Book Publishing</u>, 1973–74 ed. (New York: Bowker, 1973), pp. 270–71.

B.   Bell, James K., and Adrian A. Cohn. <u>Rhetoric in a Modern Mode</u>. 2nd ed. (Beverly Hills: Glencoe Press, 1972).
<u>Literary Market Place: The Business Directory of American Book Publishing</u>. 1973–74 ed. New York: Bowker, 1973.

17. SERIES WITH EDITOR

F.   [20]Germaine Brée, <u>Albert Camus</u>, ed. William York Tindall et al., Columbia Essays in Modern Writers, No. 1 (New York: Columbia University Press, 1964), p. 18.

B.   Brée, Germaine. <u>Albert Camus</u>. Ed. William York Tindall et al. Columbia Essays on Modern Writers, No. 1. New York: Columbia University Press, 1964.

18. MULTI-VOLUME SET

18.1 VOLUMES PUBLISHED AT THE SAME TIME

F.   [21]Jordan R. Anderson, <u>History of Aesthetics</u> (Seattle: Washington Press, 1968), III, 204.

(Abbreviations "p." or "pp." do not precede page number when volume number is included. When volumes have been published at the same time, volume number comes after publication data.)

B.   Anderson, Jordan R. <u>History of Aesthetics</u>. 3 vols. Seattle: Washington Press, 1968.

(In the footnote, reference is to a specific part of a work cited, hence mention of volume number. In the bibliography, reference is to the work in its totality. Thus total number of volumes in the set is mentioned.)

18.2 VOLUMES PUBLISHED AT DIFFERENT TIMES

F.   [22]Oswald Parkinson, <u>Philosophies of Deception</u>, IV (Chicago: Midwest Publishers, 1970), 781.

(When volumes have been published separately, volume number comes before publication data.)

B.   Parkinson, Oswald. <u>Philosophies of Deception</u>. 5 vols. Chicago: Midwest Publishers, 1970.

(Bibliographical reference is to the work in its totality, not to a component part. However, if you wish to make an exact identification, it is permissable to cite a single volume used, as in the footnote.)

18.3. SEPARATELY TITLED VOLUME IN SET

F.   [23]Percy Wharton, <u>The Renaissance</u>, in <u>History of the Western World</u>, ed. Peter Symington, XX (New York: Historical Publications, 1925), 32.

(As volumes were published separately, volume number precedes publication data.)

B.   Symington, Peter, ed. <u>History of the Western World</u>. 25 vols. New York: Historical Publications, 1925.

19. REPRINT

The MLA Style Sheet *stresses that "In a period of competitive reprinting, it is especially important to distinguish the* original date and edition *from the reprint one may happen to be using."*

19.1. A BOOK

F.   [24]Peter Jay Hudson, <u>Road to Oblivion</u> (1915; r̠ New York: Metropolitan Press, 1960), p. 14.

B.   Hudson, Peter Jay. <u>Road to Oblivion</u>, 1915. Rpt. New York: Metropolitan Press, 1960.

(In a bibliographical entry, a period normally follows title, but it is customary to place a comma before the date. Thus a comma appears in this position.)

F.   [25]Sir Charles Lyell, "Before Darwin: Conventional Scientific Opinion on the Fixity of Species," in <u>Principles of Geology</u>, II (1832; rpt. in <u>Darwin</u>, ed. Philip Appleman, New York: Norton, 1970), p. 11.

B. Lyell, Sir Charles. "Before Darwin: Conventional Scientific Opinion on the Fixity of Species." <u>Principles of Geology</u>, II, 1832. Rpt. in <u>Darwin</u>. Ed. Philip Appleman. New York: Norton, 1970.

20. CLASSICS

20.1 ACT, SCENE DESIGNATION

F.   [26]<u>Lear</u> IV. ii. 20–30.

(Use capital Roman numerals for acts, lower case Roman numerals for scenes. No punctuation occurs between title and parts. Periods are used between parts, a hyphen between page numbers.)

B. <u>Lear</u>.

(In the bibliography, reference is to the work in its totality not to component parts.)

20.2. BOOK OR PART DESIGNATION

F.   [27]Milton <u>Paradise Regained</u> I. 5–10.

(No punctuation is used between author, title, and parts. A period is used after parts. Book number is shown with a capitalized Roman numeral.)

B. Milton Paradise Regained.

(*Bibliographical reference is to the work in its totality, not to a component part.*)

20.3. CHAPTER DESIGNATION WITH LINE NUMBERS

F. [28]Aristotle Physics II. vi. 25–29.

(*Use lower case Roman numerals for chapter, capitals for book. This note reads: Book II, Chapter vi, Lines 25–29.*)

B. Aristotle Physics.

20.4 TEXT WITHOUT LINE NUMBERS

F. [29]Homer, The Odyssey, trans. W. H. D. Rouse (New York: New American Library, 1958), p. 36.

(*When there are no line numbers, the exact translation must be indicated to make page number references meaningful.*)

B. Homer. The Odyssey. Trans. W. H. D. Rouse. New York: New American Library, 1958.

21. THE BIBLE

F. [30]Psalms 15:9–10.

(*First number is chapter; second numbers are verses.*)

B. The Bible.

(*In bibliography, the reference is made to the work in its totality, not to a component part. Note that the Bible is never underlined.*)

Reference Works

1. GENERAL ENCYCLOPEDIA, ALPHABETICALLY ARRANGED

F.   [1]Aloys Fleischmann, "Irish Music," Encyclopedia
Americana, 1966.

(No place of publication and publisher are included in citations of general encyclopedias. No page number is necessary when the reference work is alphabetically arranged.)

B. Fleischmann, Aloys. "Irish Music." Encyclopedia Americana, 1966.

2. SPECIALIZED ENCYCLOPEDIA, ALPHABETICALLY ARRANGED

F.   [2]Edwin M. Borchard, "Alien Property," Encyclopedia
of the Social Sciences (New York: Macmillan, 1930).

(Include place of publication and publisher in references to specialized encyclopedias. No page number is needed in alphabetically arranged reference works.)

B. Borchard, Edwin, M. "Alien Property." Encyclopedia of
the Social Sciences. New York: Macmillan, 1930.

3. NON-ALPHABETICALLY ARRANGED REFERENCE WORK

F.   [3]Eliot Bryant, ed., The Atlantic Bibliography of
Russian Literature, IV (New York: Coastal Press, 1968),
184.

(As this is a specialized rather than general reference work, publication data is needed. As work is not alphabetically arranged, page number is necessary.)

B. Bryant, Eliot, ed. The Atlantic Bibliography of Russian
Literature. 10 vols. New York: Coastal Press, 1968.

4. UNSIGNED ARTICLE, GENERAL ENCYCLOPEDIA

F.   [4]"Tapioca," Encyclopaedia Britannica, 1910.

(No publication data is needed for a general encyclopedia.)

B. "Tapioca." Encyclopaedia Britannica, 1910.

(Normally, a period follows the title of a work in a bibliographical reference, but it is customary to precede the date with a comma.)

5. SIGNED ARTICLE, INITIALS ONLY PROVIDED

F.   [5]W[illiam] M[alcolm] B[eeson], "Livestock Judging,"
Encyclopaedia Britannica, 1962.

(*Key to initials appears at the end of the index volume in* Britannica.)

B.   B[eeson], W[illiam] M[alcolm]. "Livestock Judging."
Encyclopaedia Britannica, 1962.

6. SIGNED BIOGRAPHICAL REFERENCE WORK

F.   [6]W[orthington] C[hauncey] F[ord], "Adams, Charles
Francis," Dictionary of American Biography (1943).

(*MLA places year of biographical reference works in parentheses. Each
reference work using initials of contributors will provide a key. DAB's
key is in the front of each volume.*)

B.   F[ord], W[orthington] C[hauncey]. "Adams, Charles Francis." Dictionary of American Biography. Ed. Dumas
Malone. New York: Scribner's, 1943.

(*MLA gives publication data for bibliographical citation of biographical reference works, not for footnote. Note also that editor is included
in bibliographical entry and omitted in footnote.*)

7. UNSIGNED BIOGRAPHICAL REFERENCE WORK

F.   [7]"Andre, Carl," Who's Who in America, 1970–71.

B.   "Andre, Carl." Who's Who in America. Chicago: Marquis
Who's Who, Inc., 1970–71.

8. DICTIONARIES

F.   [8]E[ric] B[loom], "Accelerando," Grove's Dictionary
of Music and Musicians (1954).

(*The key to the initials is found in the front of the first volume. Dates
of dictionaries are placed in parentheses.*)

B.   B[loom], E[ric]. "Accelerando." Grove's Dictionary of
Music and Musicians. Ed. Eric Bloom. New York: St.
Martin's, 1954.

(*Note inclusion of publication data in bibliography.*)

Class, now we shall study periodical forms—
Wait! Where are you going?

Periodicals

1. SEPARATELY PAGED PERIODICAL

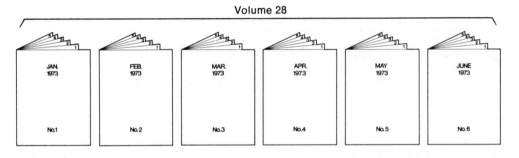

Volume 28

| JAN. 1973 | FEB. 1973 | MAR. 1973 | APR. 1973 | MAY 1973 | JUNE 1973 |
| No.1 | No.2 | No.3 | No.4 | No.5 | No.6 |

1.1. WEEK, MONTH, OR SEASON NEEDED AS PAGES ALONE CANNOT LOCATE MATERIAL

F.   [1]Peter Bartlett Emory, "Death Cults," World Views,
    28 (April 1973), 5-6.

OR

[1]Peter Bartlett Emory, "Death Cults," World Views,
April 1973, pp. 5-6.

(*Volume* may *be omitted in citations of weekly or monthly periodicals.*)

B.   Emory, Peter Bartlett. "Death Cults." World Views, 28
        (April 1973), 5-15.

OR

Emory, Peter Bartlett. "Death Cults." World Views, April
        1973, pp. 5-15.

(*Note that pages in the bibliographical citation are for article in its
entirety, not merely pages referred to in research paper.*)

1.2. ISSUE NUMBER NECESSARY IF MONTH IS NOT MENTIONED AS PAGES ALONE
CANNOT LOCATE MATERIAL

F.   [2]John Perkins, "Army and Individual," News of the
World, 20, No. 2 (1972), 7-8.

(*Abbreviation for pages "pp." is not included in note with a volume
number. Year alone is always enclosed in parentheses.*)

B.   Perkins, John. "Army and Individual." News of the World,
20, No. 2 (1972), 7-24.

2. CONTINUOUSLY PAGED PERIODICAL—ISSUE AND MONTH MAY BE OMITTED
BECAUSE PAGES LOCATE MATERIAL

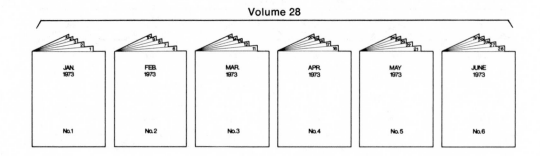

Volume 28

F.   [3]David R. Michaels, "Man and God in Combat," Theology Today, 28 (1972), 431.

(*Date is always in parentheses after volume number. Year alone is
always in parentheses. Volume number is always used with a yearly
designation though it may be omitted in weekly or monthly citations.*)

B.   Michaels, David R. "Man and God in Combat." Theology
Today, 28 (1972), 31-35.

3. WEEKLY PERIODICAL

F.   [4]Horace Sutton, "Fanon," Saturday Review, 17 July
1971, pp. 16-17.

B.   Sutton, Horace. "Fanon." Saturday Review, 17 July 1971,
pp. 16-20.

(*Volume number is generally omitted in citations of weekly periodicals.
Thus date is not put in parentheses.*)

4. MONTHLY PERIODICAL

4.1. WITHOUT VOLUME NUMBER

F.   [5]Peter F. Drucker, "The Surprising Seventies," Harper's, July 1971, pp. 35-36.

*(No volume number is necessary with a monthly periodical, though it
may be included at the writer's option.)*

B.   Drucker, Peter F. "The Surprising Seventies." Harper's,
        July 1971, pp. 35-42.

4.2. WITH VOLUME NUMBER

F.   [6]William Bevan, "Higher Education in the 1970's,"
American Pedagogue, 26 (July 1971), 537.

*(Though volume number may be omitted from popular magazines like
Harper's, it is more frequently used in references to scholarly journals
appearing monthly. Note that no "p." precedes page number when
volume number appears in the entry. The date is always enclosed in
parentheses after volume.)*

B.   Bevan, William. "Higher Education in the 1970's." Ameri-
        can Pedagogue, 26 (July 1971), 537-49.

5. SEASONAL PERIODICAL

5.1. WITHOUT ISSUE NUMBER

F.   [7]Donald Atwell Zoll, "Philosophical Foundations of
the American Political Right," Modern Age, 28 (Spring
1971), 714.

*(MLA suggests that issue number is not necessary when paging is
continuous and month or season specified.)*

B.   Atwell, Donald Zoll. "Philosophical Foundations of the
        American Political Right." Modern Age, 28 (Spring
        1971), 714-20.

5.2. WITH ISSUE NUMBER

F.   [8]Tesfaye Gessesse, "Ayee My Luck," African Arts,
40, No. 2 (1971), 17.

(MLA suggests that issue number is needed when pagination is separate—that is, beginning with "1" in each issue—and month or season is not specified. Remember that pages alone won't identify an article in separately paged periodicals.)

B. Gessesse, Tesfaye. "Ayee My Luck." African Arts, 40, No. 2 (1971), 17–25.

6. NO AUTHOR

F. [9]"Children of Hunger," Today's News, 18 March 1970, pp. 17–18.

(As this is a weekly periodical, volume number is not needed. Date is in parentheses only after volume number.)

B. "Children of Hunger." Today's News, 18 March 1970, 17–25.

7. EDITORIAL

F. [10]P. M. Erickson, "Editorial Views," News of the Week, 14 Sept. 1967, p. 71.

B. Erickson, P. M. "Editorial Views." News of the Week, 14 Sept. 1967, pp. 70–73.

Newspapers

1. SIGNED ARTICLE

F. [1]Tad Szulc, "U.S. Is Facing New Strains with Russians and Taiwan," <u>New York Times</u>, 18 July 1971, Sec. 1, p. 14, cols. 6–7.

(Note that section number and column numbers are included in citation.)

B. Szulc, Tad. "U.S. Is Facing New Strains with Russians and Taiwan." <u>New York Times</u>, 18 July 1971, Sec. 1, p. 14, cols. 6–7; p. 18, cols. 4–5.

(Note that bibliographical citation includes reference to article in its totality—hence both pages on which article occurs.)

2. UNSIGNED ARTICLE

F. [2]"Transit Authority, City and Fire Department Panels Investigate Blaze in Lexington Avenue IRT Tunnel," <u>New York Times</u>, 18 July 1971, Sec. 1, p. 29, cols. 1–3.

B. "Transit Authority, City and Fire Department Panels Investigate Blaze in Lexington Avenue IRT Tunnel." <u>New York Times</u>, 18 July 1971, Sec. 1, p. 29, cols. 1–8.

(Note that bibliographical citation gives location of newspiece in its entirety. Columns "1–8" as opposed to "1–3" in footnote indicate full space article occupies.)

3. EDITORIAL

F. [3]Editorial, <u>New York Times</u>, 18 July 1971, Sec. 4, p. 12, cols. 1–2.

B. Editorial. <u>New York Times</u>, 18 July 1971, Sec. 4, p. 12, cols. 1–4.

4. LETTERS TO THE EDITOR

F. [4]Mary E. Friel, "Letters to the Editor," <u>New York Times</u>, 18 July 1971, Sec. 4, p. 12, cols. 3–4.

B. Friel, Mary E. "Letters to the Editor." <u>New York Times</u>, 18 July 1971, Sec. 4, p. 12, cols. 3–4.

Government Documents

GUIDELINES IN CITING FEDERAL GOVERNMENT DOCUMENTS

1. U.S. always opens citation.
2. Next, government body sponsoring publication.
   U.S., Congress
   U.S., Department of State
3. Then any subsidiary bodies involved in publication
   U.S., Congress, Senate, Committee on Government Operations,
4. Then title of document
   U.S., Congress, Senate, Committee on Government Operations, *Report of the Committee on Government Operations,*
5. Include any identifying numbers appearing on document
   U.S., Congress, Senate, Committee on Government Operations, *Report of the Committee on Government Operations,* Report No. 91-809,
6. When Congressional papers are being cited, include number and session of Congress
   U.S., Congress, Senate, Committee on Government Operations, *Report of the Committee on Government Operations,* Report No. 91-809, 91st Cong., 2d sess., 1970, p. 4.
7. These and the models that follow are only guidelines. Because of the seemingly infinite variety of government papers, all problems cannot be anticipated. Ask yourself if you are providing enough information to permit a reader to locate or order the document involved.

Constitution

1. U.S. CONSTITUTION

   F.   [1]U.S., <u>Constitution</u>, Art. II, sec. 4.

           [2]U.S., <u>Constitution</u>, Amendment XVIII, sec. 3.

   B.   U.S. <u>Constitution</u>. Art. II, sec. 4.

         U.S. <u>Constitution</u>. Amendment XVIII, sec. 3.

2. STATE CONSTITUTION

   F.   [3]California, <u>Constitution</u>, Art. 1, sec. 19.

   B.   California. <u>Constitution</u>. Art. 1, sec. 19.

   (Provide date only for non-current constitution.)

See *Federal Register*, *Presidential Papers*. Check *New York Times Index* for Nixon news.

Find a statement to match each expression. See *Congressional Record*. Find a statement or bill to provoke each expression.

Executive Papers

1. PRESIDENTIAL PAPERS

   F.   [1]U. S., President, <u>Public Papers of the Presidents of the United States</u> (Washington, D.C.: Office of the <u>Federal Register</u>, National Archives and Records Service, 1971), Richard Nixon, 1969, pp. 161–163.

B. U.S. President. <u>Public Papers of the Presidents of the United States</u>. Washington, D.C.: Office of the <u>Federal Register</u>, National Archives and Records Service, 1971. Richard Nixon, 1969.

(*The first date in parentheses in the footnote is the date of publication. The second date refers to the year in Nixon's administration covered in the volume.* Federal Register *is underlined because it is the title of a government publication containing executive pronouncements.*)

2. FEDERAL REGISTER

(*The* Federal Register, *issued daily, contains presidential orders, proclamations, messages of interest issuing from the president directly or from one of the departments of the executive branch.*)

F. [2]U. S., President, Proclamation, "White Cane Safety Day, 1971," <u>Federal Register</u>, XXXVI, No. 129, July 3, 1971, 12671–72.

(*The* Federal Register *has a volume number, issue number, date, and page numbers. As paging is consecutive, there are large page numbers like 12671 above. Observe that as a volume number is used in the note, no "pp." precedes page numbers.*)

B. U. S. President. Proclamation. "White Cane Safety Day, 1971." <u>Federal Register</u>, XXXVI, No. 129, July 3, 1971, 12671–72.

(*Page numbers are given in the bibliographical citation because the proclamation, like an article in a periodical, is a part of a larger work. If source is an executive order, simply substitute "Executive Order" for "Proclamation." If source is issued by an executive agency, substitute name of agency for "President, Proclamation.")*

3. DEPARTMENTAL DOCUMENTS, EXECUTIVE BRANCH

3.1. WITH PUBLICATION NUMBER

F. [3]U. S., Department of State, <u>The Suez Canal Problem: July 26–Sept. 22, 1956</u>, A Documentary Publication No. 6392 (1956), p. 18.

B. U.S. Department of State. <u>The Suez Canal Problem: July</u>
   <u>26–Sept. 22, 1956</u>. A Documentary Publication No.
   6392 (1956).

3.2. WITH VOLUME NUMBER

F.   [4]U.S., Department of the Air Force, <u>Air Navigation</u>,
Air Force Manual 51–40, II, 14.

B. U.S. Department of the Air Force. <u>Air Navigation</u>. Air
   Force Manual 51–40, Vol. II.

3.3. WITH MICROCOPY NUMBER

F.   [5]U.S., Department of State, National Archives and
Records Service, General Services Administration, <u>Records</u>
<u>of the Department of State Relating to the Internal</u>
<u>Affairs of China, 1910–29</u>, Microcopy No. 329 (Washing-
ton, D.C.: National Archives Microfilm Publications,
1960), p. 4.

B. U. S. Department of State. National Archives and Records
   Service. General Services Administration. <u>Records</u>
   <u>of the Department of State Relating to the Internal</u>
   <u>Affairs of China, 1910–29</u>. Microcopy No. 329. Washington, D.C.: National Archives Microfilm Publications, 1960.

*(Agency and subsidiary divisions sponsoring the document are always
listed, moving from the larger to the smaller division.)*

3.4. WITH EDITION AND BULLETIN NUMBER

F.   [6]U. S., Department of Labor, Bureau of Labor Statistics, <u>Occupational Outlook Handbook</u>, 1970–71 ed.,
Bulletin No. 1650 (Washington, D. C.: Government Printing Office, 1971), p. 163.

B. U. S. Department of Labor. Bureau of Labor Statistics.
   <u>Occupational Outlook Handbook</u>. 1970–71 ed. Bulletin
   No. 1650. Washington, D.C.: Government Printing
   Office, 1971.

F. [7]U. S., Department of Interior, Bureau of Flood Control, <u>Emergency Relief Measures for Flood Disaster Areas in the Mississippi Basin</u>, by G. Q. Morgenstern, Emergency Disaster Relief Report No 8 (Washington, D.C.: Government Printing Office, 1939), p. 47.

B. U.S. Department of Interior. Bureau of Flood Control. <u>Emergency Relief Measures for Flood Disaster Areas in the Mississippi Basin</u>, by G. Q. Morgenstern. Emergency Disaster Relief Report No. 8. Washington, D.C.: Government Printing Office, 1939.

YOU ARE THE EYES OF THE PEOPLE, AND YOU ARE THEIR VOICE.

CONGRESSIONAL PAPERS

Things to Know about Congressional Papers

1. Proposed pieces of legislation are called bills. They appear in pamphlet form as slip bills in the interval before they are passed and published in *Statutes at Large*.
2. A daily, word by word transcript of congressional proceedings is published in the *Congressional Record*.
3. Each house also publishes a daily *Journal*. Unlike the *Congressional Record*, the *Journal* contains a summation or digest of proceedings rather than a verbatim record.
4. When bills have passed both houses and have become law, they are published at the end of each calendar year in *Statutes at Large*.
5. Finally, statutes are published in a compendium of public laws called *United States Code*.

Congressional Papers

1. BILL BEFORE ENACTMENT INTO LAW

F.   [1]U.S., Congress, Senate, <u>A Bill to Authorize the</u>
<u>Secretary of the Interior to Construct, Operate, and</u>
<u>Maintain the Salmon Falls Division, Upper Snake Project</u>,
<u>Idaho, and for Other Purposes</u>, S. 432, 92d Cong. 1st
sess., 1971, pp. 1–3.

B.   U.S. Congress. Senate. <u>A Bill to Authorize the Secretary</u>
<u>of the Interior to Construct, Operate, and Maintain</u>
<u>the Salmon Falls Division, Upper Snake Project,</u>
<u>Idaho, and for Other Purposes</u>. S. 432, 92d Cong.,
1st sess., 1971.

IF LIBERTY AND EQUALITY, AS IS THOUGHT BY SOME,
ARE CHIEFLY TO BE FOUND IN DEMOCRACY, THEY
WILL BEST BE ATTAINED WHEN ALL PERSONS SHARE
IN THE GOVERNMENT TO THE UTMOST.—ARISTOTLE

Check the *Congressional
Record*. Find a statement
by each of these people
on war, pollution, school
integration, or the
economy.

2. CONGRESSIONAL RECORD

F.   [2]U.S., Congress, Senate, Senator Fulbright's tribute to Warren Duffee, 90th Cong., 1st sess., Dec. 13,
1967, Congressional Record, CXIII, 36175.

[3]U.S., Congress, House, Congressman Pepper speaking
for the Amendment of the International Travel Act of
1961, H.R. 3934, 90th Cong., 1st sess., Dec. 15, 1967,
Congressional Record, CXIII, 37190.

B. U.S. Congress. Senate. Senator Fulbright's tribute to
Warren Duffee. 90th Cong., 1st sess., Dec. 13,
1967. Congressional Record, Vol. CXIII, 36175.

U.S. Congress. House. Congressman Pepper speaking for
the Amendment of the International Travel Act of
1961. H.R. 3934, 90th Cong., 1st sess., Dec. 15,
1967. Congressional Record, CXIII, 37190.

(*In references to the* Congressional Record, *central intention of a
speech is included in the documentation entry unless content is clarified
in the text of your paper.*)

3. HOUSE JOURNAL

F.   [4]U.S., Congress, House, Appropriations for Departments of Labor, and Health, Education, and Welfare—
1970, 91st Cong., 1st sess., 1968, Journal, Dec. 22,
1969, pp. 1308-1312.

B. U.S. Congress. House. Appropriations for Departments of
Labor, and Health, Education, and Welfare—1970.
91st Cong., 1st sess., 1968. Journal, Dec. 22,
1969.

4. SENATE JOURNAL

F.   [5]U.S., Congress, Senate, Study of Public and Private Housing and Urban Affairs, 91st Cong., 1st sess.,
1969, Journal, Jan. 16, 1969, p. 61.

B. U.S. Congress. Senate. <u>Study of Public and Private Housing and Urban Affairs</u>. 91st Cong., 1st sess., 1969. <u>Journal</u>, Jan. 16, 1969.

AND THEN IT IS LAW

I've never heard the constitution referred to
so often as I have in this case. . . . .
I don't know what you're talking about sir.

Jules Feiffer.

The Law is the true embodiment
Of everything that's excellent.
It has no kind of fault or flaw,
And I, my Lords, embody the Law.
— Gilbert and Sullivan

5. STATUTES AT LARGE

(Statutes at Large *contains bills and resolutions that have been passed into law. A volume is issued at the end of each calendar year. Volumes contain public laws, private laws, joint resolutions, concurrent resolutions, proclamations, and treaties. The documentation form remains the same, though each section has its own numbering system. In a 1903 volume, acts were given chapter numbers. By 1969, acts were identified as public laws with Pub. L. numbers. Proclamations have numbers, treaties article numbers; acts may have part and chapter numbers.*)

5.1. PUBLIC LAWS

F. [6]An Act to Continue for a Temporary Period the Existing Interest Equalization Tax, Statutes at Large, LXXXIII, Pub. L. 91-50, 86 (1969).

B. An Act to Continue for a Temporary Period the Existing Interest Equalization Tax. Statutes at Large, Vol. LXXXIII. Pub. L. 91-50 (1969).

(*No "p." precedes page number, 86, because volume number occurs in entry. Note omission of page number completely in bibliographical citation. The reference is to the Public Law in its entirety not to a component part.*)

5.2. PROCLAMATIONS

F. [7]A Proclamation by the President of the United States, Statutes at Large, XXXII, pt. 2, No. 3, 197 (1903).

[8]A Proclamation by the President of the United States, Statutes at Large, LXXXIII, No. 3880, 910 (1969).

B. A Proclamation by the President of the United States. Statutes at Large, Vol. XXXII, pt. 2, No. 3 (1903).
A Proclamation by the President of the United States. Statutes at Large, Vol. LXXXIII, No. 3880 (1969).

(*Note that proclamations in both 1903 and 1969 volumes are identified by proclamation numbers.*)

5.3. PRIVATE LAWS

F.   [9]An Act for the Relief of Basil Rowland Duncan,
Statutes at Large, LXXXIII, Private Law 91-1, 867
(1969).

(Private Laws are identified by a Private Law Number.)

B.   An Act for the Relief of Basil Rowland Duncan. Statutes
at Large, Vol. LXXXIII. Private Law 91-1 (1969).

> Good laws lead to the making of better ones; bad
> ones bring about worse. As soon as any man
> says of the affairs of State, "What does it matter
> to me?" the State may be given up for lost.
> — Jean Jacques Rousseau

6. UNITED STATES CODE

F.   [10]Shipping Act, U.S. Code, 1964 ed., X, secs. 801-
803 (1965).

B.   Shipping Act. U.S. Code, Vol. X (1964).

(Statutes are ultimately published in the United States Code. *Code
documentation does not use page, but section number. Most recent publications are the 1964 and 1970 editions.)*

IN ADDITION TO BILLS ORIGINATING IN CONGRESS AND
THE LAWS THAT ULTIMATELY EMERGE, GOVERNMENT PA-
PERS INCLUDE MISCELLANEOUS PAPERS IN THE FORM OF
CONGRESSIONAL HEARINGS AND COMMITTEE REPORTS.

7. CONGRESSIONAL COMMITTEE REPORTS

7.1. WITHOUT AUTHOR

F.   [11]U.S., Congress, Senate, Committee on Government
Operations, Report of the Committee on Government Operations, Report No. 91-809, 91st Cong., 2d sess., 1970,
p. 4.

B. U.S. Congress. Committee on Government Operations.
    Report of the Committee on Government Operations.
    Report No. 91–809, 91st Cong., 2d sess., 1970.

7.2. WITH AUTHOR

F.   [12]U.S., Congress, Senate, Committee on Aeronautical
    and Space Sciences, _NASA's Space Science and Applica-
    tions Program_, by Homer E. Newell (Washington, D.C.:
    Government Printing Office, 1967), p. 14.

B. U.S. Congress. Senate. Committee on Aeronautical and
        Space Sciences. _NASA's Space Science and Applica-
        tions Program_, by Homer E. Newell. Washington,
        D.C.: Government Printing Office, 1967.

_(Government papers are never catalogued by author; hence citation is
by sponsoring agency.)_

8. CONGRESSIONAL HEARINGS

F.   [13]U.S., Congress, House, Committee on Interstate
    and Foreign Commerce, _Health Reinsurance Legislation_,
    Hearings, before the Committee on Interstate and Foreign
    Commerce, House of Representatives, on H. R. 8356, 83d
    Cong., 2d sess., 1954, pp. 4–6.

B. U.S. Congress. House. Committee on Interstate and For-
        eign Commerce. _Health Reinsurance Legislation_.
        Hearings before the Committee on Interstate and
        Foreign Commerce, House of Representatives, on
        H. R. 8356, 83d Cong., 2d sess., 1954.

_(Committee before whom hearings were held must be included in cita-
tion.)_

CURSE ON ALL LAWS BUT THOSE WHICH
LOVE HAS MADE.—ALEXANDER POPE

Miscellaneous Materials

MISCELLANEOUS MISCELLANEOUS MISCELLANEOUS

1. PAMPHLETS

1.1. WITHOUT AUTHOR

F. [1]Academic Freedom and Civil Liberties of Students in Colleges and Universities (New York: American Civil Liberties Union, Nov. 1961), pp. 11–12.

B. Academic Freedom and Civil Liberties of Students in Colleges and Universities. New York: American Civil Liberties Union, Nov. 1961.

(Page numbers are not used in bibliographical references to books and pamphlets.)

1.2. WITH AUTHOR

F. [2]Robert M. Hutchins, Two Faces of Federation (Santa Barbara, Calif.: Center for the Study of Democratic Institutions, 1961), p. 15.

B. Hutchins, Robert M. Two Faces of Federation. Santa Barbara, Calif.: Center for the Study of Democratic Institutions, 1961.

1.3. AGENCY SPONSORSHIP

F. [3]The Ritual Murder Accusation, Fireside Discussion
Group of the Anti-Defamation League (Chicago: B'Nai
B'rith, n.d.), p. 21.

[4]James E. Larson, Re-apportionment and the Courts,
Bureau of Public Administration (Birmingham: University
of Alabama, 1962), p. 57.

B. The Ritual Murder Accusation. Fireside Discussion Group
of the Anti-Defamation League. Chicago: B'nai
B'rith, n.d.

Larson, James E. Re-apportionment and the Courts. Bureau
of Public Administration. Birmingham: University of
Alabama, 1962.

1.4. SERIES

F. [5]William T. R. Fox, The Struggle for Atomic Control, Public Affairs Pamphlet, No. 129 (New York: Public
Affairs Committee, Inc., 1947), p. 18.

B. Fox, William T. R. The Struggle for Atomic Control. Public Affairs Pamphlet, No. 129. New York: Public
Affairs Committee, Inc., 1947.

2. INTERVIEWS

F. [6]Interview with Peter Haskins, Dean, Grove Hills
College, Grove Hills, Calif., Jan. 18, 1970.
Interviews with Five Kendall College Students,
Evanston, Ill., February 20, 1968.

B. Interview with Peter Haskins. Dean, Grove Hills College.
Grove Hills, Calif., Jan. 18, 1970.
Interviews with Five Kendall College Students. Evanston,
Ill., Feb. 20, 1968.

3. ADDRESSES

F.   [7]R. A. Tsanoff, "Intellectual Freedom," Address presented at the Rice Institute Student Forum, Houston, 1953.

B.   Tsanoff, R. A. "Intellectual Freedom." Houston, 1953.
          (Address presented at the Rice Institute Student
          Forum.)

4. RECORDS

F.   [8]"Herman Melville's Bartleby the Scrivener," Lively Arts recording, No. 30007. Narrated by James Mason.

        [9]"Negro Prison Songs: Mississippi State Penitentiary," ed. Alan Lomax. Tradition Records, No. TLP 1020.

B.   "Herman Melville's Bartleby the Scrivener." Lively Arts
          recording, No. 30007. Narrated by James Mason.
    "Negro Prison Songs: Mississippi State Penitentiary."
          Ed. Alan Lomax. Tradition Records, No. TLP 1020.

5. TELEVISION OR RADIO PROGRAMS

F.   [10]"The Bishop Sheen Program," A.B.C. news special, Aug. 12, 1971: "Strangers in Their Own Land—The Blacks."

B.   "The Bishop Sheen Program." A.B.C. news special. Aug.
          12, 1971: "Strangers in Their Own Land—The
          Blacks."

(If a narrator is involved, end note with a period. Continue, "Narrator, Eddie Jones.")

6. BOOK REVIEWS

6.1. SIGNED AND TITLED

F.   [11]Jackson Emory Anders, "Muted Voices," rev. of Poems of Innocence and Pain, by Harlen L. Parks, Current Reviews, 24 July 1967, p. 18.

B.   Anders, Jackson Emory. "Muted Voices." Review of <u>Poems</u>
        <u>of Innocence and Pain</u>, by Harlen L. Parks. <u>Current</u>
        <u>Reviews</u>, 24 July 1967, pp. 18–22.

(No volume is needed with weekly periodicals; "p." precedes page numbers when no volume is included.)

6.2. SIGNED AND UNTITLED

F.   [12]Brooks Morgan, rev. of <u>Harcourt: Unknown Warrior</u>,
        by Theobald Armand, <u>Reviews of Best Books of the Month</u>,
        28 (1968), 401–404.

(Note that in continuously paged magazines—indicated in this case by high page numbers—issue number and month may be omitted as pages locate the material.)

B.   Morgan, Brooks. Review of <u>Harcourt: Unknown Warrior</u>, by
        Theobald Armand. <u>Reviews of Best Books of the</u>
        <u>Month</u>, 28 (1968), 401–408.

6.3. UNSIGNED AND TITLED

F.   [13]"The Decline of Grace," rev. of <u>Queries to God</u>,
        ed. Arnold L. Logan, <u>Weekly Review Anonymous</u>, 8 March
        1967, pp. 18–19.

B.   "The Decline of Grace." Review of <u>Queries to God</u>, ed.
        Arnold Logan. <u>Weekly Review Anonymous</u>, 8 March
        1967, pp. 18–21.

6.4. UNSIGNED AND UNTITLED

F.   [14]Rev. of <u>Bouquets of Poppies</u>, by Grayson Benton,
     <u>Modern World</u>, 46 (1969), 452.

B.   Review of <u>Bouquets of Poppies</u>, by Grayson Benton. <u>Modern</u>
        <u>World</u>, 46 (1969), 452–455.

MATTERS OF STYLE

Now let us consider matters of style.

Numerals

1. As a general rule, spell out one and two digit numbers appearing in the body of your paper. (Documentation numbers, of course, are never written out.)

> In the group, two boys volunteered to go. However, three were needed.

2. Use figures for three digits or more.

> John counted 104 varieties of fungi.

3. When numbers of one or two digits occur with numbers of three or more digits, use figures for *all* of them.

> Though 97 men arrived, 350 were needed.

4. Always spell out numbers at the beginning of a sentence.

> One hundred men competed against 100 women in the contest.

5. Plurals of numbers
   (a) Form plurals of numbers that are spelled out just as you would spell other plurals.

> He counted two sixes, two twenties, and three fours.

   (b) Form plurals of figures by adding *s*.

> The highest test scores were the 100s earned by the top students in the class.

6. Inclusive numbers
   (a) When referring to consecutive page numbers between one and ninety-nine, give opening and concluding numbers in full.

> Read pages 10–15.

   (b) When referring to consecutive page numbers for 100 and over, give only the last two digits of the second number.

> Read pages 100–15.

Hyphenation

1. If a word must be divided at the end of a line, use a hyphen between syllables. Consult your dictionary when you are in doubt of correct syllable division.

2. Never leave one or two letters hyphenated at the beginning or end of a line: "o-men," "rigorous-ly," and so on.

3. Check your dictionary for hyphenation practice with compound words, but remember that recently the tendency has been away from hyphenating compounds. Generally, the compounds are spelled as one word.

4. Sometimes hyphens are used between adjective noun combinations for purposes of clarity. These are called temporary compounds: "slow-moving car," "fast-talking salesman," and so on.

5. When fractions are spelled out, the numerator and denominator are hyphenated: "nine-tenths," "one-third," and so on.

6. Compounds involving use of the word *all* are hyphenated: "all-knowing," "all-embracing."

7. When a combination of words functions as an adjective, hyphenate the combination: "a do-it-right-now type," "the world's-going-to-end-tomorrow mentality." Note that no hyphen joins the adjective combination and the noun described.

8. For an extensive discussion of hyphenation practices, see *A Manual of Style*, 12th ed. rev. (Chicago: University of Chicago Press, 1969), pp. 132-40.

Titles

1. Use quotation marks around titles that are segments of larger works: poems, short stories, essays, chapters in a book.

2. Use quotation marks around titles of lectures and unpublished works.

3. Italicize (underline) titles of works in their totality: books, paintings, statues, drawings, plays, motion pictures, musical works.

4. Capitalization procedures in titles
   (a) Capitalize key words in both quoted and italicized titles: nouns, verbs, adjectives, adverbs, pronouns, subordinating conjunctions.

   > *The Man Who Died Though He Sought to Live*
   > (*Though* is a subordinating conjunction.)

   (b) Do not capitalize prepositions, articles, coordinating conjunctions.

   > *Hadley Speaks to God*   (*To* is a preposition.)
   > *Woman and Man*   (*And* is a coordinating conjunction.)
   > *Manley and the Moon*   (*The* is an article.)

   (c) Always capitalize first and last words.

   > *The Day the Earth Caved In*
   > (Preposition *in* is capitalized.)

Italicizing (underlining)

1. In titles (see page 220).

2. To call attention to words in a quoted passage.

> "The history of man is ridden with cliches, *torn by redundancies*, and mutilated by ambiguities."

However, the writer must indicate if italics have been added to the original quotation. This can be done in a footnote or in parentheses following the quotation: "italics added" or "italics mine."

3. For foreign words and phrases.

> The book is pervaded by the author's *weltschmerz*.

4. For letters used as letters.

> The letter *q* appeared forty-five times in the poem.

5. For words used as words.

> Avoid repetitive use of *and* in chains of compound sentences.

6. For names of ships.

> Captain Bligh's *Bounty* appeared on the horizon.

Plurals

1. Add *s* to capital letters used as letters and to words used as words.

> There are three *BBC*s in the Toronto directory.

> Avoid the excess use of *and*s in your composition.

2. Add *'s* to lower case letters used as letters. An *s* alone might be confusing.

> Pronounce the *th*'s carefully.

3. When your dictionary gives two plurals for a word, use the first. It generally has the wider acceptance.

4. Pluralize proper nouns by adding *s* or *es*. Never change *y* to *i* and add *es* as you would with common nouns.

> The Joneses have three Garys in their immediate family; their cousins, the Henry Smiths, have three Marys.

5. General principles of pluralizing:

   (a) Add *s* to most nouns.

   (b) add *es* to nouns ending in sibilants: *s, z, x, ch, sh:*

   > They moved boxes of topazes from the churches to the bushes.

(c) When nouns end in a *y* preceded by a consonant (outcry), change *y* to *i* and add *es:*

Their courtesies were met only with outcries.

(d) Check your dictionary for nouns ending in *o* and *i*. Sometimes *es* is added, sometimes *s* alone: echo, echoes; potato, potatoes; banjo, banjos.

Quotations

Placement of Quotations

1. Prose quotations of 100 words or less should be enclosed in quotation marks and run into the body of the text.

2. Prose quotations exceeding 100 words should be double-spaced, indented two spaces from the left-hand margin, and *not* enclosed in quotation marks.

3. Poetry quotations of two lines or less should be enclosed in quotation marks and run into the body of the text. A slash (/) should separate the two lines: "Lift not the painted veil which those who live/Call Life: though unreal shapes be pictured there."

4. Poetry quotations exceeding two lines should be double-spaced, centered on the page, and not enclosed in quotation marks.

Punctuation of Quotations

1. Place commas inside quotation marks.

"I'm seriously ill," Mary cried.

2. Place periods inside quotation marks.

Mary exclaimed, "I refuse to go to any doctor in Chicago."

3. Place semi-colons outside of quotation marks.

Mary declared, "Keith is a reptile"; Joe answered, "You're hallucinating."

4. Place exclamation and question marks inside quotation marks when they are part of the quotation itself.

"Are you defying me?" Mary's father roared.

5. Place exclamation and question marks outside of quotation marks when they are not part of quoted matter.

How can we avoid "ecological disaster"?

Anticipating and Integrating Quotations

1. Introduce the quotation with a preliminary phrase or sentence.

> Jordan's argument seriously undermines Everett's conclusions: "As men place comfort before ecological balance, as vested interest groups refuse to commit financial suicide, as profit precedes survival, efforts to save the environment are doomed to failure."

2. Or integrate quoted material into the fabric of your own sentences.

> It is hard to believe in the possibility of ecological survival as long as "vested interest groups refuse to commit financial suicide."

3. *Never* throw in a quotation apropos of nothing. Make the quotation an integral part of your paper.

4. Instructions for handling omissions from and insertions in quoted passages appear on pages 132–33.

THE TEN COMMANDMENTS OF GRAMMAR

I am the author, thy teacher, which
brought thee out of the land of error.

1. Thou shalt have no errors in case before I, for me
   alone am thy teacher. Thou and them, thy fellows,
   shalt adore I and bow down only to I.
2. Thou shalt not make thee any run-on sentences thy
   sentences shalt have periods between them.
3. Thou shalt not take the agreement of a pronoun and
   their antecedent in vain, for I will not hold him
   guiltless who denies my commandments and dese-
   crates it.
4. Use thy adverbs to modify verbs though thou writest
   hasty, as I have stern commanded thee.
5. Comma splices thou shalt abhor, thou shalt not em-
   ploy them. Thy son should abhor them with thee,
   also thy daughter and thine ox and ass should not
   abide them.
6. Honor thy subjects and thy verbs in their agreement
   that thy days is prolonged in the college that stand
   on the campus.
7. Thou shalt not shift tense in thy papers. This I com-
   mand thee. Again I commanded thee to remember
   thou art a student who obeyed my law. I will admonish thee of tenses in thy carelessness and in thy
   sloth. I have uttered my mandate and had bespoken
   thee. I thy teacher am fierce in rigor and was not
   loathe to admonish thee.
8. Neither shalt thou writing fragments. Nor shalt thou
   to know them in my presence. Nor utter them.
9. Neither shalt thou place modifiers from thy verbs a
   great distance, that are meaningful only near them.
   Neither shalt thou steal so perfectly the modifier
   from the verb it adorneth.
10. Thou shalt not create irregular verbs I hath not
    speaken, nor any partial likeness of the verbs I have
    brung thee. Thou shalt not bind thy auxiliaries unto
    verb parts I hath not chose thee, nor follow laws
    I have not gave thee. For I the author thy teacher
    am a jealous pedant, visiting the iniquity of the
    students upon the gradebook unto thine transcript
    which resideth in the filebox of the registrar's office
    forever.

These words the author spake unto all your assembly in
the classroom out of the midst of the hallways of the
college, and out of the campus, with a great voice; and
he added no more. And he wrote them in a book of paper,
and delivered them unto thee.

Which says what?
Only I hit him in the eye.
I *only* hit him in the eye.
I hit *only* him in the eye.
I hit him *only* in the eye.
I hit him in the eye *only*.

She held a ham sandwich in
one hand and a coke bottle in the
other. Then she drank it. *(Huh?)*

Mary milked the cow wearing
a pink sunbonnet.
While fishing, my toe was
bitten by a crab.
At four year's old, Father brought
me to the office.
Being a slow-witted clod, I must
explain everything to that
fool fifteen times.
Joe held the infant reciting the
second law of thermodynamics.

ON THE DANGER OF TAKING ANYTHING FOR GRANTED:

sink	drink	shrink	stink	think	wink
sank	drank	shrank	stank	thank	wank
sunk	drunk	shrunk	stunk	thunk	wunk

Spelling in a Nutshell

The English Language She Crazy

When we write the English *tongue*
Why is it not spelled like *rung?*
Why is *steak* not rhymed with *freak?*
Wherefore *meek,* and *peak,* and *clique?*
Why is *cough* not rhymed with *rough?*
Are not *though* and *sew* enough?
Must we suffer 'neath a *bough*
That mindlessly aligns with *cow?*
Do we also need to *add*
Irrationalities like *plaid?*
What oh what could yet be *worse*
Than puzzles rising out of *hearse?*
Curse and *nurse* refresh the *sense,*
But *verse* proceeds to drive us *hence,*
Pondering the ancient *source*
Of ambiguities like *coarse*
Compounded by Icelandic *Norse.*

Driven to a soothing *wood*
We'd welcome reason if we *could.*
But stumbling upon *cold* and *mould,*
We find our senses roiled and *rolled.*
Wherefore *hose* and *blows* and *clothes?*
Why can I say *goose* and *loose*
And yet court madness spelling *ruse?*
Why oh why can man not *choose*
To spell a word like *fuse* or *lose*
According to some laws of *mind?*
Instead, my fellows be *resigned*
To puzzlement and addled *brains*
O'er *foams* and *combs* and monarch's *reigns*
That testify to all who *be*
The horrid, wild autocra*cy*
Imposed on men who think they're free
When sounds and letters won't agree.

THE LOGIC OF MISSPELLING

MISSPELLINGS ARE LOGICAL.
MISSPELLINGS ARE ADAPTIONS TO PATTERNS.

The trick is *not* to analyze 10,000 commonly misspelled words, but the few that *you* habitually misspell. Try to figure out why you misspell a particular word; that is, try to figure out the rationale for your "error." If you find your personal, internal logic, you can renounce it for "illogical" correctness.

1. Analogy

The human mind perceives similarities: ice, mice, lice, vice, slice, nice, advice, *presice*. Well, why not? The correct spelling, *precise*, violates the pattern.

My fourth grade daughter came up with a nice one in this category. Correct spelling of the word *though* was pounded into her head; so she wrote: *Thoughs* stars are not in our galaxy.

One of my students used the word *wizzard* in a paper. Again, why not? We have gizzard, blizzard, frizzled, drizzled, fizzled.

FIND YOUR SYSTEM OF PATTERNING, AND VIOLATE YOUR LOGIC. YOU MUST UNEARTH THE PRINCIPLES THAT GOVERN <u>YOUR</u> SPELLING, NOT EVERYBODY ELSE'S.

2. Pronunciation
   You probably say *libary* rather than *library*.
   You probably say *generly* rather than *generally*.
   You probably say *mathmatics* rather than *mathematics*.

SOMETIMES YOUR MISSPELLINGS ARE LOGICAL RENDERINGS OF YOUR PRONUNCIATION.

3. Phonetics
   Pamflet more accurately reproduces the sounds than *pamphlet*.
   Laf more accurately reproduces the sounds than *laugh*.
   Sargent more accurately reproduces the sounds than *sergeant*.
   Shofer more accurately reproduces the sounds than *chauffeur*.

SOMETIMES YOU MAY TRY TO SPELL WORDS THE WAY THEY SOUND, FORGETTING A BASIC PRINCIPLE: "THE ENGLISH LANGUAGE SHE CRAZY."

4. Reversal
Gril represents a reversal of the *i* and the *r* in *girl*. Watch yourself for this kind of tendency.

5. Magic
If the dictionary, patterning, and logic all fail you, try "magic."

> PRINT THE DEMONIAC WORD IN BLACK MAGIC MARKER ON A BLANK WHITE PAGE. PLACE ANOTHER BLANK WHITE PAGE BESIDE IT. STARE FIXEDLY AND UNBLINKINGLY AT THE DEMON. THEN SWIFTLY SHIFT YOUR GAZE TO THE BLANK PAGE. THE DEMON SHOULD GLOW FAINTLY ON THE PAGE.

Some people argue that the after image imprints the spelling on your brain!

Now you have finished your research paper

THE NECESSITY FOR PROOFREADING

A factor in shopping decisions for students of Joplin R-8 District Schools is the R-8 dress code for students. . . . All attire shall be from obscene or suggestive writing or advertising.
— Joplin *Globe*

Some folks think it's now we live.
Others believe your word
to forgive.
But I'm sure you ment it to be
woedl t udbo eam ees.
— "Poet's Corner,"
Tri-Town News

William Tepper, resembling a young Elliott Gould, plays a starring role as a disillusioned college basketball.
— Sacramento *Union's*
"Weekender."

We would encourage both proponents and opponents of the open classroom concept to attend tonight's meeting and voice their onions.
— Alaska *Empire*

John

227

At best, research is discovery, writing is systematizing that discovery, documentation is recording the evidence, and completion is keeping what you have learned.

Have you ever wondered what the trees say?

Will you walk into the forest?

Or shall we write for the inquiring portion of you:

LOST SOMEWHERE BETWEEN SUNRISE AND SUNSET AN OPPOR-
TUNITY, AN IDEA, A CHANCE. NO REWARDS OFFERED—
FOR IN TIME THEY ARE GONE FOREVER.—SIGNS OF OUR TIMES

INDEX

Abbreviations:
  in footnotes, 181
  of books of Bible, 181
  of titles of magazines, 181–182
Abortion:
  bibliography, 5
Act:
  of play, 195
Addresses (speeches):
  in footnotes, 217
African Studies, 81
  reference works, 81–82
Agnew, Spiro, 22, 23, 205
Alphabet:
  letters of, in heading divisions, 134, 141
  principles of alphabetizing, 59
American Indians, 72
  reference works, 72–73
Analysis:
  of data, 177
Anonymous author:
  in footnotes, 188
Anthropology, 73
  reference works, 74–75
Art, 75
  reference works, 75–76
Arts, performing, 105
  reference works, 106–107
Astronomy, 77
  reference works, 77–78
Atlases, 33, 47–48
Author:
  objectivity, competency, 34
Author's name:
  anonymous, 188
  in footnotes, 183, 185, 186, 188–189,
    191, 192
  on entry card, 58
  on note cards, 131
Automation jokes, 172–173
  analysis of, 177
  bibliography, 177

Bible:
  abbreviation of books of, 182
  in footnotes, 196

Bibliographies, 32, 49–56
  of bibliographies, 48–49
Bibliography (as source), 130
  citations, 187
  compiling cards, 32, 33
  subject, 57, 62
Biography index, 67
Black literature:
  bibliography, 9
Black studies, 78
  reference works, 79–81
Books:
  out-of-print, 35
  title in footnotes, 183, 185, 186, 187,
    188, 195
Book reviews:
  indexes, 66
  in footnotes, 217
Brackets:
  use of, 133
Business, 83
  reference works, 83–84

Card catalog, 32, 50, 57, 62, 69
Center, missing, 178
Chapter:
  headings, 62
  in footnotes, 196
Chisholm, Shirley, 209
Clarity, 176
Classics:
  in footnotes, 195
Classification
  of data, 174
Classification systems:
  Dewey Decimal, 32, 60–61
  Library of Congress, 55–56
Co-authors:
  in footnotes, 188, 189
Colon:
  in footnotes, 184
Comma:
  in bibliography, 187, 194
  in footnote, 183, 184, 185, 187, 197
  placement, 222

Communes, 132, 133
  analysis of data on, 177
  bibliography, 161–163, 167–168
  data in common, 172
  framework, 174
  model paper on, 143–169
  quotations on, 135–139
  sorting data, 174
Communication, 176
Conclusion:
  of paper, 177
Congressional papers, 208
Constitution:
  in footnotes, 205
Coordination, 141, 143
Copyright:
  dates, 182

Daley, Richard, 10
  bibliography, 11
Dali, Salvador:
  "Automatic Beginning of a Portrait
    of Gala," 125
  "Dali at Age of Six," 36
  "Las Meninas," 100
Dante Alighieri
  The Divine Comedy, Inferno, 24–25, 97
Data, 172
  analysis and interpretation of, 177
  missing, 190
  reference to, 175
  sequence, 183
Dates:
  copyright, 182
David, Jacques Louis:
  "The Death of Socrates," 107
Dewey decimal, 32, 60–61
Dictionaries, 20, 25, 27, 28, 32, 33, 41
  in footnotes, 198
"Diss," 181
Division, 142, 143
  see also Subdivision
Divisions:
  of outline, 134, 135, 161
  of paper, 134, 135, 174
Documentation:
  in footnotes, 180–218
  models, 188
  of sources, 130
Douglass, Frederick, 44
Drug use, 84
  reference works, 85–86
Druids:
  as suggested topic, 33, 38–65
"Dying Gaul," 91

Ecology, 86
  reference works, 87–88
Economics, 88
  reference works, 88–89

Edition:
  of book in footnotes, 183
Editor:
  in footnotes, 183, 191, 192, 193
  preface, 190
Education, 89
  reference works, 89–91
Einstein, Albert, 119
Ellipsis:
  use of, 132–133
Encyclopedias, 25, 32, 39
  in footnotes, 197–198
Essay:
  index, 65
Exclamation mark:
  use of, 183, 222
Executive papers:
  in footnotes, 205

Factbooks, 33, 44–47
Facts:
  documentation of, 130
Feiffer, Jules, 211
Feininger, Andreas, 116
Folklore, see Mythology
Footnotes, 62, 130
  abbreviations in, 181–182
  citations, 187
  model, 164–166, 183–218
  numbering and spacing, 181–186
  numbers, 179
Framework:
  of paper, 143, 174
Fulbright, William J., 209

Goldwater, Barry, 209
Government publications, 22, 32, 35, 67–69
  in footnotes, 204–214
Graham, Billy, 23
Grammar:
  ten commandments of, 224
Gropper, William:
  "The Senate," 124
Groups:
  of cards, 135, 141, 174

Haas, Ernest:
  "New Mexico," 72
  "The Graceful Dancing Girls
    of Bali," 105
Headings, 141
  arranging, 130
  roman numerals, 134
"Heroic Gaul, The," 53
History, 91
  reference works, 91–93
Hyphen:
  in footnotes, 195
  use of, 220

"Ibid." 186
Indentation:
  in bibliography, 187
  in footnotes, 181, 187
Indexes, 32, 64
  biography, 67
  book review, 66
  essay, 65
  newspaper, 65
  pamphlet, 65
Inductive method, 172
Insertions:
  indication of, 133
Interviews:
  in footnotes, 216
Introduction:
  in footnotes, 190
I.Q.:
  literary, 25
Issue number:
  in footnotes, 185
Italicizing:
  use of, 221
  see also Underlining

Kennedy, Robert, 14, 15
Kliendienst, Richard, 23

Latin:
  reference tags, 186
Letters (of alphabet):
  in heading divisions, 134, 141
Libraries, 19, 20, 35
  card catalog, 32, 50, 57, 69
  catalogs, 35
  information desk, 37
  interlibrary loan, 35
  vertical file, 35
Library of Congress, 55–56
Line numbers:
  in footnotes, 196
Literature, 93
  reference works, 94–95
Literature, British and American, 95
  reference works, 96
Literature, world, 97
  reference works, 97–98
"loc. cit." 186
Lockiesh, M.:
  Visual Illusions, 7

McGovern, George, 209
Magazines:
  abbreviation of, 182
Manual of Style, A, 220
Mass Media, 98
  reference works, 99–100
Mathematics, 100
  reference works, 101

Max, Peter:
  "A-maze-zing Maze," 19
  "Scorpio," 17
Microfilm, 35
Mills, Wilbur D. 209
Mitchell, John, 22
Mitchell, Martha, 23
MLA Style Sheet, 186, 191, 194, 198,
    201, 202
Music, 101
  reference works, 101–103
Mythology and Folklore, 104
  reference works, 104–105

Names, see author, titles
Neanderthals, 16
  bibliography, 17
Newspapers:
  indexes, 65
  in footnotes, 202
Nixon, Richard, 22, 205
Nixon, Tricia, 23
Notes cards, 32, 33, 130, 131, 134, 135,
    141, 172, 179
  examples of, 135
  grouping of, 143
  putting in order, 134, 174, 179
  scrambles, 135
Notes:
  notetaking, 130, 131
  see also Note cards
"n.p." 190
"n. pag." 190
Numerals:
  style, 219
Numerals, Arabic:
  in footnotes, 181, 185
  in heading divisions, 134, 141
Numerals, Roman:
  in footnotes, 195, 196
  in heading divisions, 134, 141

O'Brien, Lawrence, 23
Omissions:
  indication of, 132–133
"op. cit." 186
Optical illusions, 6
  bibliography, 7
Outline:
  development, 130
  putting together, 134
  scrambled, 143
  structure, 141, 142

"P. pp."
  in footnotes, 184, 193
  use of abbreviation, 181
  when to use, 185, 186, 200, 201, 206, 212
Pamphlets:
  indexes, 65
  in footnotes, 215

Paper:
    as collage, 134–139
    central idea, 172
    conclusion, 177
    introductory passages, 172
    model, 143–164
    to begin writing, 134
Parallelism, 141, 143
Parentheses:
    in footnotes, 183, 184, 185, 187, 198,
        200, 201, 202, 206
Period:
    in bibliography, 194
    in footnotes, 184, 186, 195, 197
    in "p., pp." 181
    placement, 222
Periodicals:
    indexes, 64–65
    in footnotes, 185, 187, 199–202
Philosophy, 107
    reference works, 108
Physical education, see Recreation
Plagiarism, 131
    nature of, 179–180
Plurals:
    pluralizing, 221–222
Political science, 108
    reference works, 109–110
Preface:
    editor's, 190
Pre-writing:
    procedures, 130–143
Proofreading, 227
Psychology, 110
    reference works, 111–112
Publisher:
    use of name, 181
Punctuation, 132, 133, 181
    see also under individual marks

Question mark:
    use of, 183, 222
Quizzes, 25–29
Quotation marks:
    use of, 183, 185, 222, 223
Quotations:
    acknowledgment of, 130
    anti-youth, 22–23
    collections of, 33, 43
    dictionaries of, 43
    use of, 179

Radio programs:
    in footnotes, 217
Reagan, Ronald, 23
Records (phonograph):
    in footnotes, 217
Recreation and physical education, 112
    reference works, 113–114

Reference tools, 36
Reference works:
    biographical, 198
    guides, 49
    non-alphabetically arranged,
        in footnotes, 197
    specialized, 32, 40, 70, 72–126
Religion, 114
    bibliography, 13
    reference works, 115–116
Reports:
    documentation, 189, 205, 215
Reprint, 194
Research:
    steps, 32
    materials, 172
Rexroth, Kenneth:
    "Thou Shalt Not Kill: A Memorial
        for Dylan Thomas," 20–21
Riley, Bridget:
    "Current," 6
"Rpt." 181
Rubens, Pieter Paul:
    "Prometheus Bound," 93

Science, 116
    reference works, 117
Science, biological:
    reference works, 118
Science, physical:
    reference works, 119–120
Semicolons:
    placement, 222
Short forms, 186
Social science, 120
    reference works, 121
Sociology, 121
    reference works, 122–123
Source:
    acknowledging, 180
    designating, 131
    evaluating, 34–35
    quoting, 131, 132, 179
Speech, 124
    reference works, 124–125
Spelling, 225–227
State:
    name of in data, 189
Style:
    hyphenation, 220
    italicizing, 221
    numerals, 219
    plurals, 221
    quotations, 222
Subdivision, 142, 143, 174
    see also Division
Subgroups:
    of cards, 134, 135, 141
Subheadings, 130

Subject:
  division of, 142
Subordination, 141, 143
Subthesis:
  development of, 175
Subtitle, 187, 190
Subtopic, 131, 134
Suicide, 24

Television programs:
  in footnotes, 217
Thesis, 178
  emergence of, 172
Thomas, Dylan, 20
Thurmond, Strom, 22
Titles of works, 58
  style, 220
Topic:
  central, 134
  choosing, 3
  limiting, 32, 34, 130
  suggested, 4–17, 22, 23, 24, 38, 40, 72–126
Topic sentence, 178

Translator:
  in footnotes, 183, 192
Tree of Knowledge, The, 31

Underlining:
  in footnotes, 183, 185, 186, 192, 196,
    206, 220
  see also Italicizing
Unity:
  of paper, 178

Victimology, 14
  bibliography, 15
Vishniac, Roman, 110
Volume numbers:
  in footnotes, 185, 193, 194, 200, 201

Warhol, Andy:
  "Marilyn Monroe," 98
Women's liberation, 125, 142
  reference works, 126
Wordbooks, 33, 42

Yearbooks, 32, 40